Salvation

AND

Sovereignty

Salvation

AND

Sovereignty

A MOLINIST APPROACH

Kenneth Keathley

NASHVILLE, TENNESSEE

Salvation and Sovereignty:
A Molinist Approach

ISBN: 978-0-8054-3198-8

Published by B&H Publishing Group
Nashville, Tennessee

Dewey Decimal Classification: 234
Subject Heading: SALVATION\DOCTRINAL THEOLOGY\
PROVIDENCE AND GOVERNMENT OF GOD

Printed in the United States of America

7 8 9 10 11 12 • 18 17 16 15 14

CONTENTS

FOREWORD

When I was a child, I spoke like a child, I thought like a child,
I reasoned like a child. When I became a man,
I put aside childish things. (1 Cor 13:11)

And you know that from childhood you have known the sacred
Scriptures, which are able to give you wisdom for salvation
through faith in Christ Jesus. (2 Tim 3:15)

ARLIEST MEMORIES OF the contemplation of what had happened to me when I was saved as a nine-year-old boy arise largely from my fifteenth year. Then I contemplated fulfilling the call on my life to preach the gospel of Christ. A preacher-father, adept in theological considerations, guided his fledgling preacher-son into a program of reading that served me well. Here I was first introduced to Calvinism and authors steeped in the Reformed tradition. This reading was fodder for many a discussion with my father and eventually with other evangelists, pastors, missionaries, and theologians who visited the First Baptist Church in Beaumont, Texas, where my father served as pastor.

From the outset I was charmed by the writings of the Reformed. The appeal lay in the systematization of biblical truth, which early presented itself as essential to my mind. In addition to that, the Puritans, as a case in point, seemed to be intense in their devotion to God and to speak most about the sovereignty of God and the gentle obedience demanded of all in submitting to the providences of God.

But even to the mind of the young teenage preacher, in the Reformed writers there were also disturbing implications that troubled my soul. Initially, these were of a pragmatic and experientialist nature, which simply found the tenets of Calvinism inconsistent with what I observed in the world-mission mandate and the evangelization of the lost. Eventually I would "put aside childish things" and realize that the pragmatic and experientalist impulses must be adjudicated carefully by the revelation of God. But once I had arrived at this conclusion I was faced with certain other difficulties associated with the Reformed system. Eventually I came to recognize that these problems for me were clearly not viewed as problematic to most of the adherents of Calvinism.

At this point I concluded and continued to affirm that the problem with Calvinism, if indeed there is a problem, is the system itself and not the sincerity of those who hold it. I am still persuaded of that truth and hence join Ken Keathley, the author of this volume, in the conviction that these are my brothers in Christ; and I love and honor them, though I cannot agree with them.

The new problems focused on my reading of Scripture. Certainly I could see where my Calvinistic friends derive some of their teachings, but the botany of Calvinism seemed to me flawed by having two petals of the TULIP at best sparsely represented in Scripture. I could see that irresistible grace and limited atonement made sense to the Calvinistic system; but for the life of me, I could find little substantive witness for them in Scripture. More troubling still was my inevitable conclusion that a thoroughly consistent form of the Calvinistic message made God in some way or another the author of evil and thus called into question both the justice and the universal love of God. In fact, some Calvinists openly advocated that God created most men in order to condemn them and thus demonstrate His justice, and these advocates seemed to me to be the more consistent Calvinists.

As the years have passed and I have studied these questions more extensively, my dissatisfaction with the answer of Calvinism has become more profound. Added to this, I find myself uncomfortable with the usual definitions of three other petals of the TULIP and the fact that in order for me to endorse them I have to be certain that the definitions are correlated with what I find on the pages of Holy Scripture, not only in verses specifically on the subject but also in accounts of the nature and character of God Himself.

To these troublesome circumstances were added the frequent charges of Calvinists that non-Calvinists are guilty of not believing in "the sovereignty of God" or in the "doctrines of grace." There has never been a time when I have not believed that salvation is totally and completely by grace. The use of this argument is a classical case of attempting to win an argument by establishing the terms of the discussion in such a way that the opponent's position appears objectionable at the outset. Most non-Calvinists believe fully in the sovereignty of God, and many believe that salvation is by grace through faith alone; but they do not define these terms the same way the Calvinist does. The issue is not whether or not these are biblical concepts, but rather what do these concepts mean?

The Calvinist can answer in return that he, too, has been the subject of abuse through the calumnies of non-Calvinists. For example, some say that "Calvinists are unevangelistic and fail in their missionary commitment." While I find unavoidable both the overall historical picture and the scriptural logic that a Calvinistic soteriology is more often hurtful than helpful to the cause of evangelism, a Calvinist does not necessarily fail at this point.

Having said all of the above, fairness would dictate my admission that I experienced no end of frustration attempting to find a theological volume to defend adequately the position I personally espouse as advocated by Scripture. The Reformed tradition has been nothing if not superb in the breadth of literature produced favoring its position, while non-Calvinist authors have often fallen into inadequate argumentation, or positions that I found untenable, such as the possibility of the loss of salvation, open theism, and even universalism. Other books are not charitable and Christlike in their response and hence of limited usefulness. Non-Calvinists who see things as I do were simply guilty of not having gone to the trouble to develop a thorough biblical answer; and for this reason, I welcome the present volume, *Salvation and Sovereignty: A Molinist Approach* by Kenneth Keathley, Professor of Theology at Southeastern Baptist Theological Seminary in Wake Forest, North Carolina. This book will answer the need for all those Baptists and probably for a host of others outside of our Baptist Zion—all of whom are intensely uncomfortable with the conclusions of Calvinism, especially with the Dortian Calvinism and its logic, exegesis, and potential effect on the question of the sincere offer of salvation in Christ to all people. For those who find themselves in that position, here is an irenic proposal attempting just assessment of the proposals of the biblical text.

Professor Keathley, in the pages that follow, develops a Molinist approach to the doctrine. But even if you are not convinced that the perspective of Luis de Molina, the sixteenth-century Jesuit theologian, is the proper perspective, this book nevertheless will be of infinite value.

Keathley demonstrates why Calvinism is unacceptable to many in terms of its logic, its exegesis, and its theology. Yet, he does so with the touch of a pastor, generous toward all men, faithfully giving the positions of even those with whom he disagrees, and presenting a volume void of the vitriol often characterizing these debates.

Keathley's botanical garden uproots the TULIP and plants ROSES in its place. Using the acrostic of ROSES suggested by Timothy George, Keathley presents a far more palatable and, I believe, faithful witness to the New Testament. He has a philosopher's reasoning, a theologian's grasp of Scripture, and a preacher's clarity. The book is remarkable for the clarity of its argumentation on a subject that is otherwise often extraordinarily complicated. The complication is still there, but Keathley's ability to present it in a way that a common man can grasp is an encouragement to be sure.

In the end, Dr. Keathley's volume is a humble attempt to state soteriological truth. Keathley knows only too well the caution of Scripture, "For who has known the mind of the Lord? Or who has been His counselor?" He does not try to venture too far into the mind of God, and he does recognize that a mystery resides in the Lord. But rather than finding that mystery in the will of God, he has discovered the mystery in the omniscience of God. This coincides with a conviction I have held for many years, and I am grateful to Dr. Keathley for articulating that position with much greater clarity than I have ever been able to do. Such a position makes all the difference in comprehending how God can sovereignly elect and at the same time maintain sovereign justice in those actions of God that are known to Him in eternity. In addition to all of this, he has linked the Anabaptist theologian Balthasar Hubmaier to the text, and in so doing he not only demonstrates that Hubmaier had a view very close to Molinism, but also that the Radical Reformers, who were Anabaptists, usually held such a view. Since that is the tradition to which I give adherence and which I believe to be the most important influence on the development of modern Baptists, I was grateful to see the linking of these two.

In a word, this book is essential reading for two groups. First, for all those who are uncomfortable with Calvinism and feel that it has exceeded the actual witness of Scripture, while ignoring other major emphases in Scripture, this book is the one for which you have waited. For my Calvinistic friends, I do not believe the book will change your mind. You hold your convictions sincerely; and because I am a Baptist, I believe in the freedom of faith that enables you to do so. Of course, I hope you read the volume because I think some of you will see the wisdom presented within these pages; and those of you who do not change your minds will nevertheless have been exposed to an irenic and profoundly Christian response, which without trace of uncharitableness should move all toward taking the gospel to the world until Jesus comes. Finally, to Ken Keathley I express my deepest appreciation for writing the tome that I have long hoped someone would write.

Paige Patterson
President
Southwestern Baptist Theological Seminary
Fort Worth, Texas

ACKNOWLEDGEMENTS

THIS BOOK GOT its start in 2003 as the brainchild of Chuck Kelley, president of New Orleans Baptist Theological Seminary, who also suggested the title of *Salvation and Sovereignty*. The project originally involved Stan Norman, who at that time along with me was on the faculty of NOBTS. A number of events delayed things, not the least of which was a hurricane named Katrina. By the time writing actually commenced in earnest, Dr Norman and I had been washed to other parts of the country. Because of his new administrative responsibilities, Stan was no longer able to devote the time necessary to the project and regretfully had to drop out. I want to thank him and Chuck Kelley, because without their help *Salvation and Sovereignty* would never have gotten off the ground.

I have been blessed with a number of remarkable helpers. Special thanks must be given to the assistants who slogged through the task of typing page after page of handwritten notes and of proofreading manuscripts replete with mangled grammar and awkward sentences. Tammy Sollenberger, Tracy Lightkip, Astasha Baker, and Allison Keathley—all deserve special thanks for their patient typing. In addition, I must thank Carrie Pickelsimer and Billie Goodenough for proofreading.

Several colleagues were good enough to read various chapters of *Salvation and Sovereignty*. I thank Doug Geivett, John Hammett, Nathan Finn, Bruce Little, Ed Gravely, Bruce Ashford, Steve Lemke, and Jeremy Evans. They provided many helpful comments and critiques. Whatever errors remain are my responsibility. I also wish to thank the Lilly Foundation for a writing grant. Thanks also go to the trustees of Southeastern Baptist Theological Seminary, who allowed me to take a half sabbatical to finish the book. I give special thanks to Tom Schreiner. Even as we agreed to disagree, he was always helpful and gracious in his comments and communications.

At various times I presented chapters or significant portions of chapters of *Salvation and Sovereignty* as papers at conferences and meetings. In turn, those sections of the book were sometimes published. Chapter two, "Does God Desire the Salvation of All?" was presented at *The Mission of Today's Church* conference in New Orleans and then published by Broadman and Holman in a book by the same title. I had the privilege of speaking at both the *Building Bridges* conference at Ridgecrest, North Carolina, in 2007 and the *John 3:16* conference in Atlanta in 2008. I presented significant portions of chapter five, "S Is for Sovereign Election" at the *Building Bridges* conference and chapter six, "E Is for Eternal Life" at the *John 3:16* conference. The presentations for the first conference were published as *Calvinism: A Southern Baptist Dialogue* and as *Whosoever Will: A Biblical-Theological Critique of Calvinism* for the second (both published by B&H). The *Journal of the Grace Evangelical Society* also published chapters two and six, and I thank them for their permission to include them in the present volume.

Most of all I thank Penny, my dear wife, for her steadfast encouragement and support. "Let her works praise her!" (Prov 31:31).

Kenneth Keathley

THE CASE FOR ROSES WITHIN
A MOLINIST FRAMEWORK

*Whoever makes a whole judgment and does not lay the counter-
Scriptures on the same scale next to it, to him a half-truth is more
damaging than a whole lie.*

—Balthasar Hubmaier,
Anabaptist theologian and martyr[1]

W HAT SHALL A CHRISTIAN do who is convinced of certain central tenets of Calvinism but not its corollaries? Specifically, what if I am convinced that God elects individuals to salvation but I am also compelled by the evidence of Scripture to reject the notion that Christ died only for the elect? What if I am also convinced that the Calvinist doctrine of irresistible grace—that God gives saving grace only to the elect while withholding it from others—has little or no biblical foundation? Like someone who comes to embrace premillennialism but remains unimpressed with the standard Dispensational eschatology generally associated with it, I see salvation as a sovereign work of grace but suspect that the usual Calvinist understanding of sovereignty (that God is the cause of all things) is not sustained by the biblical witness as a whole.

Most Christians are familiar with the five points of Calvinism generally denoted by the TULIP acronym:

T Total depravity
U Unconditional election
L Limited atonement
I Irresistible grace
P Perseverance of the saints

I agree with three of the points of TULIP: total depravity, unconditional election, and perseverance of the saints. The biblical evidence seems

---

[1]Balthasar Hubmaier, "Freedom of the Will, I" in *Balthasar Hubmaier: Theologian of Anabaptism*, H. Wayne Pipkin and John H. Yoder, eds., (Scottdale, PA: Herald, 1989), 428.

clear enough. But the Bible also presents a genuine desire on the part of God for the salvation of all humanity and declares a real offer of the gospel to everyone who hears it. In addition, the biblical case for limited atonement and irresistible grace is shockingly weak. This means that "L" and "I" must go. Limited atonement and irresistible grace cannot be found in the Scriptures unless one first puts them there.

EVERYTHING IS COMING UP ROSES

ROSES Compared to TULIP			
T	Total depravity	→	Radical depravity
U	Unconditional election	→	Sovereign election
L	Limited atonement	→	Singular redemption
I	Irresistible grace	→	Overcoming grace
P	Perseverance of the saints	→	Eternal Life
R	Radical depravity	←	Total depravity
O	Overcoming grace	←	Irresistible grace
S	Sovereign election	←	Unconditional election
E	Eternal life	←	Perseverance of the saints
S	Singular redemption	←	Limited atonement

In addition to arguing that only three of the five points of TULIP can be defended scripturally, I also argue that the T, U, and P need to undergo some retooling. So the next obvious step is to recast the TULIP acronym itself. Timothy George has presented the ROSES acronym as a replacement for TULIP, and I intend to build upon it.[2] I do not claim that Dr. George and I prune roses exactly the same way (he favors reformed theology). However, we both agree that the use of the TULIP acronym tends to obscure as much as it illuminates.

There is reason to believe that the framers of the Canons of Dort would not like the TULIP formulation. The five points of Dort were an

---

[2]Timothy George, *Amazing Grace: God's Initiative—Our Response* (Nashville: Lifeway, 2000), 71–83.

ad hoc response to the five complaints presented by the followers of Arminius (called the Remonstrants) in Holland during the early seventeenth century. TULIP was not intended to be a summary of the Calvinist doctrine on salvation, and it certainly does not encapsulate Reformed theology, which is much broader and more nuanced than the TULIP formulation. Some of the terms that make up the TULIP acronym are not even in the Canons of Dort. For example, one will search in vain to find the term *total depravity* in the typical English translation of the Canons. When one reads the Canons, it becomes immediately apparent that the terms that make up the acronym in many ways misrepresent the positions taken by the Synod—this is particularly true of the term *limited atonement*. In some places the misrepresentation is so severe as to be a caricature.

Even those who describe themselves as "five point" Calvinists express regret about one or several of the terms.[3] A modern proponent of Calvinism will often subscribe to the points only after clarifying (or in some instances completely redefining) what a particular point means. In light of these facts, I suggest that the acronym has outlived its usefulness. If a set of terms must constantly be redefined, or if they tend to mislead and misinform as much as they inform and clarify, then surely those terms need to be replaced. Dr. George has done this with his proposed alternative acronym. Instead of TULIP, he offers ROSES, and I believe his approach warrants further attention.

So what are the tenets of ROSES? Without defending them at this point, let me explain them briefly as follows:

R*adical depravity*: The old term, *total depravity*, gives the impression that fallen humanity always is as bad as it possibly can be. The new term, *radical depravity*, more correctly emphasizes that every aspect of our being is affected by the fall and renders us incapable of saving ourselves or even of wanting to be saved.

O*vercoming grace*: The old term, *irresistible grace*, seems to imply that God saves a person against his will. The new term, *overcoming*

---

[3]R. C. Sproul and J. I. Packer are good examples of five point Calvinists who have expressed dislike of the TULIP formulation. See R. C. Sproul, *Chosen by God* (Wheaton, IL: Tyndale House, 1986), 103; and J. I. Packer, "The Love of God: Universal and Particular," in *The Grace of God, the Bondage of the Will,* vol. 2, eds. T. R. Schreiner and B. A. Ware (Grand Rapids: Baker, 1995), 424.

grace, highlights that it is God's persistent beckoning that overcomes our wicked obstinacy.

Sovereign election: Often the term *unconditional election* is presented in such a way as to give the impression that those who die without receiving Christ did so because God never desired their salvation in the first place. The replacement label, *sovereign election*, affirms that God desires the salvation of all, yet accentuates that our salvation is not based on us choosing God but on God choosing us.

Eternal life: The old term, *perseverance of the saints*, leads to the notion that a believer's assurance is based on his ability to persevere rather than on the fact he is declared righteous in Christ. The purpose of the new term, *eternal life*, is to stress that believers enjoy a transformed life that is preserved and we are given a faith which will remain.

Singular redemption: A particularly unfortunate concept, *limited atonement*, teaches that Christ died only for the elect and gives the impression that there is something lacking in the atonement. As we will see, many Calvinists prefer terms such as *definite atonement* or *particular redemption*. We will use the label *singular redemption* to emphasize that Christ died sufficiently for every person, although efficiently only for those who believe.

SO WHAT IS MOLINISM?

Calvinism has at least three dilemmas: (1) reconciling God's sovereign election of individuals with his genuine desire for the salvation of all; (2) adhering to a deterministic view of sovereignty without blaming God for the fall of Adam; and (3) adhering to limited atonement and irresistible grace while also affirming that the gospel is genuinely offered to everyone. There is an alternative to Calvinism—called Molinism—which provides answers to these three quandaries that are both biblical and logically consistent.

Most Christians have heard about Calvinism, but not as many are familiar with Molinism. I suspect some who embrace Calvinism do so because they recognize the Bible teaches that God is sovereign and Calvinism is the only theological system of which they are aware that attempts to do justice to God's sovereignty. Calvinism often wins by default, especially when Arminianism is understood to be the alternative. Simply put, Molinism argues that God perfectly accomplishes His will in free creatures through the use of His omniscience. It reconciles two crucial biblical truths: (1) God exercises sovereign control over all His creation, and (2) human beings make free choices and decisions for which they must give account.

So what is Molinism? Named after its first proponent, Luis Molina (1535–1600), a sixteenth-century Jesuit priest, Molinism holds to a strong notion of God's control and an equally firm affirmation of human freedom.[4] In other words Molinism simultaneously holds to a Calvinistic view of a comprehensive divine sovereignty and to a version of free will (called *libertarianism*) generally associated with Arminianism. As Doug Geivett argues, the fact that Molinism is the one proposal that tries to hold simultaneously to both is a point in its favor, since both "are *prima facie* true."[5]

Molinism teaches that God exercises His sovereignty primarily through His omniscience, and that He infallibly knows what free creatures would do in any given situation. In this way God sovereignly controls all things, while humans are also genuinely free. God is able to accomplish His will through the use of what Molinists label His *middle knowledge*. We will look at the Molinist model of God's knowledge and providence in chapter 1 and in the chapter on sovereign election (chap. 5).

So Molinism formulates a radical "compatibilism"—a Calvinist view of divine sovereignty and an Arminian view of human freedom—and for this reason is often attacked from both sides of the aisle. Calvinists such as Bruce Ware and Richard Muller consider Molinism to be a type of Arminianism, while Roger Olsen and Robert Picirilli (both card-

---

[4]According to K. R. MacGregor (*A Molinist-Anabaptist Systematic Theology* [Lanham, MD: University Press of America, 2007]), the Anabaptist theologian Balthasar Hubmaier argued for a position similar to Molinism nearly fifty years before Molina published his works. Molina certainly was not the first to argue for understanding God's knowledge in a series of three logical moments. Duns Scotus and Thomas Aquinas also used a three-moment formulation. See W. L. Craig, *The Problem of Divine Foreknowledge and Future Contingents from Aristotle to Suarez* (Leiden: Brill, 1988), 173.

[5]R. D. Geivett, "Divine Providence and the Openness of God: A Response to William Hasker," *Philosophia Christi* 4 (2002): 380.

carrying Arminians) reject Molinism for being too Calvinistic.[6] However, Molinism is attractive to many leading Christian philosophers of our day, such as Alvin Plantinga, Thomas Flint, and William Lane Craig. One of the main reasons is that it demonstrates it is logically possible to affirm divine sovereignty and human freedom in a consistent manner.[7] Even open theist William Hasker, who is no friend to Molinism, admits, "If you are committed to a 'strong' view of providence, according to which, down to the smallest detail, 'things are as they are because God knowingly decided to create such a world,' and yet you also wish to maintain a libertarian conception of free will—if this is what you want, then Molinism is the only game in town."[8]

As a matter of fact, that is exactly what I want because I believe Molinism is faithful to the biblical witness. The Molinist model is the only game in town for anyone who wishes to affirm a high view of God's sovereignty while holding to a genuine definition of human choice, freedom, and responsibility. William Lane Craig goes so far as to describe the Molinist notion of middle knowledge as "the single most fruitful theological concept I have ever encountered."[9] As we apply Molinism to the vexing questions of predestination and election, the reasons for his enthusiasm will become evident.

---

[6]See B. Ware, *God's Greater Glory* (Wheaton: Crossway, 2004), 25; R. Muller, *Post-Reformation Reformed Dogmatics* Vol. 3 (Grand Rapids: Baker, 2003), 411–36; R. Olson, *Arminian Theology* (Downers Grove, IL: IVP, 2006), 194–99; and R. E. Picirilli, *Grace, Faith, Free Will* (Nashville: Randall House, 2002), 62–63. W. Grudem (*Systematic Theology* [Grand Rapids: Zondervan, 1994], 348–49) calls Molinism a type of Arminianism but says that in many ways it more resembles Calvinism.

[7]A. Plantinga, *God, Freedom, and Evil* (Grand Rapids: Eerdmans, 1977); T. P. Flint, *Divine Providence: the Molinist Account* (Ithaca: Cornell University Press, 1998); and W. L. Craig, *The Only Wise God* (Grand Rapids: Baker, 1987).

[8]Quoted in Flint, *Divine Providence*, 75.

[9]W. L. Craig, "The Middle Knowledge View," in *Divine Foreknowledge: Four Views*, ed. J. K Beilby and P. R. Eddy (Downers Grove: InterVarsity, 2001), 125–36.

Molinism: A Middle Way between Calvinism and Arminianism:	
The five "Calvinistic" tenets of Molinism	**The five "Arminian" tenets of Molinism**
1. God controls all things.	1. God is not the author of sin.
2. Man does not contribute to his salvation.	2. God desires the salvation of all.
3. God is Author and Completer of salvation.	3. Christ died for all people.
4. Individual election is unconditional.	4. God's grace is resistible.
5. The believer is eternally secure in Christ.	5. At crucial times, humans have the ability to choose.

So why do I embrace Molinism? Because, like the Calvinist, I am convinced the Bible teaches that (1) God is sovereign and His control is meticulous; (2) man is incapable of contributing to his salvation or of even desiring to be saved; (3) God through Christ is Author, Accomplisher, and Completer of salvation (i.e., salvation is a work of grace from beginning to end); (4) individual election is unconditional; and (5) the believer is secure in Christ.

However, like the Arminian, I am also convinced the Bible teaches that (6) God is not the Author, Origin, or Cause of sin (and to say that He is, is not just hyper-Calvinism but blasphemy); (7) God genuinely desires the salvation of all humanity; (8) Christ genuinely died for all people; (9) God's grace is resistible (this means that regeneration does not precede conversion); and (10) humans genuinely choose, are causal agents, and are responsible for the sin of rejecting Christ (this means that the alternative of accepting salvation was genuinely available to the unbeliever). As we will see, there is only one position that coherently holds to all ten affirmations, and that is Molinism.

THE ARGUMENT OF THIS BOOK

What This Book Argues For and Against	
This books argues for: 1. *Molinism*—a model of divine sovereignty/human responsibility. 2. *ROSES*—a model for the doctrines of salvation.	**This book argues against:** 1. *Fatalism*—i.e., all choices are understood in terms of necessity. 2. *Determinism*—i.e., all choices are understood in terms of causation.

Two arguments will be made throughout this book: (1) the Molinist paradigm presents the best model for understanding the relationship between God's sovereignty and human responsibility, and (2) the ROSES framework provides the best way of applying Molinism to the doctrines of salvation.[10]

In addition I will argue against two concepts generally associated with Reformed theology: that (1) God's perfections and infinite attributes require that all events and choices are understood in terms of necessity, and that (2) God's sovereignty and/or man's depravity require that all choices, decisions, and actions are understood in terms of causal determinism. *Necessity*, as it relates to the matter of human choice, is the notion that since God knows beforehand whatever decisions a person will make, the possibility of choosing otherwise is never available. *Causal determinism* is a specific type of necessity that argues that the choices made by a person are determined by his particular make-up and his given setting. In other words, a person's choices are determined by his nature and environment, so he does not have the ability to choose otherwise. This work will argue that God's omniscience does not forbid contingency, and in fact, the concept of "possibility" is clearly a biblical notion. In addition, the Bible teaches that because we are created in the image of God, we are *causal agents*—we are the origin of our respective decisions for which we are morally responsible.

The Reformed view of providence which embraces causal determinism has been given the (rather misleading) label of *compatibilism* (also

---

[10]Molinism does not entail the ROSES model, but I hope to show they fit together so much like hand in glove that it is appropriate to view the first as segueing to the second.

often called *soft determinism*). Compatibilism views human freedom as compatible with causal determinism (hence the term "compatibilism"), but only after redefining free will. Human freedom is understood merely to be the *freedom of inclination* (i.e., the freedom to do what you want). Therefore many Calvinists argue for casual determinism, through which God's will is the cause of all things.

Against compatibilism, I argue for a Molinist understanding of the interaction between God's sovereignty and human choice. Molinism understands God to carry out His sovereign plans through His exhaustive foreknowledge. It views man's freedom as the *freedom to refrain* (i.e., the freedom to choose something or refrain from choosing that thing) and sees him as the causal agent of his decisions. This is known as *soft libertarianism* or *concurrence*. The attractiveness of Molinism is that it presents a logically coherent view of providence, which holds that God is meticulously sovereign, while at the same time humans are genuinely free. In short, this book affirms divine sovereignty but rejects universal necessity; it affirms the reality of human depravity but rejects causal determinism. We will discuss these matters further in the chapter on radical depravity (chap. 3).

The Molinist Balancing of Six Pairs of Twin Truths

1. God is both good and great.
2. Human freedom is both derived and genuinely ours.
3. God's grace is both monergistic and resistible.
4. God's election is both unconditional and according to foreknowledge.
5. The saved are both preserved and will persevere.
6. Christ's atonement is both unlimited in its provision and limited in its application.

As the quote by Balthasar Hubmaier which began this introduction points out, to emphasize one biblical truth to the exclusion of others is to embrace a half-truth. If one focuses on the electing decree of divine sovereignty to the exclusion of human choice, then the result is a type of Calvinism of the double-predestination variety. If one decides that human moral responsibility requires the absolute ability to choose to the contrary, then this results in a radical form of Arminianism called Open Theism, which denies that God always knows what free creatures will decide to do. The Molinist reconciliation of divine sovereignty and human freedom provides a model for affirming six pairs of twin truths that the Bible presents in tandem. And it does so in such a way that does not eclipse one truth with the other. The first pair of truths—that God is both good and great—operates as an interpretive or hermeneutical principle which necessitates the next five pairs.

First, *God is both good and great.* The fact that not all are saved raises the question of why this is so. Did God not want them saved? Was He not able to save all? Some might try to answer this question by arguing that we cannot apply human definitions of goodness to God. I agree in principle. However, that is not what we are doing when we argue that one cannot sacrifice God's character on the altar of His attributes and vice versa. God is the One who reveals Himself as good, and in addition He reveals what divine goodness is through both the Scriptures and His Son. In fact, the Incarnation indicates that we may have a better understanding of God's goodness than we have about His greatness. The Bible reveals to us much more about God's character than it does about how God's infinite attributes operate. Since we were created in His image, by grace we can bear some semblance to God's character—His love, mercy, and integrity—in spite of the fall. However, as for His omnipresence, omniscience, and other infinite attributes, we have no real way to relate to or comprehend them. In short, we cannot subsume God's love to His sovereignty and vice versa. We address the proper handling of this first pair of truths in the chapter on God's universal salvific will (chap 2).

Second, *human freedom is both derived and genuinely ours.* Scripture does not present human freedom as something absolute, unlimited, or autonomous. However, God fashioned us in His image, and one important aspect of the *imago dei* is the real ability to choose. The Bible presents freedom in two ways—as a permission and as a power. Liberty is permission to make certain choices, while free will is the ability or power to make those choices. We will examine the nature of human freedom and how the fall has drastically affected our freedom in the chapter on radical depravity (chap 3).

Third, *God's grace is both monergistic and resistible.* Now *monergism* is an important term with which many may not be familiar. Basically it means that God is the only worker and accomplisher of our redemption. The concept emphasizes the complete graciousness of our salvation. Yet generally those who hold to monergism have had a difficult time explaining why many reject the gospel or why Christians continue to commit sins after they are born again without making it appear that God secretly desires the unbelief of the Christ-rejecter or the disobedience of the Christian. In the chapter on overcoming grace (chap 4), we will look at a model that proposes that God's grace simultaneously is unilateral and resistible. God is entirely responsible for salvation; humans are entirely responsible for sin.

Fourth, *God's election is both unconditional and according to foreknowledge.* Most Calvinists affirm that God actively ordains the salvation of the elect but merely permits the damnation of the unbeliever. This book will argue that any Calvinist who uses the concept of permission is in practice already a Molinist, even if he does not know it, or else he uses "permission" in such a way that renders the term meaningless. Molinism argues that God's sovereign choice is informed by foreknowledge but not determined by it. Even Calvinists believe that foreknowledge plays some role in predestination. As Reformed theologian John Frame points out, God did not foreordain this world while in a state of ignorance.[11] Molinists agree with Calvinists that it is crucial to maintain that God did not elect on account of foreknown merit or foreseen faith. A number of self-described Arminians also identify themselves as Molinists, but when we look at how Molina dealt with election in his interpretation of Romans 9, it will be clear that Molinism is not merely a variation of Arminianism. In the chapter on sovereign election (chap 5), I argue that, relating to the difficult matter of predestination, Molinism has advantages over both Calvinism and Arminianism.

Fifth, *the saved are both preserved and will persevere.* The Bible teaches that not all who claim to be a Christian go to heaven. As we will see, formulating a doctrine of assurance of salvation which takes this fact

---

[11] J. Frame, *The Doctrine of God: A Theology of Lordship* (Phillipsburg, NJ: P&R, 2002), 338.

into account is a challenge that bedevils both Calvinists and Arminians. In the chapter on eternal life (chap 6), this book proposes a model of assurance that affirms that everyone who trusts Christ for salvation is securely preserved and that every saved person possesses a faith that is guaranteed to remain.

Sixth, *Christ's atonement is both unlimited in its provision and limited in its application*. Often, the debate over the extent of the atonement has been cast as being between the general and particular views (i.e., that Christ died universally for everyone in general or that he paid only for the specific sins of each individual believer). Usually, general atonement is associated with Arminianism while Calvinism is understood to require the particular view. However, not all Calvinists hold to limited atonement. Many Calvinists believe Christ died provisionally for the specific and particular sins of all, but that the benefits are applied only to those who believe. Generally, Calvinists of this stripe distinguish their position from the Arminian view of general atonement by calling their position "unlimited atonement." The chapter on singular redemption (chap 7) will argue for the unlimited atonement of Christ, and that it is sufficient for all but efficient only for those who believe.

As we said, the first pair of twin truths—of God's goodness and greatness—operates as a hermeneutical principle for interpreting what the Bible teaches about salvation. This book is about salvation and the sovereignty of God: the sovereign Creator lovingly saves the fallen creature by paying the creature's sin-debt on a cruel tree. The remaining five pairs of truths are the result of the application of the first pair and establish the ROSES paradigm.

SOME CAVEATS AS WE BEGIN

A Word about Mystery

I do not claim that this book is the final answer to every question concerning the mystery of salvation. Molinism is a model, a possible explanation that has abundant scriptural support. As we will see, the way it effectively synchronizes some of the most difficult biblical concepts makes Molinism very attractive. But the goal is not to explain that which

God has left unrevealed, but to demonstrate that it is not irrational to believe in the simultaneous existence of the sovereign God of the Bible and creatures endowed with genuine, responsible freedom.

At points, I will have to appeal to mystery. There is nothing wrong with that since the Bible leaves many aspects of salvation unexplained, and all approaches to soteriology eventually make the same appeal. The big difference is in where they locate mystery. There are limits to our explorations, but we cannot use our theological conclusions to negate the clear revelation of Scripture. On this both Calvinists and Molinists agree.

I concede to a number of mysteries pertaining to the matters covered in this book that will still be with us at the end. First, the mystery of evil remains. I provide no explanation for the origin of wickedness and unbelief, or why, when the real opportunity for redemption and righteousness avails itself, the majority of humanity turns it down. Unbelief amazed Jesus (Mark 6:6), so why should you and I expect to understand it?

Second, we do not know why God chose to create, or to "actualize," this particular world. Molinism posits that an infinite number of feasible worlds were available for God to create, but it provides no explanation for why He chose this one. There is good reason to believe we will have a better understanding of this mystery in the new heavens and the new earth. In the meantime, we trust in the wisdom and goodness of our Creator and Redeemer in His sovereign choice.

Third, how exactly God knows what free creatures will decide and choose remains unknown.[12] Some are bothered by this mystery, but I am not. God knows all things and omniscience is an attribute of God. God innately knows our free choices by His very nature—by the very fact that He is God. Thus asking how God knows what genuinely free creatures will choose is the same as asking how it is that God is God. The mystery of God's omniscience simply does not keep me awake at night.

However, as the approach taken by the early Church to the Christological controversies demonstrates, affirming mystery is not the same as embracing illogical contradictions. In his book, *The Logic of God Incarnate*, Thomas Morris showed that the Councils were careful to

---

[12]As we will see in the chapter on sovereign election, this mystery is known as "the grounding objection" (i.e., what are the grounds for God's knowledge of our choices?).

describe the mystery of the hypostatic union of Christ in such a way that did not involve a logical contradiction.[13] For example, the early Fathers declared Jesus to "truly" and "genuinely" possess the essential attributes of each nature, rather than saying that Christ was "totally" and "completely" human or divine. Such nuances are necessary to avoid gibberish. There is a place for mystery. However, in the divine sovereignty/human responsibility paradox, sometimes my Calvinist brethren appeal to mystery in order to avoid the harsh and contradictory conclusions of their own system. "Mystery" and "contradiction" are not synonyms.

A Word about the Nature of the Debate

In this work I take issue with my Calvinist brethren on a number of points. If in any way I am unfair or harsh, I sincerely apologize. My desire is to follow the admonition of C. S. Lewis, who said that we are to argue *towards* the truth, rather than *about* the truth.[14] In other words, the purpose of this discussion is not to win but to arrive at a better understanding of the biblical witness. We are brethren, not adversaries, working in a mutual effort. Until we cross the veil, none of us has arrived on the journey of faith. So I look forward to this cooperative effort, convinced that the end result will be that we are better and more faithful witnesses of our common salvation. Calvinism and Molinism are much more similar than they are dissimilar, so I endeavor to avoid what might be called the narcissism of trivial differences.

A Word about Getting Lost in the Theological Minutiae

There are places in this book where precise definitions and nuanced arguments become necessary. I'm sorry about that. Namely, this work contends that (contrary to the teachings of many in Reformed circles) God's sovereignty cannot be understood in terms of necessity, nor can human actions be defined in terms of causal determinism. Proponents of these positions often argue that determinism is compatible with human free will, but they have to radically redefine freedom in order to make

---

[13]T. V. Morris, *The Logic of God Incarnate* (Ithaca: Cornell, 1986).

[14]This point was made by Walter Hooper. See W. Hooper, "C.S. Lewis: Reflections about the Man." Lecture, Southeastern Baptist Theological Seminary, Wake Forest, NC. October 26, 2007. Available at http://www.sebts.edu/news-resources/multimedia.aspx?type=culture&Vid=110.

such a claim. I argue that we must affirm God's ultimate sovereignty and man's genuine ownership of his choices in such a way that does not play fast and loose with the definitions of either truth. I will make the case for a *middle knowledge* approach to God's sovereignty and a *soft libertarian* understanding of human choice—terms which hopefully will become clearer in the upcoming chapters. The arguments presented necessarily will be nuanced, but I will do my best to make my case as clearly and simply as possible.

There is a concern that the discussion of details can appear cold. Sometimes the use of precise argumentation can seem to be a detached fixation on minutiae. However, like a mother reading the fine print concerning the medicine she is about to give her sick child or a man studying the schematics for a house he is building for his family, the focus on the details can also be an act of devotion. That is my intent. God loved me while I was a stranger, and Christ died for me when I was His enemy. This is a work of "faith seeking understanding" and is written in the spirit of P. P. Bliss's hymn "Hallelujah! What a Savior."

> *Man of Sorrows!" what a name*
> *For the Son of God who came.*
> *Ruined sinners to reclaim!*
> *Hallelujah! What a Savior!*
>
> *Guilty, vile and helpless we,*
> *Spotless Lamb of God was He;*
> *"Full atonement!" can it be?*
> *Hallelujah! What a Savior!*
>
> *"Lifted up" was He to die,*
> *"It is finished," was His cry;*
> *Now in heav'n exalted high;*
> *Hallelujah! what a Savior!*
>
> *When He comes, our glorious King,*
> *All His ransomed home to bring,*
> *Then anew this song we'll sing;*
> *Hallelujah! what a Savior!*

CHAPTER 1

THE BIBLICAL CASE FOR MOLINISM

Without God we cannot, without us, he will not.
—Augustine of Hippo

*Take away free will and there will be nothing left to save; take
away grace and there will be no means left of salvation.*
—Bernard of Clairvaux[1]

MOLINISTS ARGUE THAT God perfectly accomplishes His will in the lives of genuinely free creatures through the use of His omniscience. The model they propose presents God's infinite knowledge as a series of three logical moments: God's *natural knowledge*, *middle knowledge*, and *free knowledge*.

It is important to keep in mind that these three moments are a logical sequence, not a chronological sequence. Since God is omniscient, He innately knows all things—this means He does not go through the mental processes that finite beings do of "figuring things out." God never "learns" or has things "occur" to Him. He already knows all truths. The fact that God is omniscient does not merely mean that God is infinitely more knowledgeable than us, but that His knowledge is of a different type and quality. So the three moments of God's knowledge proposed by Molinism refer to logical order, not a sequence in time.

There is nothing unique to Molinism about understanding God's knowledge in terms of moments. Reformed theologians also describe God's knowledge as a series of logical moments, as we will see in the chapter on sovereign election. Nor was Molina the first to argue for three moments. Previously, the medieval theologians Duns Scotus and Thomas Aquinas had done so in their respective presentations of divine omniscience. But Molina was the first to demonstrate that the three-moment

---

[1] Augustine quoted by D. G. Bloesch, *The Last Things: Resurrection, Judgment, Glory*. Christian Foundations, vol. 7 (Downers Grove, IL: InterVarsity, 2004), 174; Bernard quoted by T. C. Oden, *The Transforming Power of Grace* (Abingdon: Nashville, 1993), 114.

model provided a way of reconciling divine sovereignty with human freedom that genuinely did justice to both truths.

MOLINISM IN A NUTSHELL

The Three Moments of Molinism in Terms of "Could," "Would," and "Will" *God uses His omniscience to perfectly accomplish His will.*		
1st Moment: God's Natural Knowledge	*"Could"* Everything that could happen	God knows all possibilities.
2nd Moment: God's Middle Knowledge	*"Would"* Everything that would happen	God knows which possibilities are feasible.
Between 2nd & 3rd moment: *God freely and sovereignly chooses this particular world from the infinite number of feasible possibilities.*		
3rd Moment: God's Free Knowledge	*"Will"* Everything that will happen	God exhaustively knows all things.

The Three Moments of Molinism in Terms of Could, Would, and Will

So how does Molinism understand the three moments of God's knowledge to work? For the purposes at hand we are going to simplify things a bit.[2] Consider the three phases in terms of *could*, *would*, and *will*. The first moment of God's omniscience is His natural knowledge: He knows all possibilities, everything that could happen. He knows what reality would be like if He had created a world without you or me in it, or never created anything or anyone at all. These fully formed possible scenarios are generally called *possible worlds*. There is an infinite upon

---

[2]If one wishes for a more thorough yet accessible presentation of Molinism, see W. L. Craig, *The Only Wise God* (Grand Rapids: Baker, 1987). For a more technical study see T. P. Flint, *Divine Providence: A Molinist Account* (Ithaca: Cornell Univ. Press, 1998).

infinite number of possible permutations of how things could have been. Just contemplating such a notion is overwhelming for us but poses no problem for God.

Now let's jump to the third moment: God's free knowledge. This is His perfect knowledge of the world—this world—that He chose to "actualize" (i.e., create). Molina referred to this third moment as "free" because it is the result of God's free, sovereign decision to bring this particular world into existence. Of the infinite possibilities available to God, He was under no compulsion to choose this one. Yet He chose a world that contains free moral agents—angels and humans—who make genuinely free decisions. How is He able to infallibly accomplish His will in a world in which other moral agents besides Him exist? This brings up the crucial notion of God's middle knowledge.

Within His natural knowledge of all possibilities—everything that *could* happen—God possesses a perfect knowledge of all feasible worlds—all possibilities which *would* accomplish what He wanted to have happen. This knowledge of all viable possibilities is "located" (so to speak) between God's natural and free knowledge—and hence the term middle knowledge. God's middle knowledge contains all of the choices and decisions that free creatures would do if they were created in a particular world. When God chooses to actualize one of these feasible worlds, He knows certainly what *will* happen. Notice: *could*, *would*, and *will*.

So to sum up: from the infinite set of possible worlds that *could* happen (God's natural knowledge), there is an infinite subset of feasible worlds which *would* accomplish His will (God's middle knowledge). God freely chooses one of the feasible worlds, and He perfectly knows what *will* happen in this actual world (God's free knowledge). In the Molinist model, God sovereignly controls all things, yet humans possess real freedom for which they must give an account. We will give more attention to the Molinist understanding of the divine sovereignty/human responsibility relationship in the chapter on sovereign election.

Is Molinism Merely a Philosophical System?

But just how biblical is the notion of understanding God's omniscience in terms of logical moments? How strong of a scriptural case for Molinism can be made? This chapter argues two points: (1) the ingredients that seem to necessitate Molinism are provided by the Bible; and (2) rather than being exotic examples of metaphysics, "possible world" concepts are notions we use and understand in everyday life. The ideas central to Molinism—such as possible scenarios and counterfactuals—are not strange at all. Rather, we find that they are contained within the very grammar of the Bible.[3]

If Molinism were simply the overlaying of a philosophical grid on top of Scripture, then it would be a very bad idea and should not be done. Rather, Molinism is a precise philosophical system that arose out of a commitment to certain principles clearly taught in the Bible: (1) God can and has created beings with significant and genuine creaturely freedom; (2) God can and does exhaustively know what free creatures would do in every possible scenario; and (3) God can and does sovereignly and meticulously accomplish His will through His omniscience—namely that aspect of His knowledge we call middle knowledge.

The Bible teaches a high view of divine sovereignty: God has exhaustive knowledge of all things, meticulous control over all things, sovereign freedom above all things, and yet at the same time He is perfectly free from the sin and evil of this world. Scripture also declares a robust view of human freedom, choice, and agency: there are contingent events; certain contingent events are conditioned by our decisions; and God uses His counterfactual knowledge of our free decisions to accomplish His will. Molinism—and its advocacy of the concept of middle knowledge—is the one view of providence that holds to a consistent view of both biblical teachings.

---

[3]As Craig points out, middle knowledge is a reasonable inference from the witness of Scripture. He states, "Does God, then, possess middle knowledge? It would be difficult to prove in any direct way that he does, for the biblical passages are not unequivocal. Nevertheless, the doctrine is so fruitful in illuminating divine prescience, providence, and predestination that it can be presumed unless there are insoluble objections to it." W. L. Craig, *The Only Wise God*, 137.

The Biblical Teaching Concerning Divine Sovereignty and Human Freedom	
Concerning God's Sovereignty:	**Concerning Human Freedom:**
1. God exhaustively knows all things. 2. God perfectly controls all things. 3. God is free from all things. He does not choose out of necessity. 4. God is holy and righteous in all things. He is not the cause of sin.	1. Contingency—certain things could have been otherwise. 2. Conditionality—some contingent choices are placed before humans. 3. Counterfactuals—statements which predict the outcome of contingent choices, even the results of choices not made

GOD'S SOVEREIGN LORDSHIP OVER ALL THINGS

Scripture makes clear declarations concerning God's sovereignty: God rules over all His creation and is without equal or opponent. He is the unambiguous sovereign Lord over Creation. Divine sovereignty entails four biblical truths: (1) God knows all things, (2) He controls all things, (3) He is free from all things, and (4) He is holy and righteous in all things.

God Has Exhaustive Knowledge of All Things

In Hannah's prayer of dedication for her son, the prophet Samuel, she declares, "The LORD is a God of knowledge, and actions are weighed by Him" (1 Sam 2:3). The psalmist agrees and proclaims, "Our Lord is great, vast in power; His understanding is infinite" (Ps 147:5). The Bible teaches that God has omniscient knowledge of all that was, is, will be, and could have been. God knows all truths, and the extent of His knowledge is universal. First, *God has exhaustive knowledge of the present.* Whether it is about the stars in the sky (Ps 147:4; Job 38:31–33; Isa 40:26) or the creatures below (Matt 10:29–30), God has complete and comprehensive knowledge about everything in the heavens and the earth.

Nothing escapes His attentive gaze (Job 24:23; 28:12–27; Ps 33:13–15; Jer 16:17).

Second, *God has exhaustive knowledge of the future.* Through Isaiah, the Lord asserts, "I declare the end from the beginning, and from long ago what is not yet done" (Isa 46:10). The Bible contrasts the Lord's ability to foretell the future with the failure of the pagan idols and holds up fulfilled prophecy as proof that Israel's God is the one true God worthy of worship and obedience (Isa 41:21–24; 44:6–8). Moses declared that the litmus test for a prophet was his ability to perfectly forecast the future (Deut 18:22). God's perfect knowledge of the future demonstrates that history has a purpose that He is accomplishing through His Son Jesus Christ (Dan 2:36–43; Acts 2:23; 3:18; Gal 3:8; Eph 1:10; 3:9–11; 2 Tim 1:9–10; 1 Pet 1:20).

Third, *God has exhaustive knowledge of things that involve other agents.* There is nothing about you and me that God does not know. As Job asks, "Does He not see my ways and number all my steps?" (Job 31:4). God does not merely make very good guesses about us; He knows everything about us—our thoughts and our actions (1 Sam 16:7; 1 Kgs 8:39; 1 Chr 28:9; Pss 7:9; 94:11; 139:23–24; Jer 17:9–10). The Lord knows the very intent of our hearts (Acts 1:24; 15:8; Rom 8:27; 1 Cor 4:5; 1 John 3:19–20). The author of Hebrews tells us that God's knowledge of us is so comprehensive that "no creature is hidden from Him, but all things are naked and exposed to the eyes of Him to whom we must give an account" (Heb 4:13).

God Has Meticulous Control over All Things

As John Frame puts it, "Nothing is too hard for God (Jer 32:27); nothing seems marvelous to him (Zech 8:6); with him nothing is impossible (Gen 18:14; Matt 19:26; Luke 1:37). So his purposes will always prevail."[4] The Lord declares His sovereignty: "See now that I alone am He; there is no god but me. I bring death and I give life; I wound and I heal. No one can rescue from my hand" (Deut 32:39 NIV).

---

[4]J. M. Frame, *The Doctrine of God: A Theology of Lordship* (Phillipsburg, NJ: P&R, 2002), 48.

First, *God has meticulous control over big things.* Without qualification, God asserts His sovereign power over all creation. The psalmist
declares, "The LORD does whatever He pleases in heaven and on earth, in
the seas and all the depths" (Ps 135:6). He is able to perfectly accomplish
His will because He wields irresistible power and authority. Just a few
representative verses are needed to establish the teaching of Scripture
concerning His dominion:

> The LORD frustrates the counsel of the nations; He thwarts the
> plans of the peoples. The counsel of the LORD stands forever, the
> plans of His heart from generation to generation. (Ps 33:10–11)

> The LORD of Hosts has sworn: As I have planned, so it will be; as
> I have purposed it, so it will happen. (Isa 14:24)

> This is the plan prepared for the whole earth, and this is the hand
> stretched out against all the nations. The LORD of Hosts Himself
> has planned it; therefore, who can stand in its way? It is His hand
> that is outstretched, so who can turn it back? (Isa 14:26–27)

> I declare the end from the beginning, and from long ago what is
> not yet done, saying: My plan will take place, and I will do all
> My will. (Isa 46:10)

> All the inhabitants of the earth are counted as nothing, and He
> does what He wants with the army of heaven and the inhabitants
> of the earth. There is no one who can hold back His hand or say
> to Him, "What have You done?" (Dan 4:35)

> From one man He has made every nation of men to live all
> over the earth and has determined their appointed times and the
> boundaries of where they live. (Acts 17:26)

The Lord, as the sovereign most high King reigns over all creation,
which is His alone, and He does with it as He determines (1 Chr 29:11;
Pss 9; 24:1; 47:2,7–9; 93; 95:3–5; 104; 115:3; Isa 45:9–12; Ezek 17:4;
Rev 1:8; 4:8,11).

Second, *God has meticulous control over little things.* Many Christians affirm God's general providence (i.e., His control over big things) but have difficulty affirming His control over specific and mundane matters (i.e., His control over little things). However, the Bible teaches both that God has overarching control over Creation for the ultimate fulfillment of His plans and that also He exerts meticulous command of the minutest details.

Solomon declares, "The lot is cast into the lap, but its every decision is from the LORD" (Prov 16:33). This means every roll of the dice, every flip of the coin, and every seemingly random event is overseen by the fastidious providence of God. That which appears chaotic and haphazard, that which appears to be the product of meaningless chance is under the purview of divine control.

The Bible presents God's scrupulous providence as a source of comfort and encouragement. Our Savior admonishes us, "Aren't two sparrows sold for a penny? Yet not one of them falls to the ground without your Father's consent. But even the hairs of your head have all been counted" (Matt 10:29–30). It is Paul's confidence in God's sovereign control that allows him to declare, "We know that all things work together for the good of those who love God: those who are called according to His purpose" (Rom 8:28). God accomplishes His ultimate purposes, and He does so through His meticulous strategies in human history. He has determined both the means and ends of His will—over both the big and little things of life. Charles Spurgeon, the great Baptist preacher, declared:

> I believe that every particle of dust that dances in the sunbeam
> does not move an atom more or less than God wishes,—that
> every particle of spray that dashes against the steamboat has its
> orbit as well as the sun in the heavens,—that the chaff from the
> hand of the winnower is steered as surely as the stars in their
> courses,—that the creeping of an aphis over over a rosebud is as
> much fixed as the march of the devastating pestilence, and the fall
> of sere leaves from the poplar is as fully ordained as the tumbling
> of an avalanche. He who believes in God must believe this truth.[5]

---

[5]C. H. Spurgeon, "God's Providence," *The Metropolitan Tabernacle Pulpit* (Pasadena: Pilgrim Pub., [1908] 1978), 502. My attention was directed to this sermon by an unpublished paper by Thomas McCall of Trinity Evangelical Divinity School.

With Spurgeon let's also affirm our confidence in God's intricate providence.

Third, *God has meticulous control over things that involve other agents*. Again, Solomon lets us know that, not only does God have control over the littlest of details, but He even has control in matters where other free moral agents—angels and humans—are involved. Solomon declares, "A king's heart is a water channel in the LORD's hand: He directs it wherever He chooses" (Prov 21:1). The classic example of God working His will through the actions of humans—even evil actions—is that of Joseph's brothers selling him into slavery. Twenty years after they committed the deed, Joseph makes a declaration that reveals his remarkable confidence in God's meticulous control:

> And now don't be worried or angry with yourselves for selling
> me here, because God sent me ahead of you to preserve life. For
> the famine has been in the land these two years, and there will
> be five more years without plowing or harvesting. God sent me
> ahead of you to establish you as a remnant within the land and to
> keep you alive by a great deliverance. Therefore it was not you
> who sent me here, but God. (Gen 45:5–8)

Nothing about what Joseph said to his brothers absolved them from their sin. In fact, it is just the opposite. Later, he states, "You planned evil against me; God planned it for good to bring about the present result— the survival of many people" (Gen 50:20). God concurrently accomplished His plans through Joseph's brothers.

When God determined to judge Israel for its idolatry and rebellion, He used the pagan nations surrounding Israel to do it. Isaiah presents Assyria as a weapon of punishment in the hands of God:

> Woe to Assyria, the rod of My anger—the staff in their hands is
> My wrath. I will send him against a godless nation; I will com-
> mand him [to go] against a people destined for My rage, to take
> spoils, to plunder, and to trample them down like clay in the
> streets. (Isa 10:5–6)

Then, remarkably, after God accomplishes His will through the evil designs of Assyria, God in turn judges Assyria!

> But when the Lord finishes all His work against Mount Zion and
> Jerusalem, [He will say,] "I will punish the king of Assyria for
> his arrogant acts and the proud look in his eyes. For he said: 'I
> have done [this] by my own strength and wisdom, for I am clever.
> I abolished the borders of nations and plundered their treasures;
> like a mighty warrior, I subjugated the inhabitants.' . . . Does
> an ax exalt itself above the one who chops with it? Does a saw
> magnify itself above the one who saws with it? As if a staff could
> wave those who lift it! As if a rod could lift what isn't wood!"
> (Isa 10:12–13,15)

Isaiah clearly teaches that the God of Israel can and does control other free moral agents as surely as a workman controls his tools.

But the ultimate example of God's meticulous control in the decisions and actions of other moral agents is the crucifixion of Jesus Christ. On the day of Pentecost, Simon Peter declared to Israel, "Though He was delivered up according to God's determined plan and foreknowledge, you used lawless people to nail Him to a cross and kill Him" (Acts 2:23). Later, Luke records the early church as praying, "For, in fact, in this city both Herod and Pontius Pilate, with the Gentiles and the peoples of Israel, assembled together against Your holy Servant Jesus, whom You anointed, to do whatever Your hand and Your plan had predestined to take place" (Acts 4:27–28). Through sinful men, God accomplished the offering of His Son for the sins of men.

God Has Sovereign Freedom from All Things

Now here is an interesting thing: a proper understanding of God's sovereignty requires the notion of *contingency*. The Lord's sovereignty over Creation requires that it places no constraints upon Him. Contingency is the concept that things "could have been otherwise." There are at least three reasons why the notion of contingency is crucial: (1) God created freely; (2) God is not the author of sin; and (3) God permits rather than causes the damnation of the unbeliever. We will look at the first two points now and address the third in the chapter on sovereign election. The important thing to realize is that contingency is an integral, essential component to a correct view of God as Creator.

In regards to Creation, God enjoys *aseity* and *freedom*. One cannot properly conceive of these divine attributes without using the concept of contingency.[6] God's aseity is His complete independence and sufficiency within Himself. God did not create the universe because He was lonely or because He needed the world. He did not create the world to meet any need or fulfill any lack. The Triune Godhead is perfect and is perfectly self-sufficient. If the Lord had never created, it would not have detracted from the glory of any of His perfections. His act of creation was completely gratuitous. God enjoys sovereign aseity over the world. God is the necessary being; Creation is contingent.

Similarly, God's freedom is His sovereign independence from any obligation to the world. God's aseity means He did not create because of need while His freedom means He did not create because of obligation. Taken together, the doctrines teach that Creation is contingent, and could have been otherwise. When God created the heavens and the earth, He did so freely, without any necessity or compulsion upon Him. Nothing internal or external compelled Him to create this or any other world. God had the freedom to choose not to create. By definition, the ability or power to choose or to refrain from choosing is what is called *libertarian freedom*. So a proper understanding of God's sovereignty requires the corresponding concept of contingency, and this necessitates understanding God's freedom in libertarian terms. This means that it is reasonable to speak of contingencies and possibilities.

God Has Perfect Righteousness and Holiness in All Things (the Arrival of Evil)

The great mystery, of course, is how, in a world created by the God of the Bible, evil could arrive. But the existence of evil is a present reality. The Bible is explicit in its declaration that, though God is the sovereign Ruler over all, He is not the origin or cause of evil. At various times heretical groups (such as the Gnostics and the Manichees) have tried to present God as the author of sin, but the apostle John forbids such a notion, declaring that "God is light, and there is absolutely no darkness in

---

[6]J. W. Richards, *The Untamed God* (Downers Grove: InterVarsity, 2003), 15–16.

Him" (1 John 1:5b). Similarly, James tells us we can never say that God is the source of our temptations or our sins (Jas 1:13–15). Even though He is the origin of the elements that made evil possible (namely, the granting of significant freedom to morally responsible creatures), and even though He often accomplishes His will through the evil that free moral agents commit (Gen 50:20), He is perfectly righteous and holy in all things.

How can this be? This is because the Bible presents God's relationship with iniquity as one of *permission*. The notion of God's permissive relationship to evil permeates the Bible. For example, when Satan challenged Job's fidelity to God, the Lord replies, "Very well . . . he is in your power; only spare his life" (Job 2:6). God allowed Satan to attack Job within certain constraints.

The Gospels present our Lord's interaction with evil to be of permission. When Jesus cast the legion of demons out of the man of Gadara, they made a surprising request. "The demons begged Him, 'Send us to the pigs, so we may enter them.' And He gave them *permission* [*epitrepō*; emphasis added]." Then the unclean spirits came out and entered the pigs, and the herd of about 2,000 rushed down the steep bank into the sea and drowned there" (Mark 5:12–13).

The Savior very carefully uses the concept of permission in His discussion with the Pharisees about divorce. When He presents marriage as a lifelong commitment to one mate, the Pharisees ask, "Why then did Moses command us to give divorce papers and to send her away?" Jesus replies, "Moses *permitted* [emphasis added] you to divorce your wives because of the hardness of your hearts. But it was not like that from the beginning" (Matt 19:7–8). Jesus changed their description of Moses' teaching from "command" to "permit." The notion of permission is crucial for understanding that God does not necessitate or cause sin, wickedness, or unbelief. As we will see in the chapter on sovereign election, the concept of permission plays a crucial part in our understanding of the predestination of the lost (i.e., what is commonly called *reprobation*).

CREATION AND CREATURELY FREEDOM

The discussion of the arrival of evil brings us to the second biblical doctrine that points to Molinism: the bestowal of genuine creaturely freedom upon angels and humans. Scripture declares that men are morally responsible before God for their disobedience, even when the Lord had already prophesied what sins a particular human was going to commit. Consider Judas Iscariot's betrayal and Simon Peter's denial of Christ. The actions of both men had already been predicted by God (Ps 41:9; Matt 26:34). Their choices were certain, yet free. How Molinism understands God to work His will through free creatures is summed up in three concepts: *contingency*, *conditionality*, and *counterfactuals*. The Bible gives us numerous examples of all three.

Contingency

Contingency, simply put, is the notion that something could have been otherwise. A contingent truth is something that happens to be true but obviously could have been false. I am writing these words while in a cabin in the Missouri Ozarks, but I could have worked elsewhere this week, such as in my office in North Carolina. If a statement is contingently true, then that means the alternative was genuinely possible.

Philosophers and theologians often speak of contingency in terms of *modal logic*. Terms like "contingency" and "modal" seem imposing, but they really refer to ways of thinking we use in everyday life. Modal logic is the systematic study of common terms such as "might," "must," "possibly," "necessarily," "ought to," "have to," and "could not have done otherwise." We have a pretty good intuitive sense of what these expressions mean, but working out the relationship between these concepts can be difficult.[7] So sometimes when Molinists use modal logic and "possible worlds" language to present their case for middle knowledge, their arguments sound alien and stilted. But actually they are simply attempting to be precise. The underlying concepts of contingency and possibility are

---

[7] Richards, *The Untamed God*, 48–51.

familiar and universal. More importantly for the matter at hand, they are commonly used by the writers of Scripture.[8]

Old Testament Examples of Contingency   One does not have to search hard to find examples. In a number of places, the Old Testament presents God's dealings with men in contingent terms or presents certain occasions as contingent events. When the angels visited Lot in Sodom, their intention was to remain overnight in the public courtyard. They told Lot, "We would rather spend the night in the square." But he persuaded them to come to his house (Gen 19:2–3). The text indicates that an alternate scenario was possible, with the angels remaining outside.

When Samuel informed Saul that God had rejected him as king, he told him that it could have been otherwise. Samuel said to Saul, "You have been foolish. You have not kept the command which the LORD your God gave you. It was at this time that the LORD *would* [emphasis added] have permanently established your reign over Israel, but now your reign will not endure" (1 Sam 13:13–14). Samuel pointed out Saul's failure did not have to happen.

Second Kings 13 gives the intriguing account of Elisha's prophecy to King Joash while Elisha was on his deathbed. He instructed Joash to strike the ground with arrows as symbols of Israel's struggles with Syria. When the king hit the ground only three times, Elisha became furious. "You should have struck the ground five or six times," declared Elisha. "Then you would have struck down Aram until you had put an end to them, but now you will only strike down Aram three times" (2 Kgs 13:19). The opportunity for victory was genuinely offered, but Joash was too timid to take it. Elisha's reaction makes clear that Joash's hesitancy demonstrated his lack of faith in God's power and His promises. Triumph over the Aram was contingently available, but lost through unbelief.

---

[8]Molinists are not the only ones to find the concepts of contingency and permission indispensable. As Reformed theologian Herman Bavinck points out, when Calvinists address the matter of the predestination of the unbeliever and the origin of evil, they also must appeal to contingency. He states, "It also has to be granted that, though we can with good reason take exception to such terms as 'permission,' 'foreknowledge,' 'preterition,' and 'dereliction,' no one is able to come up with better ones. Even the most rigorous supralapsarian cannot dispense with these words, either from the pulpit or from behind an academic theological lectern." Bavinck goes on to say that in this matter even the staunchest Calvinist is "accordingly—and fortunately! . . . consistently inconsistent." H. Bavinck, *Reformed Dogmatics,* vol. 2, *God and Creation* (Grand Rapids: Baker, 2004), 387–88.

Isaiah 38:1–5 gives the account of King Hezekiah becoming terminally ill. Isaiah at first announced to Hezekiah that he should get his house in order. Unlike Joash, however, Hezekiah had no problem with timidity—he boldly prayed to God for a reprieve. So the Lord sent Isaiah back to inform him that his life had been given a 15-year extension.

In Amos 7:1–6, God shows the prophet his intention to judge Israel: first with a swarm of locusts, then with a consuming fire. Both times Amos interceded for Israel and as a result God relented.

New Testament Examples of Contingency   Not only is contingency a frequent theme of the Old Testament, but the Gospel records also present situations where the outcome could have been otherwise. In Jesus' hometown, miracles that He could have done were not done "because of their unbelief" (Matt 13:57–58). Mark's account of Jesus walking on the water has the surprising statement that before the disciples saw Him, Jesus "wanted to pass by them" (Mark 6:47–49)[9]. A similar comment is made about Jesus' walk with the Emmaus disciples. Luke says that when the disciples arrived at their destination Jesus "gave the impression[10] that He was going farther. But they urged Him: 'Stay with us, ... So He went in to stay with them" (Luke 24:28–29).

At times Jesus Himself declared that the opportunity for a different outcome was genuinely available. When Jesus wept over Jerusalem's unbelief He cried out, "Jerusalem, Jerusalem! The city who kills the prophets and stones those who are sent to her. How often I wanted to gather your children together, as a hen gathers her chicks under her wings, yet you were not willing!" (Matt 23:37). The way the Gospel writers place certainty and contingency side by side is remarkable.

The New Testament teaches that a Christian's relationship to sin is one of contingency. When Peter confronted Ananias and his wife concerning their deception about their offering, he asked, "Was it not under

---

[9]Although R. T. France acknowledges that the verb *thelō* "does of course denote intention," he considers that in the context "the clause is best seen not as a statement of what was in Jesus' mind but of how this approach appeared from the disciples' point of view" (*The Gospel of Mark*, NIGTC [Grand Rapids/Carlisle: Eerdmans/Paternoster, 2002], 272).

[10]According to BDAG (*A Greek-English Lexicon of the New Testament and other Christian Literature* by W. Bauer, W. F. Arndt, and F. W. Gingrich, rev. and ed. by F. W. Danker; 3rd ed.; Chicago and London: Univ. of Chicago Press, 2000), 884, the verb *prospoieō* used here means "to engage in an action or gesture that gives the appearance of conveying specific intent." The suggested translation given is "he made as though he were going farther."

your control?" (Acts 5:4 NASB). Simon's point was that Ananias possessed the libertarian ability to have chosen not to lie. Paul tells us that the ability to resist temptation is always available (1 Cor 10:13). Similarly, James declares we are not allowed to say that God causes our sin (Jas 1:13–15). Believers can never say they sinned out of necessity.

The "Foreknowledge Entails Necessity" Objection

At this point some lodge an objection against the concept of contingency, namely that God's foreknowledge of what choices an agent will make removes any possibility of that person making a different choice. If God knows you are going to choose cereal for breakfast tomorrow, then there is no possibility of you choosing otherwise. Therefore contingency must be an illusion, or at least merely hypothetical, and all choices are made of necessity. This position is called *theological fatalism.*[11]

Some theologians take this objection so seriously that they react by embracing *open theism*—which is theological fatalism's polar opposite. Open theism is the remarkable view that, in fact, God does not know what free creatures will choose or do. Some will say that, in order to have a genuine give-and-take relationship with us, God chooses to not possess exhaustive foreknowledge of all our choices. This is obviously contrary to the Scriptures we surveyed in the previous section. The Bible clearly teaches that God has comprehensive and perfect knowledge of all things, including future choices.

---

[11]Craig, *The Only Wise God*, 15. Martin Luther and Jonathan Edwards are two significant proponents of theological fatalism. Luther declared, "For I was wrong in saying that free choice before grace is a reality only in name. I should have said simply: free choice is in reality a fiction, or a term without reality. For no one has it in his power to think a good or bad thought, but everything (as Wyclif's article condemned at Constance rightly teaches) happens by absolute necessity." Quoted in R. Kolb, *Bound Choice, Election, and Wittenberg Theological Method* (Grand Rapids: Eerdmans, 2005), 11. Luther argued thusly, not because man is a sinner, but because man is a creature. Luther believed that in order to protect the freedom of God it was necessary to reject any type of creaturely freedom. He states, "Natural reason herself is forced to confess that the living and true God must be One who by His own liberty imposes necessity on us." Martin Luther, *The Bondage of the Will* (London: Camelot Press, [1525]1957), 216.

Ironically, necessity negates the very divine freedom that Luther intended to preserve. Jonathan Edwards took the next step when he argued that the logic of necessity demands that all of God's choices are determined, and even that God did not have the libertarian ability to choose otherwise. See Jonathan Edwards, "Freedom of the Will," in *The Works of Jonathan Edwards,* vol. 1 (Edinburgh: Banner of Truth, 1834), 69–75.

Molinists point out that the "foreknowledge entails necessity" objection of theological fatalism confuses necessity with certainty. Certainty is a property of persons. Necessity is a property of statements.[12] God knows all truths with certainty. In fact, God knows the contingent choices of free creatures necessarily, due to His omniscience. But God necessarily foreknowing an event does not entail or require that the event necessarily happens.

Jesus declared with certainty that Simon Peter would deny him three times, using divine knowledge He necessarily had. But it is important to have the arrow of necessity going in the right direction. God necessarily knew what decision Simon Peter would take. It was not necessary that Simon make a particular choice. Simon could have denied Christ twice or four times (or not at all), but necessarily Jesus would have correctly known Peter's response and prophesied accordingly.[13] Necessity is a property of God's ability to know all things, not of Simon Peter's choices.

A good example of the congruence of certainty with contingency is the account of Moses interceding before God on behalf of the people of Israel after they had worshiped the golden calf.

> The LORD also said to Moses: "I have seen this people, and they are indeed a stiff-necked people. Now leave Me alone, so that My anger can burn against them and I can destroy them. Then I will make you into a great nation." But Moses interceded with the LORD his God.... So the LORD changed His mind about the disaster He said He would bring on His people. (Exod 32:9–11,14)

Even when the anthropomorphic language of the text is taken into account, several things are clear.[14] God told Moses not to intercede

---

[12]K. R. MacGregor, *A Molinist-Anabaptist Systematic Theology* (Lanham: Univ. Press of America, 2007), 87–88. Cf. A. Plantinga, *God, Freedom and Evil* (New York: Harper & Row, 1974), 66–72. Craig points out that certainty, as a property of persons, does not necessarily have to have anything to do with truth. Necessity is a property of statements or propositions, indicating that a proposition cannot possibly be false. We can be certain about things that turn out to be false. By contrast, we can be uncertain about propositions, such as complex mathematical theorems, that we later discover to be necessarily true. Certainty is a property of persons. Necessity is a property of statements or propositions. W. L. Craig, "The Middle Knowledge View," in *Divine Foreknowledge: Four Views,* ed. J. K. Beilby and P. R. Eddy (Downers Grove: InterVarsity, 2001), 125–36.

[13]Molinism makes the additional claim that, if three were the exact number of times the Lord decided Peter would deny him, then Jesus knew what possible worlds to actualize that would bring about this result. However, the culpability for Peter's actions belonged to Peter alone, since he acted freely. This is a clear example of how God can control a sinful action without causing it.

[14]An anthropomorphism is an analogy or metaphor which attributes a human quality to God.

("leave Me alone"), but Moses did anyway. Even though God knew for certain what Moses would do, God's statements about destroying Israel and starting over with Moses were contingently true and described real possibilities.[15] Therefore, in order for their exchange to be genuine, this statement must have real truth content. It was God's true intention given the present situation, but God was certain the situation was about to change—i.e., Moses was about to intercede. But *if* Moses had not interceded, Israel would have perished. Therefore, the dialogue was genuine, and God's statement had real truth content. Moses' act of intercession was both certain and contingent.

Anthropomorphic language always has a referent; that is, it points to a spiritual reality in accommodated language. For example, when the Bible states, "The eyes of the LORD are everywhere, observing the wicked and the good" (Prov 15:3), it is referring to God's omnipresent and omniscient awareness. Passages that speak of God's hands or refer to "the arm of the LORD" (Isa 53:1; cf. Exod 6:6; Deut 5:15) point to His omnipotent ability. Genesis 8:1 tells us that "God remembered Noah" in the ark and by so doing emphasizes God's faithfulness in keeping His promises.

So what does the Bible mean when it speaks of God "relenting" or "changing His mind" (cf. 2 Sam 24:16; Ps 106:45; Amos 7:3–6; Jonah 3:1)? It will not do merely to describe these passages as anthropomorphisms. An anthropomorphism is a type of metaphor, and metaphors have referents (i.e., they have points of contact with our everyday understanding of things). So the label of anthropmorphism cannot be used to explain away the point of these texts. And the point being made is the contingency of the moment. The biblical authors used such language to emphasize the reality of human participation and responsibility (Gen 18:16–21).

Similarly, the anthropomorphic language used by God at Abraham's offering of Isaac points to the reality of Abraham's test. "For now I know that you fear God, since you have not withheld your only son from Me" (Gen 22:12). The outcome was both contingent and certain. *Contingently*, Abraham *could* have failed. But according to God's flawless

---

[15]God's statements were counterfactually true, i.e., they were true conditionals in the subjunctive mood. We will look at counterfactuals in the next section.

foreknowledge, *certainly* Abraham *would* not. (Remember, the event is contingent; God's knowledge is certain.)

Another example of the juxtaposition of contingency with certainty is the prophecy that none of the bones of Jesus would be broken during His crucifixion (John 19:36). Our Lord's bones were normal human bones, made of calcium. There was nothing intrinsic to their makeup that prohibited injury. *Contingently*, they *could* have been broken; but *certainly*, they *would* not be broken. Contingency speaks of the characteristics of the bones; certainty is a property of God's knowledge.

Conditional Statements

Often conditional statements are choices expressed in an "if–then" structure. "If you keep eating those donuts, then you are going to get fat" is an example of a conditional statement. The antecedent presents the possible choice or action; the consequent gives the outcome. Conditional statements are perhaps the most common way Scripture expresses contingencies. The biblical writers use conditional statements to highlight that God has placed the outcome of certain contingencies in our hands. Acknowledging this takes nothing away from God's sovereignty. He makes the sovereign choice as to what decisions are set before us. Four points concerning the biblical presentation of human choice can be noted: (1) humans are commanded to choose (Josh 24:14–15); (2) choices are set before them (1 Kgs 18:21); (3) humans are responsible for their choices (Isa 1:19–20); and (4) there are examples of humans making choices (Gen 13:9–11). Conditional statements stress that the choices are truly ours, and so is the responsibility for them. Through the prophets, God repeatedly gave Israel conditional promises and threats:

> Look, today I set before you a blessing and a curse: a blessing, if you obey the commands of the LORD your God I am giving you today, and a curse, if you do not obey the commands of the LORD your God. (Deut 11:26–28)

> If My people who are called by My name will humble themselves, and pray and seek My face, and turn from their wicked

> ways, then I will hear from heaven, and will forgive their sin and
> heal their land. (2 Chr 7:14 NJKV)

> If you are willing and obedient, you will eat the good things of
> the land. But if you refuse and rebel, you will be devoured by the
> sword. (Isa 1:19–20)

> If that nation I have made an announcement about, turns from its
> evil, I will not bring the disaster on it I had planned. At [another]
> time I announce that I will build and plant a nation or a kingdom.
> However, if it does what is evil in My sight by not listening to My
> voice, I will not bring the good I had said I would do to it. (Jer
> 18:8–10)

The verses above are just representatives of a long list of passages (1 Sam 12:15; 1 Kgs 2:4; 6:12; 2 Chr 7:17–22 *passim*). The Old Testament presents the relationship between God and Israel as conditional on a number of levels.

Often prophecies were given in conditional terms with the intent that they would succeed as warnings so that the prophecies would not have to come to pass. Occasionally the conditionality was implied rather than stated. The classic example is Jonah's prophecy to Nineveh of its impending destruction. The city responded with sackcloth and ashes, resulting in a divine reprieve (Jonah 3:1–10).

Counterfactuals

So the Bible speaks of contingencies. Often it presents our responsibility for certain contingencies as conditional statements. Remember that conditional statements are contingencies expressed in the "if→then" structure. There is a particular type of conditional statement that deserves special attention, and this type is known as *counterfactuals*.

A counterfactual is a conditional statement that has two distinctive features: (1) involves a condition that is contrary to fact (for example, "if Kennedy had not been killed in 1963, then he would have won reelection in 1964"); and (2) it expresses a truth that belongs to this actual world.

In other words, a counterfactual is a statement that is contrary to fact yet possesses truth content.

We use the truths that counterfactuals contain on a regular basis. Examples are common: "If I don't take out the cookies when the timer goes off, then they will burn"; or "If I run this red light, then I will be involved in an accident." Heeding the truth content causes the events described to not come to pass—the cookies are not burned and no accident occurs—hence the statements typically are contrary to fact (which is why they are called "counter-factual"). So they are true conditionals in the subjunctive mood. And as these examples illustrate, counterfactuals are a part of daily life. The Bible also makes frequent use of counterfactuals.

Many times when discussing Molinism or the distinctions between necessity and contingency, philosophers and theologians will employ *possible world semantics*. A possible world "is the way the world might be."[16] Think of the Christmas movie, *It's a Wonderful Life*. In it, Jimmy Stewart's character, George Bailey, is shown a state of affairs consistent with the notion that he had never been born. That scenario was a counterfactual possible world.[17] At times, the biblical authors speak of alternative possibilities in terms that justify employing possible world language.

The Biblical Use of Counterfactuals. As Jay Wesley Richards notes, counterfactual language "permeates the Bible."[18] In the Exodus passage we examined earlier, God made a counterfactual promise to Moses: "Now leave Me alone, so that My anger can burn against them and I can destroy them. Then I will make you into a great nation" (Exod 32:10). In fact, Moses interceded, God relented, and God did not make Moses the progenitor of a nation.

---

[16]"One can think of a possible world as a maximal description of reality; nothing is left out. It may be thought of as a maximal state of affairs, which includes every other state of affairs or its complement, or as an enormous conjunction composed of every statement or its contradictory." J. P. Moreland and W. L. Craig, *Philosophical Foundations for a Worldview* (Downers Grove, IL: InterVarsity, 2003), 50.

[17]"While modal logic and possible worlds semantics may appear to be ivory-tower creations of tenured logicians with too much time on their hands, their motivation resides in our common use of modal terms and ideas." J. W. Richards, *The Untamed God*, 80–85. Richards notes that Christian philosophers such as Alvin Plantinga and others developed the possible world model in the face of intense hostility from atheists who reject all notions of contingency.

[18]Ibid, 86.

The book of 1 Samuel presents God using counterfactual knowledge on more than one occasion.

> Samuel said to Saul, "You have been foolish. You have not kept
> the command which the Lord your God gave you. It was at this
> time that the Lord would have permanently established your
> reign over Israel, but now your reign will not endure. The Lord
> has found a man loyal to Him, and the Lord has appointed him as
> ruler over His people, because you have not done what the Lord
> commanded." (1 Sam 13:13–14)

Samuel told Saul the counterfactual truth that if Saul had been faithful, then his kingdom would have remained. In fact, his kingship was handed over to David.

David and Saul were later involved in what is perhaps the clearest example of God's use of counterfactual knowledge. Saul headed for Keilah when he learned that David was hiding there. As Saul approached the city, David inquired of the Lord:

> Then David said, "Lord God of Israel, Your servant has heard
> that Saul intends to come to Keilah and destroy the town because
> of me. Will the citizens of Keilah hand me over to him? Will Saul
> come down as Your servant has heard? Lord God of Israel, please
> tell Your servant." The Lord answered, "He will come down."
> Then David asked, "Will the citizens of Keilah hand me and my
> men over to Saul?" "They will," the Lord responded. So David
> and his men, numbering about 600, left Keilah at once and moved
> from place to place. When it was reported to Saul that David
> had escaped from Keilah, he called off the expedition. (1 Sam
> 23:10–13)

God told David that if he stayed in Keilah, then he would have been handed over to Saul. David promptly left and Saul gave up the chase. Divine counterfactual knowledge was used to affect the outcome in the actual world.

As the Babylonians laid siege to Jerusalem, God presented to King Zedekiah two "possible world" scenarios: what would happen if he surrendered or if he did not.

> Jeremiah therefore said to Zedekiah, "This is what the Lord, the
> God of Hosts, the God of Israel, says: 'If indeed you surrender

> to the officials of the king of Babylon, then you will live, this
> city will not be burned down, and you and your household will
> survive. But if you do not surrender to the officials of the king
> of Babylon, then this city will be handed over to the Chaldeans.
> They will burn it down, and you yourself will not escape from
> them.'" (Jer 38:17–18)

When Zedekiah expressed fear about what certain Judeans would do
to him if he surrendered, Jeremiah replied, "They will not hand you
over. . . . Obey the voice of the LORD in what I am telling you, so it may
go well for you and you can live" (Jer 38:20). Tragically, Zedekiah did
not follow Jeremiah's counsel. Of the two possible world scenarios, it
was the less disastrous one that was counterfactual. The city was burned
down and the king was handed over to Nebuchadnezzar.

When Jesus denounced the cities in which He had preached and
performed miracles, He made counterfactual statements to emphasize
their culpability.

> Woe to you, Chorazin! Woe to you, Bethsaida! For if the miracles
> that were done in you had been done in Tyre and Sidon, they
> would have repented in sackcloth and ashes long ago! But I tell
> you, it will be more tolerable for Tyre and Sidon on the day of
> judgment than for you. And you, Capernaum, will you be exalted
> to heaven? You will go down to Hades. For if the miracles that
> were done in you had been done in Sodom, it would have re-
> mained until today. (Matt 11:21–23)

These are just some of the examples of counterfactual knowledge in the
Bible. Counterfactual statements are remarkably common (Matt 26:24;
John 15:22,24; 18:36; 1 Cor 2:8; *passim*).

MOLINISM—COMBINING DIVINE SOVEREIGNTY
AND HUMAN FREEDOM

The Bible presents us with a remarkable juxtaposition: God's sovereign control and certain foreknowledge on the one hand, and contingent, conditional human choices on the other hand. At times, both
are affirmed in the same passage (Gen 50:20; Acts 2:23). We have also

seen that Scripture teaches God has perfect counterfactual knowledge of contingent human choices.

Molinism does not merely argue that God knows all counterfactual truths of creaturely freedom; it contends that God uses all such counterfactual knowledge. As Craig explains, "Thus, by employing his counterfactual knowledge, God can plan a world down to the last detail and yet do so without annihilating creaturely freedom, since what people would freely do under various circumstances is already factored into the equation by God."[19] As explained at the beginning of the chapter, Molinism posits that the best way to understand God's use of counterfactual knowledge is in a three-moment model.

First Moment: God's Natural Knowledge—Everything That Could Happen

The first moment of God's knowledge is His natural knowledge. His natural knowledge—His omniscience—encompasses all truth. There are two types of truths: necessary truths and contingent truths. Necessary truths are those propositions that are true by virtue of the nature of God Himself. Contingent truths are those propositions that possibly could be true if God so chose to bring them into existence. God knows all the possible worlds He could create, with all possible individuals, and all possible circumstances in which they could be placed. God possesses this knowledge by virtue of His very nature, hence the label natural knowledge.

Second Moment: God's Middle Knowledge— Everything That Would Happen

God's middle knowledge is a subset of His natural knowledge. It contains the contingent truths of what every possible creature *would* do (not just *could* do) in any possible set of circumstances. This moment contains the counterfactual truths concerning the contingent choices of genuinely free creatures, so it is logically prior to His creative decree and His subsequent free knowledge of what will happen. Thus middle

---

[19]Craig, "The Middle Knowledge View," 122.

knowledge, like natural knowledge, is logically prior to the divine decision to create a world.

An important note to make at this point is that God does not *perceive* what free creatures would do, but rather He *conceives* their choices within Himself. That is, God does not look forward in time to ascertain what decisions we would make; instead He innately knows all free choices due to His omniscience. So God's middle knowledge contains the knowledge of the choices and decisions made by free creatures, but the source of that knowledge is not the creature. Rather the source is God Himself. Remembering that God's middle knowledge is a subset of His natural knowledge helps to keep that in mind.[20]

Third Moment: God's Free Knowledge—Everything That Will Happen

Using His middle knowledge, God decreed to create this world. God's knowledge of this world is based on His free, sovereign decision, which is why this third moment is called His free knowledge. Remember, the three moments speak of logical sequence, not chronological, so there never was a time when God had middle knowledge but did not have free knowledge.

Employing this three-moment model, Molinism fully affirms both God's foreordination and His foreknowledge, and fully affirms both divine sovereignty and human freedom. Molinists understand everything to occur either by God's will or by His permission. God directly wills and accomplishes all that is good by His grace but permissively allows the evil that occurs. God's decree to create was also a decree of predestination—which is the subject of the chapter on sovereign election. And in the chapter on overcoming grace we examine the active role God's grace plays in all that we do that is right and good.

---

[20]Some ask how it is that God innately knows what free creatures will do. That is, they want to know the grounds or basis for this knowledge (which is why this objection is commonly called the "grounding objection"). However, as Craig points out, the burden of proof is on the objector. "But why *should* I know how God has such foreknowledge? Who are human beings that they should know how God foreknows the future? . . . Therefore, we cannot be required to demonstrate the *actual* way God foreknows; we are free to suggest a *possible* way" (emphasis original). W. L. Craig, *The Only Wise God*, 118–21.

Scripture never states explicitly that God utilizes middle knowledge to accomplish His will. But when all the disparate components of the biblical witness are brought together it becomes clear that Molinism is a reasonable proposal. Molinism addresses a significant theological issue: the way the sovereign God relates to the creatures who He fashioned as reflections of His image. Its validity must be judged by its ability to do justice to the biblical witness of the relationships between God and humans in a way that takes into account all that the Bible has to say about the subject. When one does just that—takes into account all the biblical witness on the subject of divine sovereignty and human choice—Molinism, or something close to it, is where one arrives. This is why many thoughtful Calvinists through the years have been intrigued by Molinism and have attempted to incorporate the notion of God's middle knowledge into a Reformed paradigm.[21] Grasping the full implications of God's infinite middle knowledge leads one to adoration and praise of God for His breathtaking sovereignty.

---

[21]R. A. Muller, *Post-Reformation Reformed Dogmatics*, vol. 3 (Grand Rapids: Baker, 2003), 420–21. Today a number of modern Calvinists such as Bruce Ware, John Frame, and Terrance Tiessen recognize the advantages of the middle knowledge hypothesis and are employing the logical tools of Molinism.

CHAPTER 2

DOES GOD DESIRE THE
SALVATION OF ALL?

"But he that believeth not shall be damned."
—Mark 16:16b (KJV)

WHETHER ONE HOLDS to Calvinism, Arminianism, Molinism, or some other understanding of soteriology, eventually the question of why everyone is not saved must be faced. Embedded in Mark's account of the Great Commission is the implied expectation that not everyone to whom the gospel is offered will accept it, an expectation that history has borne out. Why is this so? Is God's salvific will not done, or does God not want everyone to be saved?

There seem to be four possible answers available to us. First, *universalism*—despite present appearances eventually everyone will be saved, either in this life or the next. Historically, the church has rejected this position, but it has gained new adherents in recent days. The second possible option is *double predestination*—God does not desire nor has He ever desired the salvation of the reprobate.[1] The notion that God predestines some for hell was condemned at the Second Council of Orange (529) and has had few proponents. However, as we will see, certain "High Calvinists" hold to this view firmly.

A third possible answer is that God has *two wills—the revealed will and the hidden will.* In passages such as the Great Commission, Scripture reveals God's universal salvific will (sometimes described as what God desires, or His *preceptive* will).[2] But this option posits that God

---

[1]The reprobates are understood to be those who God, in His eternal decree, rejected or determined to pass over.

[2]J. I. Packer states, "In recent years universalism has made a remarkable comeback among mainstream Christian thinkers, and it cannot now be dismissed out of hand as a foolish fantasy in the way it once could." See J. I. Packer, "Universalism: Will Everyone Ultimately Be Saved?" in *Hell Under Fire: Modern Scholarship Reinvents Eternal Punishment,* ed. C. W. Morgan and R. A. Peterson (Grand Rapids: Zondervan, 2004), 170. For example, L. R. Baker argues for an Augustinian understanding of predestination, grace, and free will, but claims that the best way to make these doctrines "palatable" is to embrace "the possibility of universal salvation." She concludes, "Moreover, universalism allows us to retain the absolute truth of Christianity without its intolerance." See L. R. Baker, "Why Christians

also has a hidden will in which, for reasons known only to Him, He has decreed to pass by many, leaving them to determine their own destiny out of a heart enslaved to sin (i.e., God's decretive will).

The fourth option agrees with the third view that God indeed has two wills, but rather than the revealed/hidden distinction, this view argues that the two wills should be understood as *an antecedent will and a consequent will*. God antecedently desires that all be saved, but He consequently wills that faith is a condition to salvation. Only those who believe will be saved.

The first two options understand God to have only one will while the last two alternatives perceive two wills in God. The fourth position—the antecedent/consequent wills view—has been the majority position throughout church history.[3] However, theologians from the Reformed perspective generally have rejected the antecedent/consequent wills position because it seems to give the ultimate decision about salvation to man rather than God. This, they contend, denigrates God's sovereignty and threatens the gracious nature of salvation while magnifying human choice.

In this chapter we will examine the four options concerning God's salvific will. I argue that the antecedent/consequent wills position by far has the fewest theological difficulties and is more in keeping with the commands and instructions of the Great Commission. Certain passages of Scripture declare that God desires the salvation of all.

> For God so loved the world that He gave His only begotten Son, that whoever believes in Him should not perish but have everlasting life. (John 3:16 NKJV)

> This is good, and it pleases God our Savior, who wants everyone to be saved and to come to the knowledge of the truth. (1 Tim 2:3–4)

> The Lord does not delay His promise, as some understand delay, but is patient with you, not wanting any to perish, but all to come to repentance. (2 Pet 3:9)

Should Not Be Libertarians: An Augustinian Challenge," *Faith and Philosophy* 20.4 (October, 2003): 473.

[3]See J. Frame, *The Doctrine of God* (Phillipsburg, NJ: P&R, 2002), 529-38; and T. Oden, *The Transforming Power of Grace,* (Nashville: Abingdon, 1993), 82-91.

In light of the above verses, this chapter argues for a Great Commission hermeneutic (Matt 28:19–20). This hermeneutic views the Great Commission as the expression of the divine will: the gospel is to be offered to all; those who believe will be saved.

THE FIRST TWO OPTIONS: GOD HAS ONE WILL

Those who emphasize the simplicity of God generally argue that there is only one will in God.[4] This approach generally requires that God's nature is understood with one divine attribute as the controlling motif by which all other attributes are interpreted. A theology which sees God's fundamental essence as love will be much different from a system based on the assumption of the primacy of the divine will. Whether based on divine love or divine volition, the single-will approach has difficulty explaining the rationale behind all components of the Great Commission, namely, that all must hear the gospel even though all do not believe.

Option One: God Is Love and This Love Is Expressed by His Will to Save All

Obviously, affirming the universal salvific will of God poses no difficulties for the one who believes that "God is love" sums up the divine essence (1 John 4:8). However, this approach logically seems to require universalism or something close to it. This appears to be true regardless of one's position concerning the nature of the human response to the gospel. In fact, because of how Reformed theologians understand grace to work on the human will, those who affirm God's genuine love and desire of salvation for all tend to embrace universalism even more readily than their Arminian counterparts.

Some significant Arminian theologians wonder aloud if their theological starting point does not necessitate an eventual arrival at universalism. In his presidential address to the Wesleyan Theological Society, Al

---

[4]When theologians speak of the simplicity of God, they are referring to His undivided essence. This means there is no division, tension, or conflict within God. God is never in a quandary or has conflicting desires. Some presentations of divine simplicity are more problematic than others. See J. W. Richards, "Divine Simplicity: The Good, the Bad, and the Ugly," in *For Faith and Clarity*, ed. J. K. Beilby (Grand Rapids: Baker, 2006), 157–78.

Truesdale examines the question as to whether the doctrine of everlasting punishment is compatible with an affirmation that love is "the defining center of God."[5] Truesdale begins with the claim that love is the "one element of who God is that governs all the rest."[6] He proceeds with a five-step argument which deduces that the doctrine of eternal damnation is not an option for the consistent Wesleyan and suggests annihilationism or postmortem salvation as possible alternatives.[7] He concludes by admonishing the reader with a quote from Barth, "On the basis of the eternal will of God we have to think of *every human being* [emphasis original], even the oddest, most villainous or miserable, as one to whom Jesus Christ is Brother and God is Father."[8] It is noteworthy that Truesdale builds his argument on the premise that God's singular will for the salvation of all is the manifestation of God's simple, undivided essence, which is love.

There are plenty of Arminian theologians who, like Truesdale, affirm God's universal love and salvific will but do not arrive at his conclusions. And universalism is not found only in Arminianism. A few Reformed theologians, who argue that God's essential nature of love compels a singular will for the salvation of all, also arrive at universalism. Philosopher Thomas Talbott, who considers himself Reformed, serves as a prime example. Where Truesdale attempts to make a positive argument based on the loving nature of God, Talbott takes the negative approach by presenting what he believes are the consequences of denying the premise that God singularly wills the salvation of all. In a celebrated debate with John Piper that covers a series of articles, Talbott argues that belief in the universal love of God combined with a Reformed understanding of soteriology add up to universalism.[9] He denounces the traditional Reformed

---

[5] A. Truesdale, "Holy Love vs. Eternal Hell: the Wesleyan Options," *Wesleyan Theological Journal* 36:1 (Spring 2001):104.

[6] Ibid., 103. Truesdale acknowledges that not all Arminians or Wesleyans would agree with his beginning premise.

[7] Of course, universalism, annihilationism, and postmortem salvation are not identical positions. However, proponents of each position share the common conviction that the doctrine of everlasting punishment is untenable.

[8] Ibid. 112; cf. K. Barth, *The Humanity of God* (Richmond: John Knox, 1969), 53.

[9] Talbott's articles are T. Talbott, "On Predestination, Reprobation, and the Love of God: A Polemic," *Reformed Journal* 33:2 (February 1983): 11–15; "God's Unconditional Mercy: A Reply to John Piper," *Reformed Journal* 33:6 (June 1983): 9–13; and "Vessels of Wrath and the Unpardonable Sin: More on Universalism," *The Reformed Journal* 33:9 (September 1983): 10–15. Piper's replies can be found at J. Piper, "How Does a Sovereign God Love? A Reply to Thomas Talbott," *Reformed Journal*

doctrine of predestination as "blasphemy" and a "manifestation of human depravity."[10]

According to Talbott, Reformed theology, with its usual distinction between God's decrees and God's commands, produces some very unfortunate consequences for the character of God. God commands us to love our enemies but fails to love His enemies. This would mean that love is not an essential property of God. Reformed soteriology, argues Talbott, presents us with a God who is less loving than many humans and leaves us with the disturbing notion that we might love our children more than God does. Talbott confesses that he finds such a God difficult to love, much less worship. He states,

> If there be a single loved one of mine whom God *could* [emphasis original] redeem but doesn't—if it should turn out, for instance, that God fails to love my own little daughter—then I can think of no better response than a paraphrase of John Stuart Mill: 'I will not worship such a God, and if such a God can send me to hell for not so worshiping him, then to hell I will go.' Of course, this may mean simply that I am not one of the elect, or, if I am one of the elect, that God will someday transform my heart so that I can be just as calloused towards my loved ones as he is.[11]

Calloused or not, Talbott considers traditional Calvinism to be sub-Christian. Of those who rejoice in their election, he states, "In this regard their attitude is quite different from that of the Apostle Paul; and in this regard, they illustrate nicely the selfishness built right into the very heart of Calvinistic theology."[12] In one telling exchange, Talbott challenges Piper by asking him how he would react to the knowledge that God had not elected one of his sons. Piper replies,

> But I am not ignorant that God *may* [emphasis original] not have chosen my sons for his sons. And, though I think I would give my life for their salvation, if they should be lost to me, I would not rail against the Almighty. He is God. I am but a man. The Potter has absolute rights over the clay. Mine is to bow before

---

33:4 (April 1983): 9–13; and "Universalism in Romans 9–11? Testing the Exegesis of Thomas Talbott," *Reformed Journal*, 33:7 (July 1983): 11–14.

[10]Talbott, "On Predestination, Reprobation, and the Love of God: A Polemic," 11–12.

[11]Ibid., 14–15.

[12]Ibid.

> his unimpeachable character and believe that the Judge of all the
> earth has ever and always will do right.[13]

Though his commitment and candor is impressive, Piper seems to be conceding Talbott's central point that Reformed theology teaches God might not love our children as much as we do.

Talbott argues that since Reformed theology teaches God has the ability to bring salvation to all by a monergistic work of regeneration but has chosen not to do so, then classic Calvinism is guilty of a number of sins. First, Reformed theology commits blasphemy—because it attributes demonic qualities to God; second, selfishness—because it teaches us to care about our election more than the election of others; and third, rebellion—because it fails to obey the command to love our neighbors as ourselves.[14] Talbott concludes that Reformed theology can be rescued only by its adherents combining the traditional doctrines of unconditional election and irresistible grace with an affirmation of divine universal love. The result would be universalism, and that suits Talbott fine.[15]

Though one is Arminian and the other a self-proclaimed Calvinist, Truesdale and Talbott make similar arguments. God's loving nature means He has only one desire toward humanity—the redemption of all. Their conclusions exclude understanding Jesus' warning in Mark 16:16 (NKJV), "he who does not believe will be condemned," as referring to eternal punishment.

Option Two: God Is Sovereign and This Is Expressed by His Will to Save the Elect

Reformed theologians such as Francis Turretin, Herman Hoeksema, and David Engelsma are called decretal theologians because they see

---

[13]Piper, "How Does a Sovereign God Love? A Reply to Thomas Talbott," 13.

[14]Talbott, "On Predestination, Reprobation, and the Love of God: A Polemic."

[15]A number of other Reformed universalists make the same argument. Karl Barth, Neal Punt, and Jan Bonda present respective versions of a Reformed universalism. See K. Barth, *Church Dogmatis,* II/2 (Edinburgh: T and T Clark, 1957); N. Punt, *Unconditional Good News* (Grand Rapids: Eerdmans, 1980); and J. Bonda, *The One Purpose of God: An Answer to the Doctrine of Eternal Punishment* (Grand Rapids: Eerdmans, 1998). C. H. Pinnock observes, "What Augustinians have to do to reach universalism is enlarge the scope of election to include the whole race, and then theologize in their usual way." C. H. Pinnock, *A Wideness in God's Mercy* (Grand Rapids: Zondervan, 1992), 155.

the eternal decrees as the starting point for studying the works of God.[16] Like Truesdale and Talbott, decretal theologians affirm a single salvific will in God, but because they often see God's sovereignty as the defining characteristic by which all other attributes are understood they arrive at very different conclusions from those surveyed in the previous section Decretal theology teaches that God, in eternity, decreed the salvation of a select and definite group of individuals. Those chosen are the elect while those rejected are the reprobate. This approach to studying salvation produces the distinctives of Reformed theology: election and reprobation, limited (or particular) atonement, irresistible (or effectual) grace, and faith as the evidence of regeneration rather than the condition for it.

Some decretal theologians hold the choice to save some and damn others to be logically initial and primary. They see the decision to ordain all other events—the fall, the atonement, and so on—as the means by which God accomplishes His first decree to elect and reprobate. This position is called supralapsarianism because it teaches that God decreed a double predestination "before the Fall." It is worth pointing out that the original Reformers—Zwingli, Luther, and Calvin—were all supralapsarian.[17]

Most subsequent decretal theologians have not followed the Reformers down the supralapsarianism path but rather have opted for infralapsarianism. Like the label indicates, this position holds that God first decreed to allow the Fall and then from the fallen race elected those whom He would save. Infralapsarianism attempts to avoid some of the obvious ethical dilemmas inherent in supralapsarianism. In infralapsarianism, God does not damn the reprobate before they fall but damns them because they are fallen. Nor in this scheme does God actively ordain the damnation of the reprobate. Rather, when God chooses certain ones for salvation, He simply passes over the remainder of humanity. Infralapsarians do not believe the reprobate are ordained for hell; rather, they see the reprobate as omitted from heaven.

---

[16]Turretin argued from the simplicity of God that the decrees were part of the divine essence. See F. Turretin, *Institutes of Elenctic Theology* (Phillipsburg, NJ: P&R, 1992), 1:312.

[17]Calvin's supralapsarianism will be examined further in chapter five.

Infralapsarians hold to a single decree of election, while supralapsarians teach a double decree of election and reprobation. Theologians generally agree that supralapsarianism has fewer logical problems, while infralapsarianism has fewer moral ones.[18] But in the end, whether supralapsarian or infralapsarian, decretal theology teaches that God has only one salvific will and that this intent is to save only His chosen.

Decretal theology produces a distinctive set of corollaries. First, such a view of divine sovereignty requires a denial of God's universal love. Theologians like Hoeksema and Engelsma do not shrink from declaring God's "eternal hatred" for the reprobate. Engelsma declares,

> It is not at all surprising that advocates of the free offer oppose the Reformed doctrine of reprobation, for reprobation is the exact, explicit denial that God loves all men, desires to save all men, and conditionally offers them salvation. Reprobation asserts that God eternally hates some men; has immutably decreed their damnation; and has determined to withhold from them Christ, grace, faith, and salvation.[19]

Second, decretal theology denies that texts such as 1 Tim 2:4 and 2 Peter 3:9 teach that God loves all humanity and desires the salvation of all. For example, Francis Turretin (1623–1687), a Reformed scholastic and one of the first clear proponents of infralapsarianism, insists that the love expressed in John 3:16 "cannot be universal towards each and everyone, but special towards a few." It refers "only [to] those chosen out of this world."[20]

A modern-day decretal theologian, James White, takes a similar approach to the other texts that seem to describe an inclusiveness in God's salvific love.[21] He understands the "all" in 1 Tim 2:4 to mean that God desires the salvation of "all sorts of men" or "from all classes of men." Likewise, 2 Pet 3:9 means that God is not willing that any of us, i.e., the elect, should perish.

---

[18]Barth, *Church Dogmatics* II/2, 131–32.
[19]D. Engelsma, *Hyper-Calvinism and the Well-Meant Offer of the Gospel* (Grandville, MI: Reformed Free, 1994), 58.
[20]Turretin, *Institutes of Elenctic Theology,* 1:405–08.
[21]J. White, *The Potter's Freedom* (Amityville, NY: Calvary Press, 2000), 127–42.

If God loves only the elect, desires salvation only for His chosen, and has provided atonement only for the objects of His love, then a third corollary is inevitable: there is no genuine universal offer of the gospel. David Engelsma devotes an entire book to the thesis that though the gospel is preached "promiscuously" to all, it is offered only to the elect. In fact, he does not care much for the word "offer" at all. Preaching does not offer the gospel. Preaching operates as the instrument by which faith is activated in the elect. The reprobate may hear the gospel, but its message is not for them. Engelsma contends that his position is not hyper-Calvinism but consistent Calvinism.

Decretal theology has definite effects on how one understands and obeys the Great Commission, and there are consequences to such a system on preaching and missions. First, decretal theology historically has had the effect of causing many Reformed pastors to restrict who are candidates to hear the gospel. In the seventeenth century many Scottish theologians argued that the gospel should be presented indiscriminately only to members of the visible church.[22] Many English Baptists in the eighteenth century told the good news only to men whose lives gave evidence of divine grace.[23] Following the hyper-Calvinism of Daniel Parker, many American Baptists in the nineteenth century rejected "duty-faith," that is, the belief that unbelievers have a duty to repent and believe the gospel.[24] Decretal theology led these "hard-shell" or Primitive Baptists to oppose all methods of evangelism, missions, or outreach. Organized evangelistic efforts were seen as "humanly contrived devices" which presumed to do God's work. Even today, the Gospel Standard (Baptist) Churches reject any responsibility to preach the gospel to all.[25]

Second, even though most decretal theologians of today have turned away from the restrictive postures of earlier hyper-Calvinists, many still do not see preaching as an appeal intended to persuade. For them, preaching is a proclamation or an announcement which activates faith

---

[22]See J. Daane, *The Freedom of God: a Study of Election and Pulpit* (Grand Rapids: Eerdmans, 1973), 22.

[23]See P. Toon, *The Emergence of Hyper-Calvinism in English Nonconformity, 1689–1765* (London: The Olive Tree, 1967), 131–43.

[24]See T. George, "Southern Baptist Ghosts," *First Things* 93 (May 1999): 18–24.

[25]The articles of faith of the Gospel Standard Churches can be found at http://www.pristinegrace. org/media.php?id=313. See specifically articles 24–26.

in the elect. Preaching outwardly instructs all, but the inward call of the Spirit is given only to those God has chosen. Engelsma claims that several things in the typical evangelical sermon will be absent from a true Reformed message: "There are several things that will not be found in Reformed preaching to the unconverted. Reformed preaching will not approach the audience with the declaration: 'God loves all of you, and Christ died for all of you.' It will not say to every man: 'God loves you and has a wonderful plan for your life.'"[26]

Third, as James Daane points out in his examination of the effect of the doctrine of reprobation on preaching, decretal theology eviscerates the gospel of its meaning.[27] For many hearers, perhaps most, the announcement is that God has decided to remain at war with them, and He made this decision in eternity past. The gospel is supposed to be good news, but according to the doctrine of reprobation, the message is certainly not new and is not necessarily good.

Ultimately, reprobation is an unpreachable teaching. Preaching is proclaiming the truth for the purpose of calling the hearers to respond. Daane points out that this cannot be done with the doctrine of reprobation; it is a message that has no response.[28] The teaching does not apply to the elect, and as for the reprobate, there is no response to the announcement that one is rejected. The doctrine of reprobation declares that there is no saving inward call for the nonelect. No call means no response and it certainly means no preaching. Reprobation can be contemplated, taught, and discussed, but it cannot be preached.

To sum up this section: if God's will is singular, then either He desires the salvation of all or He does not. As we have seen, starting with the premise of a universal salvific will can launch one into the fantasy of universalism. But positing a denial of any type of universal salvific will can lead one into the slough of reprobation. For these reasons most theologians, Reformed and non-Reformed, have opted instead for a two-will approach.

---

[26]Engelsma, *Hyper-Calvinism and the Well-Meant Offer of the Gospel*, 88.

[27]Daane, *The Freedom of God: A Study of Election and Pulpit*, 27.

[28]Ibid. Walls and Dongell point out that in pastoral counseling the doctrine of reprobation is worse than useless. See J. Walls and J. Dongell, *Why I Am Not a Calvinist* (Downers Grove, IL: InterVarsity, 2004), 186–87.

THE THIRD AND FOURTH OPTIONS: GOD HAS TWO WILLS

Most theologians, Reformed or not, have recognized that, in John Piper's words, "God's intention is not simple but complex,"[29] or if God's will is simple, it is "fragmented."[30] If the sovereign God desires the salvation of all, provides a redemption sufficient for all, and yet all are not eventually saved although God's will is ultimately done, then God's will displays a complexity that requires understanding it in stages or phases. Theologians have employed a number of categories to describe God's two wills. God's will of precept or command is often contrasted with His decretal or sovereign will. Most positions are variations on one of two paradigms: one comprises the hidden and the revealed wills (option three), and the other the antecedent and consequent wills (option four). Generally, Reformed theologians opt for the revealed/hidden wills paradigm while non-Reformed theologians take the latter.

Option Three: The Hidden/Revealed Wills Paradigm

In their discussions about divine sovereignty and human responsibility, the writings of the Reformers regularly appeal to the hidden/revealed wills position, though Luther embraces the concept much more readily than Calvin. For Luther, the two wills of God are functions of the two ways God relates to His creation. On the one hand, as *deus revelatus*, God manifests Himself to us in Jesus Christ. On the other hand, God as *deus absconditus* hides from creation, and since nothing further can be known about the hidden God, then nothing further should be said. The revealed will of God, i.e., Jesus Christ, proclaims the good news that God graciously is for us. The hidden God, with His sovereign and secret will of election and reprobation, remains terrifyingly inaccessible.

Calvin is less than consistent in his use of the revealed/hidden wills paradigm. In theological works such as his reply to the Catholic controversialist Albert Pighius, Calvin denies a genuine universal offer of the gospel. He states, "It is a puerile fiction by which Pighius interprets grace

---

[29]J. Piper, "How Does a Sovereign God Love? A Reply to Thomas Talbott," 11.

[30]R. C. Koons, "Dual Agency: A Thomistic Account of Providence and Human Freedom," *Philosophia Christi* 4 (2002): 408–10.

to mean that God invites all men to salvation despite their being lost in Adam. For Paul clearly distinguishes the foreknown from the others upon whom God did not please to look."[31] Calvin denounces the notion that God has two wills as "blasphemy."[32]

However, Calvin's commentaries present a different story. In those works, he states that 1 Tim 2:4; 2 Pet 3:9; and Ezek 18:23 plainly teach that God desires the salvation of all humanity.[33] There Calvin appeals to the hidden/revealed wills explanation to reconcile his interpretation of the universal texts with his doctrine of double predestination. On this issue at least, one might be forgiven for wondering if Calvin the theologian ever met Calvin the exegete.

So Calvinists are left with two difficult choices: argue a distinction between the revealed and secret wills of God (which appears to abandon charge the law of noncontradiction) or declare that the Bible does not teach that God desires the salvation of all. Some Reformed theologians try to reconcile the revealed and secret wills by arguing that when the Scriptures speak of God's desire for all to be saved, this is only the expression of His conditional will. And His conditional will is that whoever believes is saved. They then contend that this conditional will is consistent with God's secret will that only a limited number are saved because according to His secret will He provides faith to those whom He has elected.

The problem with this argument is that it misses what the texts actually say. Yes, all the texts presuppose that salvation is conditioned on the sinner's repentance and faith, but they present God's desire for the salvation of all humanity as universal and unconditioned. The apostle Peter does not merely say that God desires the salvation of all who repent,

---

[31]J. Calvin, *Concerning the Eternal Predestination of God* (Louisville: Westminster John Knox, [1552]1961), 72.

[32]Ibid., 117–18. Calvin states, "For the distinction commonly made in the schools of a twofold will we by no means admit. The sophists of the Sorbonne talk of a regulative and an absolute will of God. This blasphemy is rightly abhorrent to pious ears but is plausible to Pighius and those like him."

[33]See J. Calvin, *Commentaries on the First Twenty Chapters of the Book of the Prophet Ezekiel*, vol. 2 (Grand Rapids: Baker, 1999), 246–49 and *Commentaries on the Catholic Epistles*, vol. 22 (Grand Rapids: Baker, 1999), 419–20. Calvin states, "But it may be asked, If God wishes none to perish, why is it that so many do perish? To this my answer is, that no mention is here made of the hidden purpose of God, according to which the reprobate are doomed to their own ruin, but only of his will as made known to us in the gospel. For God there stretches forth his hand without a difference to all, but lays hold only of those, to lead them to himself, whom he has chosen before the foundation of the world."

but that He is not willing that any should perish and that all would repent (2 Pet 3:9). The apostle Paul affirms that God will save everyone
who believes, but that is not all that he says. He goes a step further and
proclaims that God desires all men to be saved (1 Tim 2:4). Speaking
through the prophet Ezekiel, God does not say He desires that those who
believe be spared from death. Rather He declares that He takes no pleasure in the death of the wicked and that He wishes that the wicked would
repent (Ezek 18:23).

These statements just cited are unconditioned and unrestricted. The
condition is upon humans to repent and believe, but there is no condition
upon the part of God. The expression of the universal desire for all to be
saved is the will of God. The revealed will of God is exactly that—the
will of God. Just as sure as God's secret will is greater than His revealed
will, it certainly can never be less.

John Piper argues for the hidden/revealed wills paradigm.[34] He de-
parts from many of his Reformed colleagues when he accepts those texts
such as 1 Tim 2:4; 2 Pet 3:9; John 3:16; and Ezek 18:23 as actually
expressing a desire on God's part for the salvation of all humanity. He
recognizes that traditional Reformed exegesis of these verses convinces
only the already persuaded.

Piper argues that God genuinely desires the salvation of all, but this
desire is trumped by the even greater desire to be glorified.[35] In order for
His grace to receive the fullest expression of glory, it is necessary that He
also display His righteous wrath against sin. The full glory of His grace
is properly perceived only when seen alongside His holy judgments.
Some have been selected by God to be trophies of grace while others are
chosen to be examples of His just damnation. Why God selects certain
ones for salvation while consigning others to perdition is a mystery hidden in the secret counsels of God.

There are at least six serious problems with the hidden/revealed version of the two wills explanation. First, as Carson points out, too of-

---

[34]J. Piper, "Are There Two Wills in God? Divine Election and God's Desire for All to Be Saved,"
in *The Grace of God, the Bondage of the Will*, ed. T. R. Schreiner and B. A. Ware (Grand Rapids: Baker
Books, 1995), 107–24.
[35]Ibid., 123–24.

ten theologians use the hidden will to negate the revealed will.[36] Luther certainly seems to do this. In his discussion of Jesus' lament over Jerusalem,[37] Luther's answer is to appeal to God's hidden will.

> Here, God Incarnate says: 'I would, and thou wouldst not.' God Incarnate, I repeat, was sent for this purpose, to will, say, do, suffer, and offer to all men, all that is necessary for salvation; albeit He offends many who, being abandoned or hardened by God's secret will of Majesty, do not receive Him thus willing, speaking, doing and offering.[38]

Luther points us to the revealed God in Christ but then promptly nullifies the Savior's message by appealing to the hidden God.[39]

By definition a hidden will is unknown, so how can one speak about it? How can we use something unknown as a theological foundation? Who has the right to declare the revealed will is not God's ultimate will and base this assertion on something admittedly unknowable? Who dares to nullify God's Word? If the hidden will does exist, then could it be hidden because God does not want us to engage with it?

A second problem with the hidden/revealed wills paradigm is just as serious as the first. Christ manifests the revealed will of God, but the revealed will is not always done because it is supplanted by God's secret will which lies hidden in the Father. This leads to the disturbing conclusion that Jesus does not present God as He really is. In his discussion of the two wills in God, Luther makes this very clear: "Now, God in His own nature and majesty is to be left alone; in this regard, we have nothing to do with Him, nor does He wish us to deal with Him. We have to do with Him as clothed and displayed in His Word, by which He presents Himself to us."[40] In the hidden/revealed wills scenario, Christ no longer reveals the Father.

---

[36]D. A. Carson, *Divine Sovereignty and Human Responsibility* (Atlanta: John Knox, 1981), 214.

[37]"O Jerusalem, Jerusalem, the one who kills the prophets and stones those who are sent to her! How often I wanted to gather your children together, as a hen gathers her chicks under her wings, but you were not willing!" (Matt 23:37, NKJV)

[38]M. Luther, *The Bondage of the Will* (London: The Camelot Press, [1525] 1957), 189.

[39]Calvin takes a similar tack. See *Commentaries on Ezekiel*, 246–49 and *Commentaries on the Catholic Epistles*, 419–20.

[40]Luther, *Bondage of the Will,* 175.

The second problem leads naturally to a third one. Luther describes the secret will of God as "dreadful" and then urges his reader to look to Christ alone.[41] But as Barth points out, one cannot teach the hidden will of God and then tell people not to think about it.[42] Exhortations to pay no attention to the man behind the curtain only heighten suspicions and concerns. The difficulty the hidden/revealed wills paradigm presents to pastoral ministry is well documented.[43] If our election resides in the hidden purpose, then what assurance does the revealed Christ offer us? Barth concludes that to look past Jesus is to look into the unknown.[44]

A fourth problem with the hidden/revealed wills solution is that it seems to make the preacher appear to be hypocritical. Engelsma highlights this problem when he scolds the Reformed pastor who preaches the revealed will while quietly adhering to a hidden will.

> You can now preach to all men that God loves them with a redemptive love and that Christ died for them to save them from their sins, but at the same time you must whisper to yourself, "But He will actually save only some of you and He will not save others of you according to His own sovereign will." What you whisper to yourself makes the message of universal love, universal atonement, and a universal desire to save, which you proclaim loudly, a fraud.[45]

If what we whisper to ourselves makes what we proclaim a fraud, then indeed we are guilty of dissimulation.

---

[41]Ibid., 171. "He [Ezekiel] speaks of the published offer of God's mercy, not of the dreadful hidden will of God, Who, according to His own counsel, ordains such persons as He wills to receive and partake of the mercy preached and offered. This will is not to be inquired into, but to be reverently adored, as by far the most awesome secret of the Divine Majesty."

[42]Barth, *Church Dogmatics* II/2, 66.

[43]R. T. Kendall, *Calvin and English Calvinism to 1649* (New York: Oxford University Press, 1979); and C. Bell, *Calvin and Scottish Theology: The Doctrine of Assurance* (Edinburgh: The Handsel Press, 1985).

[44]Barth, *Church Dogmatics,* II/2, 105.

[45]Engelsma, *Hyper-Calvinism and the Well-Meant Offer of the Gospel*, 41. While Engelsma mocks the Reformed pastor who preaches the universal love of God, Carson speaks sympathetically of the conflict within many. Carson states, "This approach, I contend, must surely come as a relief to young preachers in the Reformed tradition who hunger to preach the Gospel effectively but who do not know how far they can go in saying things such as 'God loves you' to unbelievers. From what I have already said, it is obvious that I have no hesitation in answering this question from young Reformed preachers affirmatively: *Of course* [emphasis original] I tell the unconverted that God loves them." D. A. Carson, *The Difficult Doctrine of the Love of God* (Wheaton: Crossway, 2000), 80.

Worse yet, the hidden/revealed wills approach appears to make God out to be hypocritical, which is a fifth problem. God universally offers a salvation that He has no intention for all to receive. Reformed soteriology teaches that the gospel is offered to all, but efficacious grace is given only to the elect.[46] The limits of salvation are set by the sovereign and secret choice of God. Numerous times—through the prophets, the Savior, and the apostles—God publicly reveals a desire for Israel's salvation while secretly seeing to it they will not repent. Calvin, citing Augustine, states that since we do not know who is elect and who is reprobate we should desire the salvation of all.[47] Shank retorts, "But why? If this be not God's desire, why should it be Calvin's? Why does Calvin wish to be more gracious than God?"[48]

Which brings us to a sixth and fundamental objection to the hidden/revealed wills paradigm: it fails to face the very problems it was intended to address. It avoids the very dilemma decretal theology creates. Peterson, in his defense of the Reformed position on God's two wills, states, "God does not save all sinners, for ultimately he does not intend to save all of them. The gift of faith is necessary for salvation, yet for reasons beyond our ken, the gift of faith has not been given to all."[49] But then he concludes, "While God commands all to repent and takes no delight in the death of the sinner, all are not saved because it is not God's intention to give his redeeming grace to all."[50] I must be candid and confess that to me the last quote makes no sense.

Let us remember that there is no disagreement about human responsibility. Molinists, Calvinists, Arminians, and all other orthodox Christians agree that the lost are lost because of their own sin. But that is not the question at hand. The question is not, "Why are the lost lost?" but

---

[46]See T. R. Schreiner and B. A. Ware, "Introduction" in *The Grace of God, the Bondage of the Will*, 12. They affirm that efficacious grace is given only to the elect: "Our understanding of God's saving grace is very different. We contend that Scripture does not teach that all people receive grace in equal measure, even though such a democratic notion is attractive today. What Scripture teaches is that God's saving grace is set only upon some, namely, those whom, in his great love, he elected long ago to save, and that this grace is necessarily effective in turning them to belief."

[47]J. Calvin, *Institutes of the Christian Religion* (Philadelphia: Westminster, [1559] 1960), 3.23.14.

[48]R. Shank, *Elect in the Son* (Minneapolis: Bethany House, 1989), 166.

[49]R. Peterson and M. Williams, *Why I Am Not an Arminian* (Downers Grove, IL: InterVarsity, 2004), 130.

[50]Ibid.

"Why aren't the lost saved?" The nasty, awful, "deep-dark-dirty-little-secret" of Calvinism is that it teaches there is one and only one answer to the second question, and it is that God does not want them saved.[51] Molinism is sometimes accused of having similar problems,[52] but Reformed theology has the distinction of making this difficulty the foundational cornerstone for its understanding of salvation.

Option Four: The Antecedent/Consequent Wills Paradigm

Throughout church history both the Eastern and Western churches have taught that God desires the salvation of all, although He requires the response of faith on the part of the hearer.[53] This antecedent/consequent wills approach sees no conflict between the two wills of God. God antecedently wills all to be saved. But for those who refuse to repent and believe, He consequently wills that they should be condemned. In this way God is understood to be like a just judge who desires all to live but who reluctantly orders the execution of a murderer.[54] The antecedent and consequent desires are different, but they are not in conflict.

The antecedent/consequent wills position seems to be the clear teaching of Scripture. God antecedently "loved the world in this way: He gave His one and only Son," that consequently "so that everyone who believes in Him will not perish but have eternal life." Christ antecedently orders the gospel preached "to every creature," but He consequently decrees that "he that believeth not shall be damned." The antecedent/consequent wills paradigm fits very nicely with the Great Commission.

---

[51]Both the point and the phrase come from Walls and Dongell, *Why I Am Not a Calvinist,* 186–87. Cf. Daane, *The Freedom of God,* 184. Both Dort and Westminster warn about preaching decretal theology publicly. Many thoughtful Calvinists concede that the moral and logical problems with the doctrine of reprobation are irresolvable. See P. Jewett, *Election and Predestination* (Grand Rapids: Eerdmans, 1985), 76–77, 99–100; and T. R. Schreiner, "Does Scripture Teach Prevenient Grace in the Wesleyan Sense?" in Schreiner and Ware, *The Grace of God, the Bondage of the Will,* 381–82.

[52]See J. Walls, "Is Molinism as Bad as Calvinism?" *Faith and Philosophy* 7 (1990):85–98.

[53]T. Oden, *The Transforming Power of Grace* (Nashville: Abingdon, 1993), 112. Oden states that the Church arrived at this consensus concerning God's two wills through a series of councils: Ephesus (431), Arles (475), Orange (529), and Quiersy (853). Jewett, a Calvinist, concedes that only the Reformed tradition rejects the antecedent/consequent wills paradigm. See Jewett, *Election and Predestination,* 98.

[54]John of Damascus seems to be the first to use the analogy of the just judge to explain the congruence of the two wills of God. See Oden, *The Transforming Power of Grace,* 83, and Jewett, *Election and Predestination,* 98.

Oden lists four characteristics of the antecedent will of God.[55] First, it is universal. Salvation is desired for all, provided for all, and offered to all. This unconditional omnibenevolent attitude is truly antecedent in that it is directed to all humanity prior to its acceptance or rejection. Second, the antecedent will is impartial. Christ died for the sins of the whole world. Universal love logically requires unlimited atonement. Third, God's will to save all is sincere. There is no hidden will, no secret decree of reprobation. And fourth, the antecedent will is an ordinate will. It is impossible for God's desire to remain impotent or unfulfilled. The antecedent will to save all is the basis of His actions to provide the means of grace to sinners through Christ.

God's consequent will possesses three components.[56] First, it is consistent with the qualities with which He has endowed His creatures. Humans are fallen, but they are still in the image of God. God's grace is not coercive and can be refused. When the hearer encounters the gospel, he is graciously enabled by the Spirit to respond freely. The hearer's decision to accept or reject the gospel is genuinely, terrifyingly, his. Admittedly, why some reject the gospel is a mystery. But in the antecedent/consequent paradigm, the mystery of iniquity resides in man rather than God.

The second aspect of God's consequent will follows from the first. If God wills that salvation is consequent to our choice, then this will is conditional. Third, the consequent will is just. God's granting of salvation to those who believe is perfectly consistent with His holy nature because of the propitiatory work of Christ (Rom 3:21–26). His damning of all who will not believe fully accords with His righteousness. God's antecedent will is perfectly gracious; His consequent will is perfectly just.

Generally, Reformed theologians find the antecedent/consequent wills approach unacceptable. They give a number of objections of which three figure most prominently. First, the antecedent/consequent wills paradigm seems to make God's decision contingent upon man's choice. They contend that this approach subtly puts man on God's throne. Berkouwer argues that a salvation that depends upon a decision from man

---

[55]Oden, *The Transforming Power of Grace,* 83–86.
[56]Ibid., 87–89.

makes God "powerless" and "waiting."[57] Robert Shank replies that God
may be waiting, but He is not powerless.[58] In fact, the imagery of God
waiting is a rich theme found throughout the Bible (Isa 1:18–20, for example). The antecedent/consequent wills approach understands God to
be the sovereign Initiator and gracious Completer of redemption. If man
is to choose between heaven and hell, it is because the Lord of Creation
has placed the choice before him.

The second objection to the antecedent/consequent wills approach
is that it seems to smack of the notion of merit. If all hearers are equally
enabled by grace to receive the gospel, and one person accepts the message while another person rejects it, then does not this mean that in some
way the first person is more virtuous than the second?[59] This is a difficult
objection, but two points should be kept in mind. First, this objection
seems to see faith as some sort of work, while the Bible consistently
contrasts faith with works (Rom 3:21–4:8). Faith, by its very nature, is
the opposite of works because it is an admission of a complete lack of
merit or ability. The beggar incurs no merit when he opens his hands to
receive a free gift.[60] Second, the mystery is not why some believe, but
why all do not believe. This again points to the mystery of evil. There is
no merit in accepting the gospel, but there is culpability in rejecting it.
This issue warrants more attention, which is why it is the focus of the
chapter on overcoming grace (chap 4). I believe the model presented in
that chapter—that God's grace is both monergistic and resistible—goes
a long way in answering this objection.

A third objection made by Reformed theologians is that the anteced-
ent/consequent wills paradigm gives "pride of place" to human free will

---

[57]G. C. Berkouwer, *Divine Election* (Grand Rapids: Eerdmans, 1960), 229.

[58]Shank, *Elect in the Son*, 129.

[59]See T. L. Tiessen, *Who Can Be Saved? Reassessing Salvation in Christ and World Religions* (Downers Grove, IL: InterVarsity, 2004), 238–39; and T. R. Schreiner and A. B. Caneday, *The Race Set Before Us: A Biblical Theology of Perseverance and Assurance* (Downers Grove, IL: InterVarsity, 2001), 318.

[60]Geisler points out that faith can be viewed as a work only by an equivocation of the word "do." "Faith is something we 'do' in the sense that it involves an act of our will prompted by God's grace. However, faith is not something we 'do' in the sense of a meritorious work necessary for God to give us salvation. Rather, it is something we exercise to *receive* salvation because we could not *do* anything to obtain salvation" [emphasis original]. See N. Geisler, *Chosen but Free: A Balanced View of Divine Election*, 2nd ed. (Minneapolis: Bethany House, 2001), 198.

over God's glory.[61] John Piper argues that the hidden/revealed view and the antecedent/consequent view are basically the same except for one important difference.[62] Both views contend that God genuinely desires the salvation of all, both views hold that this desire is superceded by an even greater will, but the two views disagree on what that greater will is. Piper states that the hidden/revealed position sees the greater will to be God's desire to glorify Himself, while the antecedent/consequent position understands the greater will to be His giving of self-determination to humans. Piper concludes that the hidden/revealed paradigm does greater justice to the glory of God.

However, in their response to Piper, Walls and Dongell emphasize that proponents of the antecedent/consequent wills position do not affirm a graciously enabled human ability of self-determination for its own sake. Rather, the concern is to portray faithfully God's character. God holds the unbeliever accountable because the sin of unbelief truly belongs to the unbeliever. Those condemned by God are justly condemned because receiving Christ was a choice genuinely available. Adhering to genuine human choice is not an end in itself; upholding the integrity of God's character is. Rather than failing to magnify God's glory, the antecedent/consequent wills position glorifies God by maintaining that His dealings are just and consistent with His holy nature.[63] If the greatest way for humans to bring glory to God is to choose Him freely, then the antecedent/consequent wills view best fulfills this goal. Again, we will give more attention to this issue in the chapter on overcoming grace.

Interestingly, Piper uses the just judge analogy to make his case for the hidden/revealed wills scenario.[64] He gives the specific instance of when George Washington was faced with the difficult dilemma of having one of his favorite officers guilty of a capital crime. Despite his affection for the young man, Washington gave the order for his execution. Piper's illustration actually is an example of the antecedent/consequent wills paradigm, because according to the hidden/revealed wills model,

---

[61]D. Westblade, "Divine Election in the Pauline Literature," in Schreiner and Ware, *The Grace of God, the Bondage of the Will*, 69–70.

[62]Piper, "Are There Two Wills in God?" 123–24.

[63]Walls and Dongell, *Why I Am Not a Calvinist*, 8.

[64]Piper, "Are There Two Wills in God?" 128.

Washington secretly wills the crime of the officer and inclines the young man's will to commit the deed.

CONCLUSION

We have considered the four options concerning God's salvific will: God has one will that all are saved, God has one will that certain ones are saved, God has two wills—one hidden and the other revealed, or God has two wills—an antecedent will for the salvation of all and a consequent will that faith is the condition to salvation. The antecedent/consequent wills paradigm seems to me to best capture the testimony of Scripture.

The Great Commission is the expression of the divine will. His desire is that everyone in the whole world hears the good news so that those who receive the gospel might be saved.[65] Armed with a Great Commission hermeneutic and Molinist understanding of divine sovereignty and human freedom, we now look at the five points of salvation generally associated with Calvinism. However, instead of TULIP, the next five chapters present ROSES.

---

[65]At this point the question of the unevanglized arises. Molinism argues that God actualizes a world in which everyone who would receive Christ actually has the opportunity to do so. See W. L. Craig, "'No Other Name': A Middle Knowledge Perspective on the Exclusivity of Salvation Through Christ," *Faith and Philosophy* 6:2 (April 1989): 172–88.

CHAPTER 3

R OSES

IS FOR RADICAL DEPRAVITY

Depravity, yes; determinism, no.

THE BIBLE PAINTS a bleak picture of the human condition. The fall affected every aspect of our being: the mind is darkened (Rom 3:11); the will is twisted (2 Pet 2:19); and affections are disordered (Isa 57:21; Titus 3:3; 1 Pet 2:11). All relationships are distorted, strained, or broken, both with God (Gen 3:8–10) and with others (Jas 4:1–2). Scriptures portray humans as morally evil (Gen 6:5; 8:21; Matt 7:11; 12:34; John 3:19), spiritually sick (Jer 17:9; Matt 9:12), and spiritually blind (Matt 4:16; 1 Cor 2:14; 2 Cor 4:4). The lost are in bondage to sin (John 8:34; Rom 6:6) and live under the sentence of death: physical death (Rom 5:12; 1 Cor 15:22), spiritual death (Eph 2:1; 5:14), and eventually eternal death (Rom 6:23; Rev 21:8).[1]

The crucial issue at hand is how depravity affects our ability to make choices. And to understand how the fall impacted our ability to choose we must also examine the nature of human choice itself. Do fallen sinners have "free will"? External coercion is easily recognized as incompatible with free will. But what if the factors determining choices and decisions were internal, located within a person's makeup? Would we call that person's will free or determined, or somehow both? Unfortunately, many within Calvinism do not just hold to depravity but determinism.

To get an idea how character "determines" choices, consider this example. In 1521, Martin Luther was summoned by Emperor Charles V to the Diet of Worms to answer charges of heresy. When pressured to recant, Luther replied, "My conscience is bound by the Word of God. I

---

[1] See B. Demarest, *The Cross and Salvation* (Wheaton: Crossway, 1997), 292–93.

cannot and will not retract. . . . I can do no other."[2] In taking his stand,
Luther described himself as incapable of doing otherwise in no less than
three different ways—his conscience was "bound" so that he "cannot"
retract and "can do no other." Was he making another of his famous ex-
aggerated statements (Erasmus often referred to Luther as "Dr. Hyperbole")? Or was he revealing an important insight into the relationship
between choices and character? If he really was not able to act in this
situation in any other way, were his actions *free?*

The principle that character determines choices is generally understood to be a fundamental tenet of *soft determinism*, but this chapter
will argue that it can also be a central plank of a position sometimes
called *soft libertarianism.*[3] Soft libertarianism contends that interaction
between character and free choice is a two-way street, providing for a
better model of human responsibility. It affirms the two great scriptural
truths concerning free will: choice is a power (1 Cor 10:13) and one's
choices are a manifestation of who he is (Matt 7:17–18).

In order to have a proper understanding of the effects radical depray-
ity has on human choice, we are going to have to spend a little time sur-
veying the issues involved. Traditionally, there have been two approaches
to the question of free will: *determinism* and *libertarianism.* For the most
part, adherents of either position qualify their respective arguments to the
point that it is appropriate to add the modifier "soft" to distinguish their
views from hard-line versions. Therefore, philosophers and theologians
speak of "soft" libertarianism and "soft" determinism.

Comparison of Determinism and Libertarianism	
Determinism—choices are caused by prior conditions.	*Libertarianism*—choices originate within persons.
Hard determinism—free will is an illusion.	*Hard libertarianism*—persons always have free will.
Soft determinism—free will is com-patible with determinism.	*Soft libertarianism*—persons have free will at significant times.

---

[2]J. H. Merle D'Aubigné, *The Triumph of Truth: A Life of Martin Luther* (Greenville, SC: Bob Jones Univ. Press, 1996), 327.

[3]Both terms, *soft determinism* and *soft libertarianism*, will be defined in the next section.

DETERMINISM

The view that Luther's decision was completely determined by his character and his situation, and that he lacked the ability to do otherwise, is a philosophical position appropriately called *determinism*. Determinism argues that since a person's character (or nature, according to some determinists) determines his choices, then in any given situation one and only one choice is actually possible. Whenever a person makes a decision, the prior conditions (i.e., the external circumstances and the internal character of the person) dictate so that no other choice can be made.

As stated earlier, determinists fall into two camps: *hard determinism* and *soft determinism*. A hard determinist believes that determinism is incompatible with free will. Since he is convinced that determinism is true, the hard determinist concludes no such thing as free will exists. This is the argument of Richard Double in his book, *The Non-reality of Free Will.*[4]

Most determinists opt for soft determinism, which argues that determinism is indeed compatible with free will, which is why it is often referred to as *compatibilism*. Many in the theological world use the label ambiguously to affirm the compatibility of free will and divine sovereignty—a position even open theists affirm. Rather, compatibilism affirms that free will is compatible with causal determinism. The above point is important, especially when Calvinists insinuate that any affirmation of libertarian freedom simply is human depravity rearing its rebellious head (One often hears, "Every man is born Arminian; grace makes him a Calvinist"). This is an odd claim indeed, in light of the fact that most determinists are not Calvinists, but atheists and Muslims.[5]

---

[4]See R. Double, *The Non-reality of Free Will* (Oxford: Oxford University Press, 1990).

[5]Theological determinism is only one of a variety of "determinisms." The ancient pagans held to fatalistic and physical determinism, while enlightenment and modern thinkers embraced psychological and logical determinism in addition to physical determinism. Islam strongly advocates a theological determinism in which the ultimate goal of the Muslim is to submit to the irresistible, all-encompassing will of Allah. See R. Kane, *The Significance of Free Will* (Oxford: Oxford University Press, 1998), 5–9; and C. Sedgwick, "Predestination, Pauline and Islamic: A Study in Contrasts," *Vox Evangelica* 26 (1996): 69–91.

The quintessential presentation of determinism and its compatibility with free will is Jonathan Edwards's *Freedom of the Will*.[6] My students can affirm that when I teach about Edwards, it is with appreciation and respect. Edwards is America's premiere philosopher-theologian. But not everything he taught should be accepted wholesale. It is primarily through Edwards's *Freedom of the Will* that causal determinism became part and parcel of Calvinism's doctrine of divine sovereignty, and this is not a good thing.

Richard Muller contends that among the post-Reformation theologians prior to Edwards there was "not even a tendency toward metaphysical determinism."[7] They resisted the works of men such as Thomas Hobbes, who in his *Leviathan* (1651) demonstrated that materialism logically requires a mechanical determinism which views the human will merely as the product of a chain of prior physical events.

A number of eighteenth-century divines took refuge from determinism by embracing Arminianism. Edwards considered this a greater threat than Hobbes's materialism. Allen Guelzo demonstrates that Edwards baptized Hobbes's determinism by co-opting his definition of the will and resetting it in a theological framework. The result was theistic causal determinism. As Guelzo notes,

> Edwards was thus, in technical terms, a compatibilist: free will
> *and* necessity can work together—but it was a compatibilism
> in which divine determinism clearly had the upper hand, and
> in which a great deal depended on an acceptance of Edwards's
> claim to define *liberty* and *necessity*. And if this still looked to

---

[6] J. Edwards, "A careful and strict enquiry into the modern prevailing notions of that freedom of will," in *The Works of Jonathan Edwards,* vol. 1 (Edinburgh: Banner of Truth, [1754]1990).

[7] R. Muller, *Post-Reformation Reformed Dogmatics,* 2nd ed., vol. 1 (Grand Rapids: Baker, 2003), 128–29. The expanded quote reads, "Both Beza and Perkins assume, moreover, a category of divine permission and the existence, as well, of contingent events and free will in the world. There is not even a tendency toward metaphysical determinism: when we enter the world of seventeenth-century theological debate, it is the purportedly predestinarian Reformed who take up the defense of human free choice and secondary causality against the more deterministic tendencies of Cartesian metaphysics, specifically the occasionalist conclusion, resting on the conception of necessary divine concursus, that God is the sole cause of all motion in the universe."

The Westminster Confession (1646) seems to endorse a libertarian view of the will and reject determinism when it states, "God has endued the will of man with that natural liberty, that is neither forced, nor, by any absolute necessity of nature, determined good, or evil." (Art 9.1 "Of Free Will")

the Arminian too much like making human beings into machines, then better to be a machine than an Arminian.[8]

So the Calvinism of today is often equated with causal determinism because many of its leading pastors and theologians explicitly follow Edwards on this point.[9] Theological determinists of today could more accurately be called "Edwardseans" rather than Calvinists. But Edwardsean is so difficult to say that I doubt the label would stick.[10]

Soft determinists affirm the *principle of universal causality*. That is, all things that happen are caused by sufficient prior conditions such that nothing else could have happened. Everything that happens is the result of cause and effect and could not have happened in any other way.[11] This is often called *event causation*, which posits a chain of events where each

---

[8]A. C. Guelzo, "The Return of the Will: Jonathan Edwards and the Possibilities of Free Will," in *Edwards in Our Time: Jonathan Edwards and the Shaping of American Religion* (Grand Rapids: Eerdmans, 1999), 94. According to Guelzo, Edwards's determinism becomes the paradigm of Calvinism in America. He states, "Over the century after Edwards's death, *Freedom of the Will* became almost a cultural synonym for Calvinism: Herman Melville's narrator in 'Bartleby' looks into 'Edwards on the Will' for direction on how to deal with the will-less scrivener; Longfellow's Killingworth parson does not need to be called a Calvinist for us to know what he is when we find out what he reads:

> …a man austere
> The instinct of whose nature was to kill;
> The wrath of God he preached from year to year,
> And read, with fervor, Edwards on the will. (p. 95)

[9]Men such as John Gerstner, R. C. Sproul Sr., John Feinberg, Bruce Ware, and John Frame all follow Edwards in his commitment to determinism. But none follow more diligently than John Piper, who also embraces Edwards's position on occasionalism. See J. Piper, *God's Passion for His Glory: Living the Vision of Jonathan Edwards* (Wheaton: Crossway, 1998), 95–96. Occasionalism is the view that God is the *direct* and *sole* cause of every event that happens.

[10]Richard Muller, whose expertise in post-Reformation theology is unquestioned, argued against determinism in his contribution in Ware and Schreiner's two-volume work on Calvinism. The response of his fellow Calvinists was to treat him like the crazy uncle at the family reunion. See R. Muller, "Grace, Election, and Contingent Choice: Arminius' Gambit and the Reformed Response," in *Grace of God, the Bondage of the Will*, vol. 2, ed. T. R. Schreiner and B. A. Ware (Grand Rapids: Baker, 1995), 251–78.

One could plot the trajectory of Reformed thought concerning free will by looking at the titles of three significant books on the subject: M. Luther, *The Bondage of the Will* (1525); J. Calvin, *The Bondage and Liberation of the Will* (1543); and J. Edwards, *Freedom of the Will* (1754). Reading the three together shows that the question boils down to whether "certainty" is synonymous with "necessity." Luther and Edwards both answer "yes," while Calvin is ambiguous. Luther denied free will; Edwards redefined it.

[11]J. S. Feinberg, "God Ordains All Things," in *Predestination and Free Will: Four Views of Divine Sovereignty and Human Freedom*, ed. D. Basinger (Downers Grove, IL: InterVarsity, 1986), 19–28; and J. L. Walls and J. R. Dongell, *Why I Am Not a Calvinist* (Downers Grove, IL: InterVarsity, 2004), 96–118.

cause is the effect of a prior cause, much like a chain of dominos. A person's choice is simply the effect of a complex nexus of prior causes.

If determinism is true, then obviously a redefinition of freedom is in order, at least a definition different from the way most people understand freedom. And compatibilists provide one: human freedom is redefined as the *freedom of inclination*. Freedom of inclination is the ability to do what one wants, but one does not have power over his inclinations. Bruce Ware defines compatibilist freedom to be the "freedom of one's strongest inclination, desire, and volition. That is, our freedom consists in our choosing and doing according to what we are inclined most, or what we desire most, to do."[12]

The Two Tenets of Soft Determinism	
The law of choice	A person's choices are dictated by his desires.
The causal necessity of choice	A person must choose the way he does; no other choice was possible.

Armed with this definition of freedom, determinism argues two central tenets. First, *a person's choices are dictated by his desires*, a point that inescapably follows from accepting freedom as the freedom of inclination. A human being may be free to choose *as* he desires, but he is not free to choose *what* he desires. In fact, determinism argues he *must* choose what he desires to be able to choose at all. R. C. Sproul Sr. labels this tenet *Edwards's Law of Choice*: "The will always chooses according to its strongest inclination at the moment."[13] Freedom is the ability to obey one's desires, but freedom does not include power over one's desires.

This leads to the second tenet, which is that all *choices are causally necessary*. In his defense of compatibilism, Bruce Ware explains,

---

[12]B. A. Ware, *God's Greater Glory: The Exalted God of Scripture and the Christian Faith* (Wheaton: Crossway, 2004), 25.

[13]R. C. Sproul Sr., *Chosen by God* (Wheaton: Tyndale, 1986), 54.

> Compatibilist freedom . . . insists that regardless of what strug-
> gles we go through in making our choices or deciding what action
> to perform, in the end, when we choose and act, we do so from
> prevailing desires which explain exactly why *this* choice and not
> another is made. This obviously means, however, that when we
> choose, all things being just what they are, we *must* choose as we
> do![14]

As Ware indicates, it is the claim that causal determinism can "exactly
explain" free will and human choice that makes it so attractive to its adherents. Compatibilism teaches that the ability to do otherwise is merely
hypothetical. When we make a choice, if we had wanted to do differently, we could have. However, given who we are and given a particular
situation, we do not have the ability to want differently, so the ability to
do otherwise is only hypothetical, not actual.

The example of Luther at Worms shows us that the relationship between responsibility and freedom gets complicated in a hurry. Soft determinism, or compatibilism, provides many helpful insights, but it also
has serious problems. It is not so much wrong as it is incomplete. It provides an inadequate view of human choice and by so doing it misleads
at crucial points. And it has a problem even its proponents recognize:
compatibilism appears to make God the author of sin (a problem we will
shortly explore further).

LIBERTARIANISM

Libertarianism is the view that the morally responsible agent is in
some sense the origin of his choices, and that prior conditions such as
circumstances are not the final determiner for that agent. Like determinism, libertarianism can be divided into hard and soft versions. A *hard
libertarian* argues that, in order for a person to be genuinely free, he
must always have the ability to choose the contrary, or must be free from
external influences.[15] Some hard libertarians, such as a number of open

---

[14]Ware, *God's Greater Glory,* 25. Emphasis original.

[15]Steve Lemke makes the distinction between the two approaches to libertarianism when he explains, "Agent causation is the view that 'if a man is responsible for a particular deed . . . there is some
event, or set of events, that is caused, *not* by other events or states of affairs, but by the man himself, by
the agent.' Agent causation thus presupposes at least what I shall call a soft libertarian view of freedom

theists, are willing to sacrifice the traditional understanding of God's omniscience in order to preserve a version of hard libertarianism.

Soft Libertarianism

Soft libertarianism, or *concurrence,* is very similar to soft determinism in many ways but views human responsibility differently in several crucial aspects. On the question of how character frames our choices, soft libertarianism holds ideas comparable to its counterpart soft determinism. Both believe that a person's character governs his choices. But a soft libertarian does not believe this tells the whole story.

Soft libertarianism has two distinctive features that distinguish it from soft determinism. First, *character determines the range of choices, rather than a specific choice itself.* This means that within the parameters of a person's makeup, a wide range of choices is available.

An example of how this principle works in practice is the way in which the nature and character of God determine the set of His possible options. The Bible teaches that God always operates within the metaphysical and moral realities of who He is. God always acts within the constraints of His holy nature, which is why we can depend on His faithfulness (Mal 3:6). God's attributes such as His wisdom and power are infinite, while His moral qualities are absolute. These perfections have the paradoxical effect of placing certain choices outside the scope of possibility. For example, the author of Hebrews tells us that because of His omnipotent nature, it is impossible for God to swear by anyone greater than Himself (Heb 6:13). And just as God's nature imposes upon Him metaphysical constraints, God's character also places upon Him

---

in which humans exhibit a creaturely freedom to choose within limited alternatives without being predetermined by prior events, states of affairs, desires, or judgments. A *soft libertarian* view of freedom, like all libertarian views, defines freedom as the ability to do otherwise in any given decision. The label 'soft' libertarian is to differentiate it from hard libertarian views in which persons are said to determine events entirely on their own without external influence. A soft libertarian perspective acknowledges the incredible influence that external forces exert on our decision making process, but still insists that the final decision remains with the agent. To cite Leibniz's famous phrase, these external influences 'incline the will without necessitating it.'" See S. Lemke, "How to Be a Soft Libertarian," http://www.nobts. edu/Faculty/ItoR/LemkeSW/Personal/Agent-Causation-Or-How-to-Be-A-Soft-Libertarian-Dr.-Lemke. pdf. The one place I amend Lemke's definition of soft libertarianism is that I do not hold that an agent must have the ability to do otherwise "in any given situation," but, as we will see, "at significant will-setting moments."

moral limits. God, declares Paul, "cannot lie" (Titus 1:2; cf. Heb 6:18).
So God's nature and character place metaphysical and moral limits, respectively, on the decisions made by God.

Yet an array of choices is still genuinely available to Him. For example, a central component of the doctrine of creation is that God created
freely, without constraint or necessity. If God had chosen not to create,
He would have suffered no lack, nor does creation provide something He
was missing. God created freely, and in order for God's act of creation
to be unconditional and gracious, His decision had to be free in a libertarian sense. The same reasoning holds true concerning His decision to
elect or not to elect, to save or not to save certain individuals. Calvinists
generally agree that God is under no compulsion to save any particular
individual.[16] So God's choices are congruent with who He is, yet within
the parameters of His nature are alternative possibilities truly within His
power.

I make this point because some determinists, namely John Feinberg
and Steven Cowen, argue against libertarianism by denying that God has
libertarian freedom.[17] They base their argument on facts such as that God
cannot sin or choose to cease to exist. Since He cannot sin, they reason
that even God does not have the power to do otherwise. If God does not
have libertarian freedom then there is no reason to believe that humans
have it either. That's quite a claim to make, for they are saying not just
that determinism is true, but that God's choices are determined also.[18]

Contrary to determinism, Thomas Flint argues that God indeed has
libertarian freedom. If God does not, then He created because He had
to—or more specifically, He had to create this particular world. Then
this is the only possible world, and "all true distinctions between necessity and contingency . . . collapse, as [does] the gratuitousness both of

---

[16]W. G. T. Shedd, *Calvinism: Pure and Mixed* (Edinburgh: Banner of Truth, [1893] 1986), 70–71.
Shedd argues that God's sovereign choice in election "denotes *optional power*; that is, the power to act
or not to act in a given instance. It is more particularly with reference to this latter characteristic of free
alternative decision, that 'the sovereignty of God in election' is spoken of. In his election of a sinner to
salvation, God as supreme, independent, and sovereign, acts with entire liberty of decision, and not as
obliged and shut up to one course of action" (emphasis original).

[17]See J. S. Feinberg, *No One Like Him* (Wheaton: Crossway, 2001), 730–31; and S. B. Cowan,
"God, Libertarian Agency, and Scientific Explanations," *Philosophia Christi* 4.1 (2002): 125–37.

[18]The claim is in keeping with Edwards's view that all of God's choices are necessary.

God's creation and our existence."[19] This clearly conflicts with Christian doctrine, so God must enjoy freedom of a libertarian variety. Flint argues that humans, who are created in God's image, have reflections of this same type of freedom.

So both Feinberg and Flint use God's freedom to illustrate the determinist and the libertarian positions respectively. If possible, it would seem that some type of combination of the two positions is in order, which is what soft libertarianism attempts to do. Soft libertarianism argues that God has a libertarian freedom that is restricted by the parameters of His nature. The notion of a limited ability to choose to the contrary seems reasonable, since soft libertarianism does not require that the ability to choose the contrary is absolute. As we will see shortly, some of the conclusions of R. C. Sproul Jr. will show the dangers of rejecting the notion that God has libertarian freedom. So soft libertarianism contends that character provides the set of possible choices, but character does not determine the specific choice itself.

The second distinctive feature of soft libertarianism is the contention that *the relationship between free choices and character is a two-way street.* Your choices manifest who you are, but they also change who you are. Choice and character interact in a feedback loop. A person's character indeed limits his choices, but the present condition of one's character is the way it is because of the previous free decisions made during certain important "will-setting" moments. We will explore the notion of will-setting again shortly.

According to soft libertarianism, or concurrence, Luther's earlier free decisions to search the Scriptures resulted in the Word fashioning his convictions and molding his character. Those earlier choices were freely made. As a result, Luther's moral fiber was shaped in such a way that would not allow him to renounce the truth, but this "inability to do otherwise" was an outcome of his previous free choices. The give-and-take interaction between free choices and character is just one difference between soft libertarianism and soft determinism, but it is a significant difference.

---

[19]T. P. Flint, *Divine Providence: the Molinist Account* (Ithaca: Cornell University Press, 1998), 26–30.

The Five Tenets of Soft Libertarianism	
Ultimate responsibility (UR)	Ultimate responsibility indicates the ultimate origin of decisions.
Agent causation (AC)	A person is the source and origin of his choices.
The principle of alternative possibilities (AP)	At crucial times, the ability to choose or refrain from choosing is genuinely available.
The reality of will-setting moments	A person does not always have the ability to choose to the contrary. Certain free choices result in the loss of freedom.
The distinction between freedom of responsibility and freedom of integrity	The Bible presents freedom as a *permission* (the freedom of responsibility) and as a *power* (the freedom of integrity).

The Five Tenets of Soft Libertarianism

From the works of libertarian philosophers such as Hugh McCann, Timothy O'Connor, and particularly Robert Kane, five central tenets of soft libertarianism can be gleaned.[20] Thus equipped, soft libertarianism provides a more complete picture of human choice than soft determinism, and thus a more accurate one. Soft libertarianism, or concurrence, holds that a moral agent has the power to choose in a libertarian sense, but the limits of this ability are decided by his character. While a determinist argues a person's choice is determined by his character, soft libertarianism contends a person's character simply determines what sets of choices are available. Outside influences and internal dispositions are factors, but the agent has the ability to take any one of the choices within

---

[20]H. J. McCann, *The Works of Agency: on Human Action, Will, and Freedom* (Ithaca: Cornell University Press, 1998); T. O'Connor, *Persons and Causes: the Metaphysics of Free Will* (Oxford: Oxford University Press, 2000); and R. Kane, *The Significance of Free Will* (Oxford: Oxford University Press, 1998).

the set. Possessing libertarian freedom means we genuinely choose, but we dwell in a fallen world so it is not an easy, even, unslanted choice. And we are finite creatures, so the range of choices is limited.

The first tenet of soft libertarianism is *ultimate responsibility* (UR). Question: how does a person know the ultimate source of his sins or the ultimate source of his salvation? Answer: whoever is ultimately responsible. And the Bible makes clear that we are responsible for our sins and God is responsible for our salvation. We receive all the blame and He receives all the credit. As Kane states, "The basic idea is that the *ultimate responsibility* lies where the *ultimate cause* is."[21] Ultimate "buck-stopping" responsibility indicates ultimate origin.

Kane argues that libertarians make a mistake by focusing too quickly on the criteria of alternative possibilities (AP), i.e., the ability to do otherwise, and contends rather that we should begin with the notion of ultimate responsibility. UR focuses on the grounds or the sources of a person's actions or choices. UR, rather than AP, should be the initial feature of soft libertarianism. And unless one wants to posit an infinite regress of past causes or (for the theist) he wants the chain of responsibility to go back to God, then he has to understand that moral agents are responsible in an ultimate sense. Kane concludes, "Therein, I believe, lies the core of the traditional 'problem of free will.'"[22]

Significantly, the UR condition does not require that every act be done of our own free will (thus, to an extent "partially vindicating" the compatibilist position). However, it is only a partial vindication, because UR argues that we "could have done otherwise" with respect to some past choices that formed our present character.

UR implies the second tenet: *agent causation* (AC). If a human being is found guilty when he stands before God, it is because he is the origin of his sins. His sins belong to him—he *owns* them. This is why everyone outside of Christ is damned. Though we inherited Adam's corruption and are judged federally in him, in a real way each person is the source and origin of his own rebellion.

---

[21] Kane, *The Significance of Free Will*, 35. Emphasis original.
[22] R. Kane, "Some Neglected Pathways in the Free Will Labyrinth," in *The Oxford Handbook of Free Will*, ed. R. Kane (Oxford: Oxford University Press, 2002), 407–9.

When the question is asked, "Why did Adam sin?" the soft libertarian answer is, "Because he chose to sin." No other or further answer is needed. God placed him in an environment where sin was possible, but God is not the cause of Adam's sin. In fact, God is not culpable in any way. Satan is certainly guilty of enticing the original couple, but in the final analysis the blame for the actual sin they committed does not fall on him. No, Scripture consistently testifies that "by one man sin entered into the world" (Rom 5:12 KJV).

AC stands in contrast to event causation.[23] Rather than functioning simply as a link in a chain of events, a causal agent operates as the impetus for new causal chains. This creative ability reflects the *imago dei*. As Robert Saucy states, "The human being is like God in that he has the ability to create thoughts and actions that have no determinative cause outside of the self." In other words, humans are causal agents with the capacity to originate choices. Saucy goes on to say that this ability constitutes what might be termed "a little citadel of creativity *ex nihilo*."[24]

After establishing the tenets of UR and AC, then and only then are we ready to consider the third tenet: *the principle of alternative possibilities* (AP). A necessary component for liability is that, at a significant point in the chain of events, the ability to choose or refrain from choosing had to genuinely be available.

Compatibilists work from the intuition that if a choice is undetermined then it must be capricious.[25] Indeterminism is equated with inexplicable choices in which an agent's will is disconnected from the rest of his person, resulting in random and chaotic choices that bewilder even the agent. In this scenario, free will resembles something akin to Tourette syndrome or epilepsy rather than a moral ability. But as determinists admit, in this field intuitions must be questioned.

Kane responds by arguing, "It is a mistake to assume that *undetermined* means 'uncaused.'"[26] Rather, one must think of the effort to choose

[23]See T. O'Connor, "Agent Causation," in *Agents, Causes, and Events: Essays on Indeterminism and Free Will*, ed. T. O'Connor (Oxford: Oxford University Press, 1995), 173–74.

[24]R. Saucy, "Theology of Human Nature," in *Christian Perspectives on Being Human: A Multidisciplinary Approach to Integration*, ed. J. P. Moreland and D. M. Ciocchi (Grand Rapids: Baker, 1993), 28.

[25]Sproul Sr., *Chosen by God*, 53.

[26]Kane, "Some Neglected Pathways in the Free Will Labyrinth," 421.

and indeterminism as "fused," not that indeterminism is something that occurs before or after the choice. The fact that the choice is indeterminate doesn't make it any less the agent's choice, nor does it make the choice simply a matter of chance or luck. So the objection that undetermined choices are "happenings" is question-begging. It assumes what the objector wishes to prove: that all choices are determined.[27] However, concurrence does not require AP to always be present, which leads to the next point.

The fourth tenet of soft libertarianism is the recognition of *will-setting moments*. This point sets soft libertarianism apart from libertarianism as generally understood. I argue, like Kane, that libertarian freedom does not entail that a person must always have the ability to choose to the contrary. Certain free choices result in the loss of freedom. An obvious example is someone jumping off a cliff. Halfway down he might change his mind, but he does not possess the ability to choose otherwise. AP does not always have to be present, but only during those times when the choices we make form us into who we are. Only then do we need to be free in a libertarian sense. The "will-setting" or "self-forming" actions occur at those crucial, difficult, or critical junctures.

Consider how we are torn during times of moral indecision. However, whether it is Luther submitting to the authority of Scripture or Pharaoh hardening his heart, those soul-searching moments are also times of self-formation. During these times the outcome is uncertain because our wills are divided by conflicting desires. Yet the decision made at that time affects who we are as persons, so that later similar decisions do not produce a similar conflict.[28] How we choose *changes* us so that, for better or worse, that choice no longer affects us in the same way. This is the fundamental principle underlying the practice of utilizing the spiritual disciplines for character formation. The reality of will-setting moments implies the next tenet.

The fifth tenet of soft libertarianism is *the distinction between the two types of ability: freedom of responsibility and freedom of integrity*. As stated earlier, freedom can be understood in two ways: as *a permission* and as *an ability*. The Bible often presents freedom as a permission,

---

[27]Ibid., 423.
[28]Ibid., 417.

a privilege, or a right to choose. An example of freedom of permission is when Paul instructs that a Christian widow is "free to be married to anyone she wants," as long as she marries a believer (1 Cor 7:39). This is what we would generally call "liberty," and the Bible provides many examples of this type of freedom (2 Cor 9:7; Phlm 14).

Freedom of permission presupposes that a person has the second type of freedom, i.e., the ability to make a reasonable choice. This is why the Bible also presents freedom as a power or ability to make a choice. As an ability, the Bible teaches that there are types of ability: *freedom of responsibility* and *freedom of integrity*. Freedom of responsibility is the ability to be the originator of a decision, choice, or action. Because a human being is the agent or cause of an action, he is responsible for the moral nature of that action and its consequences. When a situation arises that requires a decision, by definition the freedom of responsibility is the ability to respond. Take for example, if a man hears someone in the lake calling for help. Someone who cannot swim has a different level of responsibility from the one who simply chooses not to respond.

This brings up the notion of *freedom of integrity*, an important concept to soft libertarianism. Freedom of integrity is the ability to act in a way that is consistent with what a person knows to be the right thing to do. This category consists of the freedom to be the kind of person one wants to be. It is the ability to translate one's values into action. It speaks of the level of development one must reach to be a fully functioning and mature person. This is a crucial component to our understanding of freedom. More than anything else, the Bible presents freedom to be *the ability to do that which is right.*[29]

This concept of freedom pays more attention to the concept of "person" than to free will because ascriptions of personal integrity depend on an analysis of personal identity. The doctrine of the "age of accountability" is based on the notion of freedom of integrity. It is the belief that a child must reach a certain point of mental, emotional, and spiritual development before he is accountable.

---

[29]D. M. Ciocchi, "Human Freedom" in Moreland and Ciocchi, *Christian Perspectives on Being Human: A Multidisciplinary Approach to Integration*, 101–4; and J. P. Moreland and W. L. Craig, *Philosophical Foundations for a Christian Worldview* (Downers Grove, IL: InterVarsity, 2003), 268.

The notion of the freedom of integrity speaks to the conflict one often has between his values and his desires (see Romans 7). Unless one is completely pathological, sin and failure to live according to his values will result in the loss of peace of mind that comes from living with integrity.

It is easy to understand the freedom of integrity on a trivial level: freedom of integrity enables one to exercise as he should, or to not procrastinate about an assignment. The principle of freedom of integrity indicates that self-discipline is actually a profound type of freedom. As such, the relationship between free will and freedom of personal integrity can be confusing. It is commonplace to be morally responsible but lack freedom of personal integrity. Free will addresses the minimal conditions for responsibility, while freedom of personal integrity goes beyond that.

Here is the truly dangerous thing: a person can have enough freedom to be responsible yet lack (or lose) the freedom of integrity. The Bible says all have the freedom of moral responsibility but not all have the freedom of integrity.

For example, in Rom 7:13–25, Paul describes the condition of being morally responsible but lacking in moral integrity. Other clear examples are the addicted and the pathological. Heroin addicts, compulsive gamblers, and pedophiles may have lost the integrity to say no to these vices, but they are still responsible for their actions. As drug addicts illustrate, it is possible to lose this type of freedom. This loss does not exempt the person from accountability for his actions. Loss of this ability means that a person can still be morally responsible even though he is no longer capable of choosing otherwise. In fact, in the very important area of the ability to respond to God, this is the exact condition of every lost person outside the grace of God.

The progressive sanctification of a believer and his growth in grace can be understood in terms of freedom of integrity. In many ways, the process of being conformed to the image of Christ is an incremental restoration of the freedom of integrity. Sanctification is the restoring of a Christian's ability to bring his life into conformity with the will of God. This is true freedom—the ability to live a life that is pleasing to God.

Christ promises the freedom of integrity (John 8:36), which is the ability to obey the will of God.

The incremental nature of progressive sanctification should be a hint to us about the incremental nature of the freedom of integrity. That is, freedom of integrity is not something which operates like a light switch—all or nothing; on or off. Rather, it seems to be something gained or lost in increments. There appear to be gradations of the freedom of integrity.

THE FOUR STAGES OR STATES OF HUMAN EXPERIENCE

So how does soft libertarianism work? Following the Formula of Concord (1577), most theologians recognize four stages of human experience: (1) the state of Adam as originally created, (2) the present state of fallen humanity, (3) the state of the believer while still in this present age, and (4) the eventual state of the saints in glory. When the way soft determinism and soft libertarianism handle each stage is compared and contrasted, the advantages of soft libertarianism become evident.

The Four Stages of Human Existence	
Adam as Originally Created	Able to sin or not to sin. Freedom of permission with probational freedom of integrity.
Humanity as Fallen	Able to sin but not able to not sin. Morally responsible but freedom of integrity is lost (i.e., in bondage to sin).
The Present Condition of Believers	Able to sin and graciously enabled to not sin. The freedom of integrity is progressively being restored.
The Saints in Glory	Not able to sin because not able to be tempted. The fully redeemed enjoy the perfect freedom of integrity.

Stage One: Adam as Originally Created

Any attempt to describe human choice must face the question of Adam's decision to eat the forbidden fruit. The dilemma facing the soft determinist is illustrated well by comparing the views of the father and son theological team, R. C. Sproul Sr. and R. C. Sproul Jr., both noted Reformed theologians and strong proponents of compatibilism. It appears to be Sproul vs. Sproul.

In his book, *Chosen by God*, R. C. Sproul Sr. devotes a chapter to Edwards's compatibilistic understanding of free will, in which he rejects libertarianism in favor of determinism.[30] He affirms that our choices are produced by our desires and that one and only one choice is truly possible.

However, in his discussion of Adam's abilities prior to the fall, Sproul Sr. uses what only can be described as libertarian language. He states, "Before the fall Adam was endowed with two possibilities: He had the ability to sin and the ability not to sin."[31]

Sproul Sr. as much as admits that determinism fails at this point, when he states,

> Herein lies the problem. Before a person can commit an act of sin he must first have a desire to perform that act. The Bible tells us that evil actions flow from evil desires. But the presence of an evil desire is already sin. We sin because we are sinners. We were born with a sin nature. We are fallen creatures. But Adam and Eve were not created fallen. They had no sin nature. They were good creatures with a free will. Yet they chose to sin. Why? I don't know. Nor have I found anyone yet who does know.[32]

Sproul Sr. concludes that he does not know why Adam sinned and that the compatibilistic paradigm provides no answer.

But does it really provide no answer, or does Sproul Sr. simply find the deterministic answer unacceptable? Sproul Sr.'s son, R. C. Sproul Jr.,

---

[30]Sproul Sr., *Chosen by God*, 51–57. Sproul Sr. describes libertarian freedom as *"the ability to make choices without any prior prejudice, inclination, or disposition. For the will to be free it must act from a posture of neutrality, with absolutely no bias"* (p. 51, emphasis original) This is a definition of hard libertarianism, and not the position of most libertarians.

[31]Ibid., 65.

[32]Ibid., 30.

approaches Adam's fall with a consistency that his father could not bring himself to follow. In a chapter titled "Who Dunit" in his book, *Almighty Over All: Understanding the Sovereignty of God*, Sproul Jr. doggedly applies causal determinism to the bitter end.[33] The son rushes in where the father has feared to tread.

Sproul Jr. begins his examination with a challenge to his fellow determinists by declaring that any appeal to mystery is an attempt to avoid the mental labor involved, and any refusal to accept the logical implications of determinism is just "false humility."[34] He observes that it is easy to understand why God judges sinners, but "the difficult question is how men came to be sinners in the first place."[35] He reiterates the soft determinist position of Jonathan Edwards, that our choices are determined by our greatest inclination. Sproul Jr. emphasizes he is simply taking Edwards's thought to its logical conclusion.[36] He reasons that there can be only five suspects for the fall: Eve, Adam, the surrounding environment, Satan, and finally, God.

First, Sproul Jr. examines suspect 1, Eve. Since, as Edwards says, one always acts according to his or her greatest inclination, and since God created Eve originally as good, Sproul Jr. reasons that sometime between Creation and the serpent's temptation she stopped being good. In other words, someone changed Eve's inclinations. And since Eve could not change her own inclinations "any more than a leopard can change his spots," she could not have been the origin of sin. Eve did not have the means, declares Sproul Jr., because she did not have a motive. "Something outside of her must have been the agent of change, that which changed her inclinations from good to bad."[37] He concludes that though Eve is the one who first ate from the tree, "she cannot be the one who introduced evil into the world."

The next to be scrutinized are suspects 2 and 3: Adam and the surrounding environment.[38] Sproul Jr. determines that Adam was unable to

---

[33]R. C. Sproul Jr., *Almighty Over All: Understanding the Sovereignty of God* (Grand Rapids: Baker, 1999), 43–59.

[34]Ibid., 44.

[35]Ibid., 45.

[36]Ibid., 46–47.

[37]Ibid., 49.

[38]Ibid.

change Eve's inclinations, so "he slips quickly off the suspect list." He also concludes that the setting of the garden, which was impersonal and merely material, lacked the power to determine the desire of humans.

As far as possible candidates go, Sproul Jr. describes suspect 4, the devil, as the "crowd favorite."[39] However, Sproul Jr. argues that the devil could not be the one to introduce evil because though he tempts and entices, he can appeal only to inclinations which are already twisted.

This leaves only suspect 5: God. Who introduced evil into the world? God did. Sproul Jr. declares that God Almighty is "the culprit" (his term).[40] "Of course it's impossible for God to do evil. He can't sin," reasons Sproul Jr. "This objection, however, is off the mark. I am not accusing God of sinning; I am suggesting that he created sin."[41]

Why would God do such a thing? Sproul Jr. explains that wrath is a divine attribute just like the other eternal qualities of God—except that God cannot enjoy it within Himself. His wrath, in order for it to be displayed properly, must have an object worthy of wrath. Sproul Jr. speculates that though the Triune God enjoyed His strength, power, and other excellencies, He was not able to demonstrate the glory of His wrath. In fact, Sproul Jr. does not hesitate to say that God *had* to induce the fall. Why? Because, "like man, God always acts according to his strongest inclination."

Many determinists, following John Calvin and the framers of the Westminster Confession, have tried to absolve God from blame by distinguishing between primary and secondary causes. But Sproul Jr. does not bother. After all, "we recognize that hiring a hit man does not shift the blame from the hirer to the hiree."[42] Both the hit man and the one who hired him are equally guilty. "And both can hang for it." So, Sproul Jr. reckons, God may not have personally pulled the trigger, but He is the one who caused Eve to sin by providing her with the depraved inclinations—"the trail ultimately leads back to God."[43]

---

[39] Ibid., 50.
[40] Ibid., 51.
[41] Ibid., 54.
[42] Ibid., 57.
[43] Ibid.

R. C. Sproul Jr.'s position is distressing, to put it mildly, and a number of objections must be lodged. First, he does not provide one scintilla of evidence for his position from the Genesis account. He bases his conclusions not on careful exegesis or even a close reading of the Genesis text, but on a fierce commitment to causal determinism.

Second, to say that God created sin is astounding. Sproul Jr.'s position flies in the face of the teaching of Scripture, historical Christian doctrine, the major Reformed confessions, other Calvinist theologians, and, notably, the statements of his father. In his discussion of compatibilism's inability to account for the fall, R.C. Sproul Sr. states, "In spite of this excruciating problem we still must affirm that God is not the author of sin. The Bible does not reveal the answers to all our questions. It does reveal the nature and character of God. One thing is absolutely unthinkable, that God could be the author or doer of sin."[44]

One of the most significant Reformed theologians of the twentieth century was John Gerstner. He was also R. C. Sproul Sr.'s teacher. Even though he was a staunch Calvinist, Gerstner cautioned his fellow Calvinists that when it came to the matter of the cause of Adam's sin, Reformed formulations sometimes hovered perilously close to the "abyss of blasphemy," and he warned against making God the author of sin.[45] Like most Calvinists, R. C. Sproul Sr. has heeded his mentor's warning, but it appears that Sproul Jr. has taken the plunge.

Third, to say that God had to create, that he lacked the ability to do otherwise, is also astounding. At this point the irony must be noted. Even though proponents of causal determinism advocate their position for the purpose of promoting the glory of God's sovereignty and freedom, in the end determinism teaches that God's choices are just as determined as ours. Sproul Jr. does not hesitate to say that in any given situation only one choice is truly available to God, and that decision is determined by His greatest inclination. If God's choices are determined, then this means that He does all things by necessity, a point that Jonathan Edwards acknowledged.[46] As noted earlier, this would mean that His decisions to

[44]Sproul Sr., *Chosen by God*, 31.

[45]J. Gerstner, "Augustine, Luther, Calvin and Edwards on the Bondage of the Will," in Schreiner and Ware, *The Grace of God, the Bondage of the Will*, vol. 2, 281.

[46]Edwards, *Freedom of the Will*, 4.7.

create and to redeem were not contingent but necessary. The God of the determinist is not free to refrain or do otherwise. And to rob God of His freedom is to rob Him of His glory.

Fourth, the notion that anything in creation supplies God with something He lacked is problematic. The God of the Bible is self-sufficient and has no needs. The Triune Godhead of Father, Son, and Holy Spirit exists in a complete relationship of love and holiness that experiences no deficiency. In addition, Sproul Jr.'s assertion that wrath is an eternal attribute is also a problem. Perhaps it would be better to say that God is eternally holy, and that this holiness manifests itself in time as wrath against the sin and unbelief of this world.

While saying that anything in creation meets a need in God is astounding, Sproul Jr.'s claim goes beyond that. It is *what* creation supposedly supplied for God that is the fifth problem. Creation provided God with sinners. God needs the wicked! As Sproul Jr. explains, "It was his desire to make his wrath known. He needed, then, something on which to be wrathful. He needed to have sinful creatures."[47] Maybe my reading list is not as well-rounded as it should be, but this is the first time I've ever heard of an evangelical theologian claiming that God needs sin.

Sixth, Sproul Jr.'s argument reveals that the problem of evil is particularly acute for theists who adhere to causal determinism. In determinism, a person's choice is determined, or caused, by the factors immediately preceding his decision. In other words, in determinism our choices are simply effects caused by complex chains of cause and effect. The causal chains may pass internally through a person via the forces that shaped his inclinations, but it is a chain nonetheless. But this means all decisions, including Adam's choice to commit the original sin, was the effect of a prior chain of causes. If 10,000 dominoes are in a row with each one falling one after the other, then the main question is about who tipped over the first one. So it is with determinism and the existence of evil. If determinism is true, then God is the first cause of sin. The logic of R. C. Sproul Jr. demonstrates this.

---

[47]Sproul Jr., *Almighty Over All*, 57.

However, since God is not the cause of sin, then causal determinism cannot be true. If a starting assumption logically compels one to a conclusion outside the boundaries set by Scripture, then the starting assumption must be wrong. The vast majority of Calvinists who hold to soft determinism reject the notion that sin originated with God, but they do so by a sheer act of will. The logic of their system leads to such a conclusion, but most have the good sense not to accept it.

In contrast to the compatibilist version of the fall we just surveyed, the concurrence view of soft libertarianism argues that the biblical text of Genesis 1–3 establishes Adam and Eve's responsibility on the principles of the *imago dei*, genuine freedom, and genuine participation.

First, Gen 1:26 informs us that God bequeathed to humanity a very special gift, the image of God, by which in a number of ways we reflect Him. This speaks again of Saucy's observation that humans are causal agents with the capacity to originate choices within "a little citadel of creativity *ex nihilo*."[48]

Second, the principle of genuine freedom was established by the very first recorded words of God to man, in which God grants freedom to Adam. "You are free to eat from any tree of the garden" (Gen 2:16). This freedom was not absolute or autonomous. It was circumscribed in that they could not eat from the Tree of Knowledge, and it was derived in that it was granted by God. The first couple's freedom was limited but real freedom nonetheless. Inherent with the ability to choose is the responsibility for the choice, which is established in the warning in Gen 2:17.

Third, human responsibility is also established by the principle of genuine participation. Man is to work the garden and be a steward over it. Before God provides Eve for Adam, God parades a variety of creatures before him. Genesis intriguingly states that God "brought each to the man to see what he would call it" (Gen 2:19). What does it mean for God to be curious about Adam's answers? This is obviously anthropomorphic language, but labeling it as such does not explain why Moses uses this type of language in the first place. Why does the Bible say it that way? It seems to be because Moses wants to emphasize the reality and

---

[48]Saucy, "Theology of Human Nature," 28.

contingency of the event itself. Human choices are not merely something scripted in a novel.

The soft libertarian model fits very well with the garden account. The ultimate responsibility for eating the forbidden fruit points very clearly to the origin of the sin: Adam and Eve. Soft libertarianism puts the original back in original sin. Adam is the causal agent of his sin. Regardless of the setting and temptation of the Serpent, one does not look for prior causes to account for Adam's choice. Adam is the creator of his choice.

This means that alternative possibilities were truly available to the original couple. They could have refrained from eating. However, when they chose to sin it was a radical will-setting moment. Their moral character was terribly malformed by the decision. The effects of the fall illustrate the interplay between the freedom of responsibility and the freedom of integrity. By choosing to do the wrong thing, the ability to choose the right thing was lost.

Stage Two: Humanity as Fallen

Much could be said about the state of fallen humanity, but we will focus only on the issues that relate to human responsibility. Scripture teaches at least three truths about the human condition: (1) the lost are in bondage to sin (John 8:34; Rom 3:10–13; 5:12–18; 6:19–20; 1 John 5:19), yet (2) humanity exhibits a spectrum of relative moral behavior (Luke 12:46–48; Acts 10:22), and (3) even the best person is unable naturally to respond to God (John 6:44,65; 1 Cor 2:14; 2 Cor 4:3–4). Soft libertarianism provides a model that does justice to all three truths.

We inherit Adam's corrupt state, so our choices are inevitably twisted toward sin. The radical depravity model, by arguing that character provides the range of limited libertarian choices, presents humanity's plight as analogous to imprisonment. We are free to choose within the strictures of our fallen natures. We are like inmates free to roam about a prison but never to leave.

Lynyrd Skynyrd's "Free Bird" is a southern rock anthem to irresponsibility. Explaining to his girlfriend why he wouldn't commit to their relationship, lead singer Ronnie Van Zant declares his wanderlust with, "Cause I'm as free as a bird now." However, the song may reveal more than he realized. The lyrics end with a repeated refrain which admits,

> And this bird you can not change.
> Lord knows, I can't change.
> Lord help me, I can't change.

Some freedom: he is free to do anything except be different. This highlights how humanity has radically lost the freedom of integrity. In this way, the lost really should not be described as "free." A willing slave is still a slave. As Calvin puts it, if a man is free only to sin, then what kind of freedom is that? He states, "Man will then be spoken of as having this sort of free decision, not because he has free choice equally of good and evil, but because he acts wickedly by will, not by compulsion. Well put, indeed, but what purpose is served by labeling with a proud name such a slight thing?"[49]

So fallen humanity still possesses freedom as a permission but lacks it as a power. The biblical definition of freedom is the ability to do what is right, to choose and obey the will of God. This is the true freedom of integrity, and it is the crucial aspect lacking in the human condition. Ron White, a member of the "Redneck Comedy Tour," explained a drunken altercation he had with police: "I knew I had the right to remain silent; I just didn't have the ability." Exactly.

However, southern rock stars and Texas comedians aside, many times unregenerate persons do change their behaviors and habits. Some lost people quit smoking and stop drinking, and this brings up the second point. Soft libertarianism allows for how there is a spectrum of moral behavior exhibited by unsaved humanity, and how there can be relative changes within actions and attitudes of lost individuals. Within the malformed and marred fallen nature exists a range of choices and behaviors, while the ability to choose or do that which is pleasing to God lies outside that range. The point is that even the lost are capable of some relatively good actions. As Sproul Sr. notes, even Hitler loved his mother.[50]

---

[49]J. Calvin, *Institutes of the Christian Religion* (Philadelphia: Westminster, [1559] 1960), 2.2.7.
[50]R. C. Sproul Sr., *Chosen by God*, 104.

Soft libertarianism also contends that though depravity makes sin inevitable, it does not make any particular sin necessary. This is true even when a lost person is tempted. The fellow who robs a convenience store had the ability to refrain from doing so or in a previous will-setting moment had the ability to refrain. For that reason, he is morally responsible for his crime. Because of the pervasive nature of depravity, even the good choices we make are tainted with sin. But in a particular instance in which a person is tempted, at some significant point the choice of whether or not to give in is there.

This leaves the third point: man, in his natural state, is incapable of responding to God. He must have grace in order to receive grace. The Lord Jesus declares, "No one can come to Me unless the Father who sent Me draws him" (John 6:44). This is because, as the apostle Paul explains, "But the unbeliever [lit. "natural man"] does not welcome what comes from God's Spirit, because it is foolishness to him; he is not able to understand it since it is evaluated spiritually" (1 Cor 2:14).

The way God's grace works within the heart of the hearer during the presentation of the gospel is a unique event (or, more precisely, a unique process) and requires special attention. The next chapter is devoted to this crucial question. Accept for now the assertion that soft libertarianism allows for a surprising view of effectual grace which holds to a gracious work of God that is simultaneously monergistic[51] and yet resistible.

Stage Three: The Present Condition of Believers

Most determinists are aware of the problems associated with their position as it relates to Adam's fall, but there seems to be less attention given to the dilemma of reconciling causal determinism with the continued presence of sin in the believer. If salvation is a monergistic work of God, and the good that a believer does is God's grace working through him, then why does a Christian still sin? If a person chooses according to his greatest inclination, and godly inclinations are provided to the elect by the regenerating work of the Holy Spirit, then why does temptation

---

[51]Monergism is the view that God's grace alone is the efficient cause of our salvation; that salvation is the work of God from beginning to end. Synergism argues that our cooperation is also necessary.

still cause that person to sometimes stumble?[52] One might dismiss the tension between determinism and Adam's fall as an abstract theological question with only limited present-day application. But this is not so concerning the problems determinism has with the doctrine of sanctification. Here the pastoral implications are obvious.

In an interview before a live audience, John Piper acknowledged the logical problems compatibilism has with sanctification. He stated,

> My sin is my greatest burden. Why? Why? Why is the process
> of sanctification so slow? And the first answer is because I am so
> evil. But the comeback is: but God, your God, is sovereign. He
> can do whatever he wants. And if he's most glorified in us when
> we're most satisfied in him and he cares about his glory infinitely,
> why doesn't he advance your satisfaction in him, cut the roots
> of more sins, and therefore get more glory for himself more
> quickly? And that is an absolutely crucial question.[53]

Reformed theology often argues that God has two wills: His revealed will (i.e., His Word) and His hidden will (i.e., His decree). Piper answers his own question with the recognition that "the logical inference" is that our sins are actually in accordance with God's secret will. Piper wisely warns his listeners against drawing such a "dangerous" conclusion and exhorts them to obey the prohibitions and exhortations of God's revealed will.[54]

Yet such a deterministic notion is difficult to square with the Bible's repeated affirmation that Christians enjoy real spiritual freedom. Jesus declared, "Therefore if the Son sets you free, you really will be free" (John 8:36). This freedom is a genuine power over sin (Rom 6:6–14). In every particular instance, a believer possesses (or at a significant opportunity he had access to) the ability to say "no" to temptation (1 Cor 10:13).

---

[52]Some of Edwards's followers would, in fact, argue for perfectionism. See A. Guelzo, *Edwards on the Will* (Middletown, CT: Wesleyan University Press, 1989), 113–17.

[53]J. Piper and J. Taylor, "An Interview with John Piper," in *Suffering and the Sovereignty of God*, ed. J. Piper and J. Taylor (Wheaton: Crossway, 2006), 234. My attention was brought to this text by an unpublished paper by T. McCall, "The Metaphysics of Sanctification and the Problems of Pastoral Care: Questioning Theological Determinism." Paper presented at the annual meeting of the Evangelical Theological Society, San Diego, November 15, 2007.

[54]Piper and Taylor, "An Interview with John Piper," 235.

Let me be clear: I believe that there is much about God's ultimate will we do not know, and that God often works through the evil deeds of humans (Gen 50:10; Isa 10:5–15; Acts 2:23). However, I do not believe that when a Christian commits a specific sin it is because God inscrutably withholds sufficient grace. The Bible teaches that, while we may not achieve sinless perfection in this age, victory over any particular sin is always a real prospect for the believer (Gal 5:16).

At this point a number of compatibilists decide to be inconsistent with their advocacy of determinism by affirming that believers have a limited ability to choose to the contrary. R. C. Sproul Sr. and Robert Peterson both affirm that the redeemed regain a measure of the freedom of integrity.[55] Sproul Sr. explicitly depends on Augustine rather than Edwards when he declares that the regenerate regain what Adam lost, i.e., the simultaneous abilities to sin and to not sin. Surprisingly, he goes beyond accepting libertarianism in sanctification and embraces synergism. He states, "Sanctification is not monergistic. It is *synergistic*. That is, it demands the cooperation of the regenerate believer. We are called to work to grow in grace. We are to work hard, resisting sin unto blood if necessary, pummeling our bodies if that is what it takes to subdue them."[56]

This inconsistency has been noticed by other determinists. Terrance Tiessen recognizes that Calvinists are uncomfortable attributing our sins to God, but he sees no other choice. He argues, "We must approach the inclusion of sins committed by believers within the will of God's eternal purpose, just as we do all the evil that occurs within the history of the world by the sovereign will of God." Otherwise, he warns, "we commit theological suicide as monergists."[57] So like Piper, Tiessen concludes that a Christian succumbs to a particular temptation because, for reasons hidden within the divine secret will, God withholds sufficient grace for him to overcome.

---

[55]Sproul Sr., *Chosen by God*, 62–67; and R. A. Peterson, *Election and Free Will* (Phillipsburg, NJ: P&R, 2007), 129–30.

[56]Sproul Sr., *Chosen by God*, 158 (emphasis original).

[57]T. L. Tiessen, *Who Can Be Saved?* (Downers Grove, IL: InterVarsity, 2004), 253–54. Tiessen claims the support of Thomas Schreiner and Ardel Caneday for his position.

In contrast, the soft libertarian model provides for a view of sanctification that neither resorts to synergism nor attributes our sins to God. The concurrence model argues three points: (1) The ability to overcome sin is genuinely available to believers (John 8:36; Rom 6:6–14; 1 Cor 10:13). (2) Regrettably, Christians still retain the capacity to sin (1 John 1:8–2:2). And (3) God's grace gets all the credit for whatever good a Christian does while the Christian incurs all the blame for his sin, and never vice versa (1 Chr 29:14; John 15:5; 1 Cor 15:10; 2 Cor 3:5; 12:9; Phil 2:12–13). In other words, the concurrence paradigm argues that God's sanctifying grace is monergistic yet resistible.

The soft libertarian model also gives a very good platform for understanding the role of the spiritual disciplines in character formation. The New Testament teaches that a Christian can (and must) decide to put off the old man and put on the new man (Col 3:1–11) because though he has been liberated from the binding power of sin (Romans 6), he still dwells in a body of flesh (Gal 5:13–17). So in any particular instance of trial or temptation, how is the outcome decided? At this point, one must acknowledge some type of libertarian freedom within the believer. If I choose rightly, it was God's grace working within me, so whatever merit and glory of it goes to Christ (Gal 2:20). If I choose wrongly, it was a choice made in the flesh, and I alone bear the responsibility (1 Cor 3:1–4). Ultimate responsibility points to the proper causal agent. God is the cause of whatever I do that is right; I am the cause of all my sins.

It is at this point that soft libertarianism provides a powerful paradigm for understanding the interaction of habits, discipline, and choices, and how spiritual formation relates to human responsibility. We are creatures of habit. If one establishes the discipline of having an accountability partner or joining an accountability group, or of regular Bible reading and quiet time, or of involvement in a ministry of some type—outreach, teaching, etc.—then this gives a person the opportunity to develop the spiritual habits that will sustain him during times of temptation and difficulty.

However, if someone engages in harmful habits, then this leads to addictive behaviors that are destructive. Just ask any member of Alcoholics Anonymous or someone who cannot stop looking at Internet pornography. These habits are death spirals, and anyone who is whirling around in one cannot stop the nosedive by himself. To say that our habits decide our responses to certain situations sounds very deterministic, and this fact is the reason why many Calvinists embrace causal determinism. But my habits are the result of prior free choices. The ability (or inability) to respond to a particular temptation is determined by my earlier free decision about what habits I wanted to develop. This means that our choices and our disposition interact in a two-way fashion. It also means that both mere determinism and mere libertarianism are overly simplistic. The concurrence model of soft libertarianism addresses the two-way complexities of choice and character in a more nuanced fashion.

Stage Four: The Saints in Glory

Will we be free in heaven? Yes. Will we sin, or will it even be possible for us to sin? No. The soft libertarian model explains how both can be true. At that time we will enjoy true freedom: the perfect ability to do what is right. We will have complete freedom of integrity.

Consider how God cannot be tempted, much less sin (Jas 1:13). Why is He incapable of being enticed? It is because He dwells in a state of perfect, absolute freedom of integrity. Think of some sin so repulsive that it holds no allure for you. I suspect if someone offered you an opportunity to set babies on fire, the invitation would receive from you a visceral reaction. I submit that all sin is similarly odious to God, and no sin can tempt Him anymore than you and I can be tempted to torture infants. When we are in heaven with God, like Him we will see all evil in the same fashion. We will see all sin as repugnant and hideous as He does, and we will have the perfect ability to react to it properly. In that day, we cannot sin because we will not.[58]

Paradoxically, the power of the freedom of integrity is easier to express as an inability, i.e., it is easier to understand negatively. In our glorified state, we cannot be tempted; we cannot sin. But this is not a lack or loss of something we enjoyed on earth. Rather, it is the opposite. We will

---

[58]See J. F. Sennett, "Is There Freedom in Heaven?" *Faith and Philosophy* 16:1 (January, 1999): 69–82.

have a power then that we have only in a limited way now—the absolute ability to do what is right.

According to the soft libertarian model, we will operate within a perfected character that supplies the parameters for our choices. Within this glorified state, we will choose, decide, and act in a libertarian manner. This will be a magnificent state of existence.

CONCLUSION

We have explored the differences between compatibilism and concurrence (i.e., soft determinism and soft libertarianism) and have looked at how both approaches deal with the four stages of human experience. I believe that concurrence provides a better model, particularly in understanding the nature of Adam's fall and the continued presence of sin in the believer.

Conclusions Concerning Determinism

Determinism seems to be open to a number of criticisms. *First, determinism is simplistic.* Remember that the determinist understands freedom to be the freedom of inclination, i.e., one is free if he is able to do what he wants to do. However, this definition labels some as free who obviously are not—addicts and the pathological. No reasonable person would describe a heroin addict or a pedophile as free.

Determinism seems to confuse desires with purposes or intentions. In order to understand the difference between desires and intentions, consider the simple illustration of a man lost in the woods for several days. His strongest desire probably would be for food, and he may decide to act on that desire in a number of ways: forage for bugs; hunt small animals; use the stars to plot a course; create a bonfire to draw attention— these are all "intentions" or "endeavorings." Whatever course the man takes, to say that he acted according to his strongest inclination fails to describe fully the decision he finally makes. Desires are not decisions.

By defining choice as the freedom of inclination, determinism seems to be guilty of employing a tautology. If my will is simply my greatest

desire, then this definition does not say anything.[59] Of course my greatest
desire is my will. But that statement does not provide any new information or logically move the ball forward. The question is how one comes
to have a particular desire. And when determinists try to explain where
desires originate, the second problem surfaces.

Second, determinism is mechanistic. Determinism sees everything
in terms of cause and effect, and by so doing turns humans into appara-
tuses. This criticism may seem harsh, but compatibilists such as Bruce
Ware use the term "mechanism" to describe how human choices are
causally determined. In his discussion of the relationship between divine providence and human freedom, Ware asks, "What mechanism best
explains just how God may reign sovereign over the affairs of human
beings and yet those humans remain free in their choices and decisions?
One might consider this question, then, as a sort of *mechanical question*"
(emphasis original).[60]

But we are not machines; we are persons created in the image of
God. The fall distorted our moral compass, darkened our spiritual understanding, and severed our relationship with God, but it did not turn
us into equipment. Timothy George warns his fellow Calvinists against
using causal language to describe how God accomplishes His will. He
states,

> Arminians are right to protest the notions of mechanical neces-
> sity and impersonal determinism suggested (and sadly sometimes
> taught) under the banner of *irresistible grace.* God created human
> beings with free moral agency, and He does not violate this even
> in the supernatural work of regeneration. Christ does not rudely
> bludgeon His way into the human heart. He does not abrogate
> our creaturely freedom. No, He beckons and woos, He pleads and
> pursues, He waits and wins.[61]

---

[59]This criticism was made by Edwards's contemporaries. See A. Guelzo, "From Calvinist
Metaphysics to Republican Theory: Jonathan Edwards and James Dana on Freedom of the Will," *Journal of the History of Ideas* 56 (July 1995): 409. See also Geisler, *Chosen, But Free,* 19–37. Geisler
calls the compatibilist approach "victory by stipulated definition," since Edwards's definition of will
is unfalsifiable.

[60]Ware, *God's Greater Glory,* 19. Fesko contends both Calvin and Beza presented God's sovereignty in terms of mechanical causality. See J. V. Fesko, *Diversity within the Reformed Tradition:
Supra- and Infralapsarianism in Calvin, Dort, and Westminster* (Greenville, SC: Reformed Academic,
2001), 147–48.

[61]T. George, *Amazing Grace: God's Initiative—Our Response* (Nashville: Lifeway, 2000), 74.

I would simply add to his statement by observing that many non-Arminians, such as Molinists and moderate Calvinists, also reject a mechanistic understanding of human choice.

Determinism fails to fully account for agent causation and therefore runs the danger of understanding everything in terms of event causation—similar to billiard balls bouncing around a pool table or a line of dominoes falling in fashion. Some argue that since the forces that compel the person to perform a certain act were internal rather than external, then the action should be considered as free. Yet an internal mechanism is just that—a mechanism. If everything is "cause and effect," then the causal chain goes back to God. Not only does that make our decisions illusory but, as we have seen, it also makes God the author of sin.

Third, determinism is materialistic. The strongest advocates of determinism are often not Calvinists but atheists. Historically, the most ardent proponents of compatibilism have been skeptics such as Thomas Hobbes, David Hume, Pierre LaPlace, and more recently, the evolutionist Daniel Dennett. Calvinists need to realize that their historical allies have been Darwinists. One of the most important reasons for affirming the reality of genuine human freedom is that it provides a powerful moral response to materialistic atheism. Almost all non-Christian philosophers are determinists who deny human freedom in a libertarian sense.

Why do most Christian philosophers advocate some type of libertarianism? Perhaps one reason is because they spend a great deal of time and effort engaging with non-Christian philosophers. Non-Christian philosophers generally accept causal determinism instead of agent causation because determinism can be explained in purely physical terms. Enlightenment philosophers argued for "LaPlace's Demon," the hypothesis that, if a sufficient intellect knew the precise location and momentum of every atom in the universe, then it could use Newton's laws to reveal the entire course of cosmic events, past and future. Early determinists held to mechanical determinism while recent determinists argue for biological determinism.

At this point theological determinists often protest that this criticism amounts to guilt by association and that it is unfair to group them together with materialistic determinists. Yet the logic of causal determinism is a stubborn thing. If God causes all things, then He does so either directly or by secondary causation. If He does so directly, then God is the sole cause of all events and secondary causation is an illusion. This position, called *occasionalism*, was embraced by Edwards, and it posits that not just the initial moment of creation but every subsequent moment that has followed is the distinct, discrete creation of God. Like a cartoon in which one character hits another toon with a tomato, it appears that the characters are causing the actions, but this is an illusion occurring only in the observer's mind. The animator draws one frame after another; the missile leaves the hand and frame-by-frame moves toward the head. It may seem that Bugs Bunny splattered Elmer Fudd with the tomato, but the real causal agent is the animator. In occasionalism, God is the animator. Edwards embraced occasionalism, but few Calvinists followed him.[62]

So if God is not the primary cause then He must use secondary means. But what secondary means are available? The only candidate left is a metaphysical determinism that operates through physical events. And this option puts the theological determinist in the same boat with the materialists.[63]

It is not really surprising when materialists advocate determinism. Materialists reject any notion that human beings possess immaterial components such as the soul or spirit. Humans merely have brains but not minds. Human decisions are reduced to biochemical reactions. Feelings of love, outrage, or tenderness are simply appropriate hormones, chemicals, and synaptic neurons interacting in a certain way. Materialists often understand moral issues in deterministic terms whether it is alcoholism, compulsive gambling, or sexual orientation. This is why these behaviors are often treated as diseases rather than moral failings.

Many materialists consider the notion of free will to be a "useful fiction." Biochemical reactions in the brain are perceived by us to be moral choices—choices whether or not to sacrifice, love, and give care. But in

---

[62]Two critiques of Edwards's advocacy of occasionalism from a Reformed perspective are C. J. Collins, *The God of Miracles: An Exegetical Examination of God's Action in the World* (Wheaton: Crossway, 2000); and O. D. Crisp, "How 'Occasional' Was Edwards's Occasionalism?" in *Jonathan Edwards: Philosophical Theologian*, ed. P. Helm and O. D. Crisp (Aldershot, UK: Ashgate, 2003), 61–78.

[63]This point was made by T. McCall, "Rejoinder to Allison," 5–6. Paper presented at the annual meeting of the Evangelical Theological Society, San Diego, November 15, 2007.

reality they are all Darwinian "just-so" stories, or illusions, used by evolutionary forces to insure the survival of the species. Determinists such as Saul Smilansky argue for *illusionism*, i.e., the view that denies free will but believes society is better served with the illusion that it exists.[64]

Fourth, determinism is reductionistic. Reductionism is the "nothing but" approach. In the way a painting by Rembrandt can be reduced to "nothing but" colored oils on canvas, decisions are reduced to "nothing but" the strongest inclinations. As John Lennox points out, reductionism reduces humans down either to the level of machines or to the level of animals. We have several similarities with animals and some with machines, but humans are much more than either one.[65] And when determinism views human decisions to be "nothing but" one desire triumphing over competing desires, it reduces humans to the level of Pavlov's dogs, salivating on command. Materialists like David Hume and Daniel Dennett see determinism as a reinforcing argument for skepticism toward belief in the Christian God. Atheist Richard Dawkins declares that biology is destiny when he states, "DNA just is. And we dance to its music."[66]

Again, one might think it unfair to direct this criticism against theological determinists, but unfortunately they are the ones who open themselves to this charge. For example, Bruce Ware illustrates how determinism works by telling about his daughter choosing ice cream.[67] She thinks she is freely selecting the flavor, but actually it is her most powerful desire at work. She chooses according to her strongest inclination. Theological determinists often make a distinction between moral and natural ability, but in practice they reveal that this is a distinction without a difference. I would argue that our minds are more than just the overlaying aggregate of desires and inclinations.[68]

Fifth, causal determinism wreaks havoc with our understanding of God and how He relates to the world. The obvious problem of making

---

[64]See S. Smilansky, "Free Will, Fundamental Dualism, and the Centrality of Illusion," in *The Oxford Handbook of Free Will*, 489–505.

[65]J. Lennox, Carver-Barnes Lecture. Presented at Southeastern Baptist Theological Seminary, Wake Forest, NC, March 12, 2008. http://www.sebts.edu/news-resources/multimedia.aspx?type=culture&Vid=115.

[66]R. Dawkins, *River Out of Eden*, (New York: Basic Books, 1995), 133.

[67]Ware, *God's Greater Glory*, 87. Sproul Sr. uses a similar illustration in *Chosen by God*, 56.

[68]Guelzo argues that mechanical determinism has its origins in theological determinism. "From Edwards to Dennett, we have been locked in a wordy embrace with the same gargoyle." See A. Guelzo, "The Return of the Will: Jonathan Edwards and the Possibilities of Free Will," 108.

God the first cause of sin has been discussed. But it has to be noted that compatibilists do not employ determinism consistently to describe God's actions, especially in their use of primary and secondary causation and the incurring of merit or blame.[69] They declare that when God (the primary cause) caused Adam (the secondary cause) to sin, all guilt belonged to Adam. But when God (the primary cause) causes the Christian (the secondary cause) to believe and to obey, all merit belongs to God. If God is the primary cause of sin, but yet is free from its guilt, then He also is free from the glory of salvation. Of course, this is unacceptable.[70]

For the reasons listed above, among others, a number of Calvinists reject causal determinism. Paul Jewett states that "since [God] has made us as *persons*, we can assume that his will for us is not realized in the form of 'destiny'—that is, he does not determine our wills in the same way that he determines the color of our skin or the pattern of our hair."[71] Likewise Timothy George declares that "the Bible never presents God's providence as a scheme of strict determinism. God 'makes room' for the creatures He has made in His own image. He endows them with creaturely freedom, even though He knows in advance that they will misuse it to their own detriment."[72]

However, in his work *Divine Election* the Dutch Reformed theologian G. C. Berkouwer presents an even more scathing attack against causal determinism.[73] He warns Reformed theology about the "frightening idol" of "mechanistic-deterministic causality" and that causal determinism brings "disrepute" to the biblical doctrine of election and turns the gospel "into something dark." Rather than determinism, he argues that biblical passages such as Jer 20:7 teach that God's grace overcomes by persuasion.

Berkouwer understands why many turn away from Calvinism when it is presented in terms of causality. Determinism obscures God's real

---

[69]The Westminster Confession declares that God is the cause of all things, but then claims that God is not the author of sin (Art. 3.1). How so? It distinguishes between primary and secondary causation.

[70]See J. Daane, *The Freedom of God: A Study of Election and Pulpit* (Grand Rapids: Eerdmans, 1973), 65–72.

[71]P. Jewett, *Election and Predestination* (Grand Rapids: Eerdmans, 1985), 49.

[72]George, *Amazing Grace*, 36–37.

[73]G. C. Berkouwer, *Divine Election* (Grand Rapids: Eerdmans, 1960), 10, 13, 28, 48, 153–54, 175–76, 180, 189, 201–2, 215–16, 220, 244–45, 274.

relationship with humanity and turns God into "something menacing." Historically, Berkouwer argues, determinism has given way to fatalism which in turn has led to nihilism. Yet, he continues, it is easy to see determinism's attraction. The temptation of causal determinism is that it "seems to explain everything." But in so doing sin and unbelief are given metaphysical explanations rather than moral ones. When causality becomes "the all-explaining principle," it explains too much and, as a result, not enough.

Berkouwer is relentless in his denunciation of the practice of interpreting God's actions through the lens of causality. Though more restrained, Paul Jewett and Timothy George also give compelling reasons for rejecting causal determinism. These criticisms are all the more telling when it is noted that they come from self-confessed Calvinists.

Radical Depravity, Soft Libertarianism, and Moral Responsibility

Concurrence holds that humanity is condemned before God for its sinful unbelief. Humans are ultimately responsible for their moral decisions in a way the other creatures of the earth are not. This is because, as causal agents, they are in a limited, derived way, the originators of their respective choices. This ability is a gift bestowed by God and is a way in which humans reflect the divine image. At certain significant will-setting moments, persons possess the real ability to choose or refrain from choosing. However, even though we retain the freedom of responsibility as causal agents, our choices affect our freedom of integrity.

The soft libertarian understands Adam to have possessed the ability to choose to sin or to refrain from sin, but views fallen humanity to be in the bondage of sin. Christians in the present age have, similarly to Adam, the ability to not sin. This ability is perfected in the glorified saints so that they will never sin. An individual's character sets the parameters for his choices, but a set of choices within those boundaries are available to him. In this present age, we make choices and in turn our choices make us.

As the example of Luther at the Diet of Worms illustrates, possessing the freedom of integrity is often paradoxically presented as an inability. Luther's "inability" to recant was actually freedom in the truest

sense of the word. By God's grace, he had the liberating strength to follow his convictions. The way soft libertarianism distinguishes between
the different types of ability—freedom of responsibility and freedom of
integrity—helps us understand the very intricate relationship between
ability and accountability. Luther declared his conscience bound, but according to the soft libertarian paradigm, on that day he was the freest
man in Europe.

CHAPTER 4

O

IS FOR OVERCOMING GRACE
Salvation is all of grace; damnation all of sin.

W E FACE A dilemma. On the one hand, when a person responds to the gospel, we understand that it is because of a work of grace in his heart. But what about those who do not believe? Did God choose not to do a similar work in them? If God simply passes over them, then it seems difficult to affirm that He really desired their salvation or that the gospel was genuinely put forward to them.

Historically, this is what is known as Calvinism's "problem of the well-meant offer." In other words, the typical Calvinist model of irresistible grace seems to render disingenuous the numerous invitations in the Bible. When God said, "Come now, and let us reason together, . . . though your sins are like scarlet, they shall be as white as snow; though they are red like crimson, they shall be as wool" (Isa 1:18, NKJV), did He really mean it? Was it offered in good faith? Or was He extending an olive branch which Israel lacked the capacity to accept? To offer salvation while withholding the necessary ability to respond seems like offering healing to any quadriplegic who can get up to receive it.[1]

On the other hand, we can solve the above dilemma by holding that exercising faith is the necessary condition for receiving redemption (i.e., *sola fide*). This would mean that salvation—and more specifically, the ability to receive salvation—is genuinely available to all hearers of the good news. This has been the position of virtually all non-Calvinists.

---

[1] Some respond by pointing out that God is under no obligation to provide salvation to anyone, but this is beside the point. The issue is that God *has* offered salvation to the hearers. The problem with the Calvinist position is that it makes God appear to be disingenuous.

But this solution contains its own problem. If I freely believe, but my neighbor freely does not, does not this imply that somehow I was nobler than my neighbor? Did I not use my freedom to a higher end? Yes, salvation is a free gift, and receiving redemption incurs no merit, but is not the one who accepts it in some way wiser, more humble, more virtuous, more appreciative, more aware of his need, or more sensitive to sin than the one who rejects it? Calvinist theologian Terrance Tiessen makes this point when he observes,

> From numerous conversations with Arminians and Wesleyans, I know that this perception is difficult for them to understand. It is argued that believers cannot boast because they simply accept a free gift. I acknowledge the significance of grace in most synergistic theologies. But the fact remains that the critical difference between those who believe and those who do not is found in the believers rather than in God's gracious work. Since God enables all equally, the outcome is determined by the people who must respond to God's initiative. I fail to see why believers should not be commended for having responded to grace. However small their contribution has been, it was the decisive factor.[2]

If Arminians and other non-Calvinists have not given much attention to the matter, the problem has not been lost on Calvinists. In fact, a commitment to an entirely gracious salvation, rather than allegiance to divine sovereignty, may be the primary reason for many who turn away from some other theological system to embrace Reformed theology. Perhaps more than any other point (including election), the crucial component of Calvinism is effectual calling or, as it is sometimes called, irresistible grace.[3]

So historically Calvinism has struggled with the issue of the "well-meant offer" while Arminianism has had to deal with the specter of semi-Pelagianism.[4] However, Scripture teaches both that salvation is

---

[2] T. L. Tiessen, *Who Can Be Saved?* (Downers Grove, IL: InterVarsity, 2004), 239.

[3] "Thus it comes about that the doctrine of monergistic regeneration—or as it was phrased by the older theologians, of 'irresistible grace' or 'effectual calling'—is the hinge of the Calvinistic soteriology, and lies much more deeply embedded in the system than the doctrine of predestination itself which is popularly looked upon as its hall-mark." B. B. Warfield, "Calvinism," in *The Works of Benjamin B. Warfield,* vol. 5 (Grand Rapids: Baker, 2003 [1932]), 359.

[4] Pelagianism argues that man has it within his natural power to obey God. Semi-Pelagianism recognizes that man cannot be saved apart from grace but contends that man has the natural ability to turn to God.

completely the work of God and that the sin of rejecting the gospel belongs entirely to the unbeliever. How do we formulate a theological system that genuinely gives God all the credit for grace and the sinner all the blame for unbelief? This chapter argues for the *overcoming grace* position, a view which attempts to do justice to both truths. The great nineteenth-century Baptist preacher Charles Spurgeon expressed the tension that the overcoming grace model attempts to preserve:

> If any of you want to know what I preach every day, and any stranger should say, "Give me a summary of his doctrine," say this, "He preaches salvation all of grace, and damnation all of sin. He gives God all the glory for every soul that is saved, but he won't have it that God is to blame for any man that is damned." That teaching I cannot understand. My soul revolts at the idea of a doctrine that lays the blood of man's soul at God's door. I cannot conceive how any human mind, at least any Christian mind, can hold any such blasphemy as that. I delight to preach this blessed truth—salvation of God, from first to last—the Alpha and the Omega; but when I come to preach damnation, I say, damnation of man, not of God; and if you perish, at your own hands must your blood be required.[5]

"Salvation all of grace, and damnation all of sin" sums up the overcoming grace model. It affirms that both are radically true. But how can it do so in a logically consistent manner? This model builds on the arguments put forth by Richard Cross in his article "Anti-Pelagianism and the Resistibility of Grace."[6] He argued for a *monergistic* view of overcoming grace, but that this grace is resistible. Monergism (*mono*—"one," *ergon*—"work") is a term that means God is the only worker in salvation.[7] This chapter agrees with Cross that such a model is not only rationally coherent but best expresses the teaching of Scripture on the subject, and we will explore the ramifications of this position.

---

[5]C. H. Spurgeon, "Jacob and Esau," in *The New Park Street Pulpit* (Pasadena: Pilgrim, 1981 [1859]), 119.

[6]R. Cross, "Anti-Pelagianism and the Resistibility of Grace," *Faith and Philosophy* 22:2 (April 2005), 199–210. Cross presents seven possible models. I am arguing for the fifth one he presents, which appears to be the model he also advocates.

[7]Monergism is the view that God's grace alone is the efficient cause of our salvation; that salvation is the work of God from beginning to end. Synergism argues that our cooperation is also necessary.

AN AMBULATORY MODEL OF OVERCOMING GRACE

So how does the overcoming grace position understand the workings of the Holy Spirit in bringing a lost person to faith in Jesus Christ? This view can also be called "an ambulatory model" because it understands the sinner's coming to faith as a process by which the Spirit of God carries a person to the point of saving trust. In fact, perhaps an illustration using an ambulance will help. Imagine waking up to find you are being transported by an ambulance to the emergency room. It is clearly evident that your condition requires serious medical help. If you do nothing, you will be delivered to the hospital. However, if for whatever reason you demand to be let out, the driver will comply. He may express regret and give warnings, but he will still let you go. You receive no credit for being taken to the hospital, but you incur the blame for refusing the services of the ambulance.[8]

In this illustration you do not *do* anything to arrive at the hospital. The only thing you have the ability to do is *resist*. Any "contribution" made by you is hurtful. Now let the ambulance serve as a metaphor for the work of the Spirit in conversion. If you believe, it is because (and only because) the Holy Spirit brought you to faith. If you do not believe, it is only because you resisted. The only thing you are able to "do" is negative. Thus the ambulatory model provides for a monergistic work of grace that leaves room for the sinner to refuse to accept.[9] As Cross explains,

> It might be thought that the concession that a person can impede God's bringing about *a* in her by preemptively doing not-*a* somehow makes her salvation wholly up to her after all, since God's doing *a* is still dependent on her not doing not-*a*. My proposal, however, is that her doing not-*a* at a time *t* simply prevents God from bringing about *a* at her *t*, provided that God does not coercively prevent her from doing not-*a*. This amounts to a kind of

---

[8]Cross, "Anti-Pelagianism," 207. Eleonore Stump proposes a similar position that she calls a "quiescent view of the will." See E. Stump, "Augustine on Free Will," in *The Cambridge Companion to Augustine* (Cambridge: Cambridge Univ. Press, 2007), 124–47.

[9]Kevin Timpe explains that this model is "neither deterministic nor Pelagian....The resulting view allows one to maintain both (i) that divine grace is the efficient cause of saving faith and (ii) that humans control whether or not they come to saving faith." See K. Timpe, "Controlling What We Do Not Cause," *Faith and Philosophy* 24:3 (July 2007): 284–99.

> Augustinianism: damnation is, and salvation is not, something
> which is brought about by the creature.[10]

The point of Cross's rather technical explanation is that the overcoming grace model simultaneously affirms both *monergism* and *resistibility*. It is monergistic because all that is necessary in this scenario is that a person *refrains* from acting.[11] It upholds resistibility in the genuine sense of the word in that the unbeliever rejects grace that was truly available. As Cross points out, the overcoming grace model is rather Augustinian. The only thing we have the capability to do is produce damnation by our resistance.

The Two Tenets of the Ambulatory Model	
Grace is *monergistic*.	God is the only worker in salvation. The person merely refrains from resisting.
Grace is *resistible* .	God's grace is truly offered and available. The difference between the saved and the lost is the continued rebellion of the unbeliever.

In this model the question at hand has been turned around. In the earlier quote by Terrance Tiessen, he states, "The critical difference between those who believe and those who do not is found *in the believers*" [emphasis added]. This, I contend, is the fundamental error of his complaint. The overcoming grace model holds that the difference between those who believe and those who do not is found *in the unbelievers*.[12]

---

[10]Cross, "Anti-Pelagianism," 206–7.

[11]At this point some might object that refraining is a choice, and as such, we are back to the original problem. But as a number of philosophers point out, omissions are not efficient causes. Timpe calls such omissions "quasi-causal" because they control events but do not cause events. See Timpe, "Controlling What We Do Not Cause," 290-99. Cf. P Dowe, "A Counterfactual Theory of Prevention and 'Causation' by Omission," *Australasian Journal of Philosophy* 79:2 (June 2001): 216-26; J. J. Thomson, "Causation: Omissions," *Philosophy and Phenomenological Research* 66:1 (January 2003): 81-103; and S. McGrath, "Causation by Omission: A Dilemma," *Philosophical Studies* 123 (2005): 125-48.

[12]To his credit, Tiessen acknowledges the problems created by the typical Calvinist understanding of effectual grace and offers a position he calls the "sufficient grace" model. His proposal is helpful, but it highlights the dilemma of working with irresistible grace as a starting assumption. See Tiessen, *Who Can Be Saved?* 230–58, 493–97.

God's drawing grace should and would be efficacious for all. The only thing that could stop it is if, inexplicably, a person decides to refuse. As Robert Picirilli puts it, overcoming grace "is so closely related to regeneration that it *inevitably* leads one to regeneration unless finally resisted."[13]

The question is no longer "Why do some believe?" but "Why doesn't everyone believe?" The evil of unbelief remains a mystery, but this model moves this evil from God to the unbeliever.

In the overcoming grace model, God is the Evangelist. We—the Church collectively and Christians individually—are the instruments and means by which He accomplishes the task of bringing lost humanity to Himself. Salvation is completely and only a work of God: initiated, accomplished, and completed by the Triune Godhead. If you are saved, it is because of the sovereign, gracious, and monergistic work of God. If you are lost, it is your fault. The saved are delivered entirely by grace. The lost are lost entirely by their own rebellion. There is every reason to believe that the interaction between God's gracious call and the hearer is complex and drawn out, and Scripture indicates this process can be resisted.

If we are going to make our case for overcoming grace, we must answer the leading arguments given by Calvinists for their doctrine of irresistible grace. In short, they contend that the lost do not have the capacity in their natural state to turn to God. So far, so good; on this point there is universal agreement.[14] Because of human inability Calvinists reason further that the Holy Spirit must be the one who brings a person to saving faith. Again, so far so good. But many do not come to saving faith. So, conclude Calvinists, the Holy Spirit must have passed over these without drawing them as He did the elect. Here is where the disagreement is

---

[13]R. Picirilli, *Grace, Faith, Free Will* (Nashville: Randall House, 2002), 156. Emphasis added.

[14]See the Second Council of Orange, A.D. 529 (canons 5, 10, and 18) and the Council of Trent, A.D. 1546 (Decree on Justification, chaps. 5, 6, 8, and 13). See R. C. Sproul's argument, however, that Trent was ambiguous on semi-Pelagianism, which finally "triumphed" in the new Catechism of the Catholic Church (1994). See R. C. Sproul Sr., *Willing to Believe: The Controversy over Free Will* (Grand Rapids: Baker, 1997), 77–80, 83–84. Historically, semi-Pelagianism (the view that man has it within his power to make the first move towards God) has been rejected by the Roman Church, Eastern Orthodoxy, and all major varieties of Protestantism. Demarest, however, argues that Catholicism "is Semi-Pelagian in its belief that 'man really cooperates in his personal salvation from sin'" (B. Demarest, *The Cross and Salvation* [Wheaton: Crossway, 1997], 100).

located. Calvinists believe this conclusion is necessary to preserve the graciousness of salvation.

Calvinism understands conversion to be the result of *effectual calling*, a work of the Holy Spirit done only in the hearts of the elect. This grace is always effective, so it is also called irresistible grace. Many Calvinists find the term "irresistible" unfortunate because it gives the impression that a person is compelled to believe against his will. Rather, Reformed theology holds that effectual grace transforms the sinner's will, so that he gladly comes to Christ. However, TULIP requires the word "irresistible," so as long as the acronym is used so will be the term.

Besides, I am not sure the term "irresistible" can be so easily dismissed. Sproul Sr. calls the label "misleading," but at times he uses it himself. This is how he describes the sinner reaching for Christ: "By the irresistible work of grace, he will do nothing else except stretch out his hand. Not that he cannot not stretch out his hand even if he does not want to, but that he cannot not want to stretch out his hand."[15] Calvinists argue that God does not force a sinner to believe against his will but by regeneration changes the sinner's will. Yet this would mean that this regenerating act was unrequested and unwanted (i.e., it was done against the sinner's will—those whom Paul describes in Rom 5:10 as God's "enemies"). Their solution does not solve the problem of coercion; it simply moves it back a step.

By contrast, the overcoming grace model understands God's grace to operate in terms of persuasion. The Holy Spirit appeals, persuades, and wins. And the elect find the drawing "irresistible." As Timothy George puts it, "I like the term *overcoming grace* because it conveys the truth witnessed by so many Christians: Despite their stubbornness and rebellion, they say, God did not give up on them. Like a persistent lover, He kept on wooing until, at last, His very persistence won the day. His love and mercy overcame their rebellious resistance."[16]

Reformed proponents give three arguments against the notion that the decision to believe or not believe resides in the one hearing the gospel. First, they sometimes make the odd claim that "faith" to the

---

[15]Sproul, *Willing to Believe,* 120, 133–34.

[16]T. George, *Amazing Grace: God's Initiative—Our Response* (Nashville: Lifeway, 2000), 74.

non-Calvinist is actually a type of work. Second, they contend that faith is a gift. And third, they argue that faith is a virtue. These three points, taken together, are said to demonstrate that saving faith is a gift irresistibly given by the Holy Spirit only to the elect. In response, we will argue that faith is not a work and agree with our Reformed brethren that faith is indeed both a gift and a virtue. However, we contend that it is a gift available to every hearer.

CALVINIST ARGUMENT #1:
NON-CALVINIST FAITH IS A WORK

The first argument we will examine is the rather surprising claim made by some Calvinists that faith is actually a type of work within a non-Calvinist soteriology. They contend that if faith is the human condition to salvation, then in effect the act of trusting merits the receiving of salvation. Though exercising faith is a rather small act of obedience, it is an act nonetheless. R. C. Sproul Sr. expresses it this way:

> The Arminian acknowledges that faith is something a person does. It is a work, though not a meritorious one. Is it a good work? Certainly it is not a bad work. It is good for a person to trust in Christ and in Christ alone for his or her salvation. Since God commands us to trust in Christ, when we do so we are obeying this command. But all Christians agree that faith is something we do.[17]

Several responses can be made. *First, the ambiguity of the word "do" must be noted.* Isn't exercising faith something we do? Yes, it is, but what many fail to notice is that in saying this there has been a subtle equivocation of the word "do." As Geisler points out, all works are actions, but not all actions are works.[18] Faith is an action in the sense that it involves an act of the will, but it is not a work.[19] We exercise faith to receive redemption for the precise reason that we cannot *do* anything to

---

[17]Sproul Sr., *Willing to Believe*, 25–26. Note once again that Sproul lumps all who disagree with Calvinists on this point as Arminians.

[18]N. Geisler, *Chosen But Free: A Balanced View of Divine Election,* 2nd ed. (Minneapolis: Bethany House, 2001), 198.

[19]"Work" is understood in the sense of "good works," i.e., meritorious actions. See "Works," in *Evangelical Dictionary of Theology,* 2nd ed., ed. W.A. Elwell (Grand Rapids: Baker, 2001), 1296.

earn salvation. Faith is not a meritorious deed. How does receiving a gift make the gift less gracious? The challenge for Calvinists is to demonstrate from Scripture that receiving grace equates to deserving grace.

Second, the Bible does not present faith as a work. In a number of places Paul equates "by faith" with "by grace." For example, in Rom 4:16 he says "the promise is by faith, so that it may be according to grace." Then in Rom 11:6 he states that if salvation is "by grace, then it is not by works; otherwise grace ceases to be grace." At other times he juxtaposes works-righteousness with the righteousness that is received by faith (Phil 3:9). In Rom 10:3–6, Paul contrasts the righteousness that comes through the works of the law with the righteousness obtained by faith. He makes a similar claim in Gal 2:16, where he says that justification is by faith and not by works.

In short, the biblical authors understood faith and works as mutually exclusive opposites. The argument that salvation by faith is gracious simply because faith itself is a gracious gift misses the point made by Paul. He clearly views the act of exercising faith as nonmeritorious—period. As Robert Picirilli observes, whatever faith is, it is not works.[20] This means that salvation by faith is not salvation by works, and that salvation by faith roughly equates to salvation by grace. Anyone who wishes to contend that faith is a type of work finds the burden of proof is on them.

CALVINIST ARGUMENT #2: FAITH IS A GIFT

The second argument is much more substantial and has many more proponents. Therefore it will receive more of our attention. Basically, Reformed theology argues that faith is a gift given only to the elect, and they receive this gift when they are regenerated. The spiritually dead cannot exercise faith. To say that fallen humans have a natural ability to believe or respond is to embrace Pelagianism or at least semi-Pelagianism. Since not everyone believes, this must mean that the gift of faith is given only to the elect. According to this view, faith is not the instrument to receive salvation. It is evidence we are saved.

---

[20]Picirilli, *Grace, Faith, Free Will,* 179.

Three Calvinist Views of Irresistible Grace	
The nonconversionist or presumptive regeneration view	Children of the Covenant are regenerate and do not need to be converted
The regeneration precedes conversion view	The elect believe because they have been regenerated
The effectual call view	The elect believe when they receive an irresistible inward call

Calvinists differ as to when and how the gift of faith is bestowed. There are three major views: the nonconversionist position, the "regeneration precedes conversion" position, and the effectual call position. David Engelsma, R. C. Sproul Sr., and Millard Erickson will serve as the representatives of each position respectively.

The Nonconversionist Position: Children of the Covenant are regenerate and do not need to be converted.

Many Baptists who identify themselves as Calvinists along the lines of the five points of Dort often overlook what in fact the Synod said about the children of believers. Canon 1, Article 17 of the Synod states that those born into the church already enjoy the covenant of grace.[21] This provides the rationale for many within the Reformed tradition to practice infant baptism. The early Puritans followed Dort in this matter but disagreed among themselves about the role baptism was supposed to play in an infant's salvation. A few argued that baptism effected regeneration while more saw baptism as a statement or sign of faith signifying that regeneration had occurred.[22] What all classic Calvinists agreed upon

---

[21]"Since we are to judge of the will of God from his Word, which testifies that the children of believers are holy, not by nature, but in virtue of the covenant of grace, in which they together with the parents are comprehended, godly parents have no reason to doubt of the election and salvation of their children whom it pleaseth God to call out of this life in their infancy." Synod of Dort, "The Canons of the Synod of Dort, 1618–19," in *Creeds and Confessions of Faith in the Christian Tradition*, vol. 2, ed. J. Pelikan and V. Hotchkiss (New Haven: Yale University Press, 2003), Canon 1, Art. 17.

[22]R. P. Roberts, "The Puritan View of Children in the Church," in *Diversities of Gifts: Papers Read at the 1980 Conference* (London: Westminster Conference, 1980), 57–69.

was that children within the church did not need to be converted, at least
in the same way as those outside the church, because "they are the sol-
diers of Christ from their infancy."[23]

David Engelsma is a modern proponent of nonconversionist Dortian
Calvinism, or "Old Light" Calvinism as it has come to be known. He
rejects any notion that equates the spiritual condition of children born to
believers and those born to non-believers. He also dismisses the idea that
the primary advantage children of Christian parents enjoy is simply that
they are in a privileged position to regularly hear the gospel and to have
it modeled before them. Engelsma even rejects the view that children
born within the church must eventually choose Christ for themselves.
Faith, declares Engelsma, is not a condition to salvation.[24] The children
of the elect do not believe in order to be saved; they grow up believing
because they are saved. They are already regenerate and are experiencing
a gradual, life-long conversion.[25] They do not need to be won to Christ as
if they were heathen. In fact, attempts to evangelize children within the
church only have the effect of "distressing Christ's lambs."[26]

As for the typical evangelical understanding of conversion, Engelsma has no time for it. He states, "Speaking for myself, to the brash,
presumptuous question sometimes put to me by those of a revivalist,
rather than covenantal, mentality, 'When were you converted?' I have
answered in all seriousness, 'When was I not converted?'"[27] He further
declares, "As a Reformed minister and parent, I have no interest whatever in conversion as the basis for viewing baptized children as God's
dear children, loved of him from eternity, redeemed by Jesus, and promised the Holy Spirit, the author of faith. None!"[28] Engelsma is nothing
if not clear.

Engelsma argues that he is simply following Calvin on this point.
And he appears to be right. In his *Institutes,* Calvin denounced the

---

[23]Ibid., 61. Roberts is quoting the eighteenth-century English divine, George Swinnock.

[24]D. J. Engelsma, *The Covenant of God and the Children of Believers: Sovereign Grace in the
Covenant* (Grandville, MI: Reformed Free., 2005), 13–16.

[25]Ibid., 82.

[26]Ibid., 70–78. And what about children who are not born to Christian parents? Engelsma declares
that the children of unbelievers who die in infancy are reprobate and go to hell.

[27]Ibid., 39.

[28]Ibid., 86.

Anabaptist notion of the age of accountability and argued instead for infant regeneration, stating, "Now it is perfectly clear that those infants who are to be saved (as some are surely saved from that early age) are previously regenerated by the Lord."[29] Calvin viewed regeneration as a lifelong process which began in infancy or perhaps even in the womb.

In contrast to Calvin and Old Light Calvinists, Baptists universally have rejected the notions of infant regeneration and infant baptism as errors that have done serious damage to the cause of Christ by granting church membership to the unconverted. Southern Baptist evangelist Vance Havner probably summed up the suspicions of many Baptists when he observed, "I could have led many people to Christ—if only they hadn't joined the church first."[30]

Nonconversionist Calvinist doctrine, particularly as advocated by the Synod of Dort and the English Puritans, associates regeneration with baptism rather than conversion, and David Engelsma is a modern-day representative of this view. However, most Calvinists broke away from this position over two centuries ago. The mid-eighteenth century saw the Great Awakening, perhaps the greatest revival ever to come to Great Britain and America. Lead by Calvinists such as the evangelist George Whitefield and the pastor-theologian Jonathan Edwards, the Great Awakening resulted in multitudes having dramatic conversion experiences and staid churches undergoing dynamic growth and transformation. Calvinism in America divided into "New Lights" and "Old Lights." The New Lights embraced the revival and stressed the necessity of a clear conversion experience—and they proclaimed that conversion was an experience required for those who grew up in the church, too.[31] In sermons such as *The Nature and Necessity of Our New Birth*, Whitefield expressed the New Light conviction that conversion and regeneration were inseparable. The Old Lights, however, rejected the revival and its theology as enthusiastic innovations. David Engelsma is a modern example of Old Light Calvin-

---

[29]J. Calvin, *Institutes of the Christian Religion* (Philadelphia: Westminster, 1960), 4.16.17.

[30]D. Hester, *The Vance Havner Quote Book* (Grand Rapids: Baker, 1986), 41.

[31]P. Toon, *Born Again: A Biblical and Theological Study* (Grand Rapids: Baker, 1987) 156–65. Toon gives a brief but helpful history of the doctrine of regeneration.

ism, but he is in the minority even in Reformed circles. The overwhelming majority of Calvinists today are of the New Light variety.[32]

New Lights affirm the necessity of conversion, and generally understand it to be simultaneous with regeneration. However, within New Light Calvinism there is disagreement as to which one results in the other (i.e., whether regeneration produces conversion or if conversion logically precedes being born again). This leads to the next two Calvinist views of irresistible grace.

The "Regeneration-precedes-faith" Position: The elect believe because they have been regenerated.

Most Calvinists believe that regeneration precedes conversion. Speaking for the majority, R. C. Sproul Sr. succinctly states, "A cardinal point of Reformed theology is the maxim: 'Regeneration precedes faith.' Our nature is so corrupt, the power of sin is so great, that unless God does a supernatural work in our souls we will never choose Christ. We do not believe in order to be born again; we are born again in order that we may believe."[33] But can Calvinism affirm such a "cardinal point" and still maintain without contradiction that justification and even salvation are by faith? According to their *ordo salutis,* faith is just one tiny piece of a salvation process that begins with regeneration, or even with sovereign election. In such a case, does Calvinism have sufficient warrant for joining with other Protestants in proclaiming that "salvation is by faith"?

Furthermore, what is regeneration? Berkhof states, "regeneration is that act of God by which the principle of the new life is implanted in man, and the governing disposition of the soul is made holy."[34] And Grudem defines regeneration as "the act of God awakening spiritual life within

---

[32]However, along with the resurgence of Reformed theology there has also been a strong reappearance of nonconversionist Calvinism. See the *Summary Statement of AAPC's Position on the Covenant, Baptism, and Salvation (Revised),* http://www.auburnavenue.org/documents/summary-statement-on-baptism.htm.

[33]R. C. Sproul Sr., *Chosen by God* (Wheaton: Tyndale, 1986), 72–73. In fact, Bruce Ware argues for the doctrine of regeneration preceding conversion as the foundational basis for unconditional election rather than the other way around. He states, "Effectual calling, then, entails unconditional election." See Bruce Ware, "Divine Election to Salvation," in *Perspectives on Election: Five Views* (Nashville: B&H, 2006), 15–22.

[34]L. Berkhof, *Systematic Theology* (Grand Rapids: Eerdmans, 1996), 469.

us, bringing us from spiritual death to spiritual life."[35] If regeneration means to receive new life and a holy disposition of the soul, how can one understand that event as preceding faith without denying in effect that salvation is *by faith*?

At the popular level, most evangelicals would find the Calvinist position of conversion as the fruit of regeneration surprising. Citing John Gerstner's critique of Billy Graham, Sproul Sr. takes issue with Billy Graham for teaching that the "new birth is something that God does for man *when man is willing to yield* to God" [emphasis original].[36] Sproul Sr. criticizes Billy Graham for teaching "decisional regeneration" (i.e., that a person is born again when he trusts Christ for salvation).

Those who adhere to regeneration preceding faith also hold to a corollary, which is that there is a distinction between a general call to salvation and a special call. The general call is given to every hearer of the good news, but the special call is a secret, inward call directed only at the elect. This special call is understood simply to be another term for regeneration.

A second corollary naturally follows the first: the special call always succeeds. The nonelect will ignore or reject the general call because they do not have the ability to accept the gospel. But according to the regeneration-before-faith view, the gospel was never really meant for them anyway. God passes over the reprobate, and for reasons known only to Him, He does not give the gift of faith to them. But for the elect, their hearts are unilaterally transformed. The secret, inward call cannot fail.

Proponents of the regeneration before faith position appeal to a number of texts that seem to support their case. For example, John 3:5 states that unless a person is born again, he cannot enter the kingdom of God. We enter the kingdom of God when we are converted, but we must first be "born of the Spirit" in order to believe. Another passage is John 6:44, when Jesus declares, "No one can come to Me unless the Father who sent Me draws him." Sproul Sr. uses James 2:6 and Acts 16:19 to point out

---

[35] W. Grudem, *Systematic Theology* (Grand Rapids: Zondervan, 1995), 702.

[36]Sproul Sr., *Willing to Believe*, 200–201; cf. Billy Graham, *How to Be Born Again* (Waco: Word, 1977). Even the title of Graham's book is problematic for the traditional Calvinist.

that the word for "draw" often means "dragged."[37] First John 5:1 states, "Everyone who believes that Jesus is the Messiah has been born of God," and the apostle John is understood to be saying that faith in Christ is the product of being born of God (i.e., being regenerated).

The work of regeneration-producing faith is said to be illustrated by the conversion of Lydia, of whom Acts 16:14 states, "The Lord opened her heart to pay attention to what was spoken by Paul." The secret, inward call of regeneration allowed her to respond to the general call being issued by the apostle.

The Effectual Call Position: The elect believe when they receive an irresistible, inward call.

A number of Calvinists such as Millard Erickson recognize that, despite the verses just surveyed, many more passages clearly teach that conversion logically precedes regeneration.[38] Erickson distinguishes between the effectual call and regeneration and does not see them as synonyms. He presents the order of salvation as:

$$\text{Effectual calling} \rightarrow \text{Conversion} \rightarrow \text{Regeneration}$$

He continues the Calvinist differentiation between the general call of gospel preaching and the secret call of the Holy Spirit. The gospel presentation is outward and is presented to all indiscriminately; the secret call is inward and is given only to the elect. This irresistible call is effectual, not merely in that it succeeds, but in that it always succeeds.

According to Erickson, certain New Testament texts imply that not everyone who hears the gospel is called (Luke 14:23; Rom 1:7; 8:30; 11:29; 1 Cor 1:23–24,26; Eph 1:18; Phil 3:14; 1 Thess 2:12; 2 Thess

---

[37]Sproul Sr., *Chosen by God*, 69–70. F. W. Danker (*Greek-English Lexicon* by Bauer, Danker, Arndt, and Gingrich, Chicago: Univ. of Chicago Press, 2000) gives the first meaning of *elko* (used in John 6:44; 12:32; 18:10; 21:6; 21:11; Acts 16:19; 21:30; Jas 2:6) as "to move an object from one area to another in a pulling motion, draw, with implication that the object being moved is incapable of propelling itself or in the case of pers. is unwilling to do so voluntarily, in either case with implication of exertion on the part of the mover." But he assigns to John 6:44 the second, figurative meaning found several times in the Septuagint and elsewhere: "to draw a pers. in the direction of values for inner life, draw, attract." This meaning fits the overcoming grace model.

[38]M. Erickson, *Christian Theology*, 2nd ed. (Grand Rapids: Baker, 2004), 944–45; see also Demarest, *The Cross and Salvation*, 211–16.

2:14; 2 Tim 1:9; Heb 3:1; 2 Pet 1:10).[39] Similarly, Calvin understood Jesus to be teaching a general/secret distinction when He said, "Many are called, but few are chosen" (Matt 22:14 NKJV).[40]

Erickson's position is much closer to the overcoming grace model proposed in this chapter in that it does not equal enabling grace with regeneration. However, the crucial differences remain over whether this grace is resistible and whether it is offered only to the elect.

A number of responses are in order. *First, faith is indeed a gift from God, but this does not entail that the gift is irresistible.* The Calvinist view that the components of conversion—repentance and faith—are grace gifts is undoubtedly correct. The problem lies in the claim that this logically requires irresistible grace. Acts 18:27 declares that the disciples "believed through grace," while Paul tells the Philippians that their ability to trust the Lord was a gift given to them by God for Christ's sake (Phil 1:28–29). Likewise, Scripture teaches that repentance is a gift that God grants (Acts 5:31; 11:18; 2 Tim 2:25).

In other places the Bible uses comparable language to indicate that conversion (repentance and faith) is a graciously enabled gift from God. It is the Lord who "opens hearts" (Acts 16:14) and His Word that produces faith (Rom 10:17). God does not believe for us, and repenting from sin is something we do, but sinners convert only because God enables them to do so.

So the Bible presents us with a paradox: we are required to exercise faith in order to receive salvation, but this disposition of trust is a divine gift. Yet there is nothing in the graciousness of salvation that entails (i.e., logically requires) that the opportunity to believe be withheld from all but the elect. In fact, the overwhelming preponderance of Scripture teaches the very opposite. And that is the next point.

Second, rather than make a general/secret distinction between calls, the Bible presents the offer of salvation as universal and genuine. As we have seen, from the Calvinist perspective even Erickson has to argue that only the elect receive the call that really matters—an inward, secret call. But Isaiah presents God as offering salvation to all Israel and

---

[39]Erickson, *Christian Theology*, 943.
[40]Calvin, *Institutes*, 3.24.8.

the whole world. God pleads with Judah, "Come now, and let us reason together. . . . Though your sins are like scarlet, they shall be as white as snow; though they are red like crimson, they shall be as wool" (Isa 1:18 NKJV). The scope of the appeal is broadened when the Lord declares, "Turn to Me, and be saved, all the ends of the earth!" (Isa 45:22). God invites all without qualification, "Come, everyone who is thirsty, come to the waters; and you without money, come, buy and eat! Come, buy wine and milk without money and without cost!" (Isa 55:1). These appeals are real and in good faith.

Calvin declared that God created certain persons whom "it was his pleasure to doom to destruction."[41] Yet the Lord, speaking through Ezekiel, explicitly rejects such a conclusion. First, he asks the question, "Do I take any pleasure in the death of the wicked? . . . Instead, don't I take pleasure when he turns from his ways and lives?" (Ezek 18:23). Then he answers himself by declaring, "For I take no pleasure in anyone's death. . . . So repent and live! (18:32). Later, to make sure we get the point, God swears an oath, proclaiming, "As I live . . . I take no pleasure in the death of the wicked, but rather that the wicked person should turn from his way and live. Repent, repent of your evil ways! Why will you die, house of Israel?" (33:11). These offers of mercy and forgiveness were obviously authentic and were tragically ignored by Israel.

The Bible ends with a universal invitation: "Both the Spirit and the bride say, 'Come!' Anyone who hears should say, 'Come!' And the one who is thirsty should come. Whoever desires should take the living water as a gift" (Rev 22:17). The bride here takes part in issuing the appeal, so the invitation of this verse cannot be narrowed to only the elect.

What about our Lord's statement, "Many are called, but few are chosen" (Matt 22:14 NKJV)? As I. Howard Marshall demonstrates, the context shows that "chosen" is not a reference to a decision made in the past, but a judgment that will be made in the future.[42] Jesus ends two parables—the parable of the Vineyard Workers (Matt 20:1–16) and the parable of the Wedding Feast (Matt 22:1–14)—with this declaration.

---

[41]Ibid, 3.21.7.

[42]I. H. Marshall, "Predestination in the New Testament," in *Grace Unlimited*, ed. C. H. Pinnock (Minneapolis: Bethany, 1975), 127–43.

As the judgment upon the man without the wedding garment illustrates (22:11–13), many are "called" (i.e., invited; cf. HCSB), but in the last day only those robed with the righteousness of Christ will be "chosen" (i.e., accepted). Rather than being a proof text for an inward call given only to the elect, the saying reinforces the notion of human responsibility for not being chosen.

The general/special distinction of the irresistible grace position has the effect of rendering the universal calls disingenuous. When God asks, "Why will you die?" the Reformed answer must be that God mysteriously withholds the necessary grace to repent. On this point, Calvinists need to face the implications of their theological system. "Mystery" is not a universal Band-Aid to which one can appeal every time his conclusions appear to contradict the Bible.

Hyper-Calvinists and Arminians generally react to the dilemma created by the Reformed position as one would expect. Arminian Robert Shank accuses Calvinists of worshipping a dishonest God, as he hammers them for failing to provide a consistent case for affirming the genuineness of God's invitations. He declares,

> If God alone has power to act to reverse men's wayward course, if men can exercise no authentic personal decision for God and salvation, if men have no power of responding affirmatively to God apart from an immediate particular act of enabling which God in His sovereignty grants unconditionally to some and withholds from others, then in the case of every man who does not turn to Him, God's appeals to men to "turn ye from your evil ways . . . turn you at my reproof . . . turn thou unto me . . . let the wicked forsake his way . . . let him return unto the Lord . . . seek ye the Lord . . . why will ye die?" and all such appeals and admonitions constitute the most abhorrent, the most reprehensible, the most malicious and despicable deceptions that ever can be conceived, and God Himself constitutes the most abominable curse that ever can be visited on His own creation.[43]

Shank takes off the gloves in the above quote, and I do not believe he is being entirely fair to the vast majority of Calvinists. But he hits on a central point that the debate at hand is really a debate about the character

---

[43]R. Shank, *Elect in the Son* (Minneapolis: Bethany, 1989), 173–74.

of God. Calvinists by and large affirm that God invites in good faith, even though they cannot reconcile this with their theological system. They simply decide to be inconsistent on this point and I, for one, am thankful.

Hyper-Calvinists, in contrast to Calvinists, are viciously consistent. Ultra-Reformed theologians such as David Engelsma and Herman Hoeksema run rampant with the doctrine of irresistible grace. To them, irresistible grace proves there is no general call of the gospel. God's withholding of efficacious grace demonstrates His eternal hatred of the nonelect. They argue that there is no distinction between the general and special calls because no grace is offered to those whom the Lord despises. Engelsma and Hoeksema dismiss those who make the general/secret distinction as flaccid Calvinists and charge them with loss of nerve. They claim that they are the ones who are pursuing a consistent Calvinism. Arminians such as Shank are more than happy to agree that they have found it.

Third, the Bible does not merely present faith as the evidence of regeneration or effectual call but as the condition to receiving salvation. Salvation is by faith. Therefore, regeneration cannot precede conversion, for regeneration is the beginning of eternal life (i.e., salvation), and faith, along with repentance, is a component of conversion. When Calvinists such as Sproul Sr. argue that regeneration leads to conversion, they reverse what the Scriptures actually say.

Scripture repeatedly presents the benefits of Christ as contingent and conditioned on faith. For example, in Rom 5:18–19 Paul teaches both universal depravity and universal atonement. He contrasts Adam and Christ by saying, "So then, as through one trespass there is condemnation for everyone, so also through one righteous act there is life-giving justification for everyone. For just as through one man's disobedience the many were made sinners, so also through the one man's obedience the many will be made righteous." Paul teaches that Christ atoned for those who have fallen in Adam—which is everyone. So why isn't Paul a universalist? Because in the preceding verse he declares that there is a condition for receiving salvation—the condition of faith. The benefits of Christ are bestowed on "those who receive the overflow of grace and the gift of righteousness" (Rom 5:17).

Another example of the conditional nature of salvation is 2 Cor 5:19, in which Paul teaches that God has reconciled the world to Himself in Jesus Christ. Then, based on this truth, in the next verse (v. 20) he issues the call to be reconciled to God. Similarly, John declares that because God loves the world He gave His Son (John 3:16), but that the benefits of salvation are bestowed only on whoever believes. Christ came so that "the world might be saved through Him" (3:17), but God requires each individual to receive Christ in order to escape condemnation (v. 18).

In addition to teaching that the benefits of Christ are conditional, the Bible also spells out that the various aspects of salvation are not received until we place our trust in the Son of God. For example, Scripture declares that a person is justified upon believing in Christ, not the other way around. Paul states, "Through [Jesus] forgiveness of sins is being proclaimed to you, and everyone who believes in Him is justified" (Acts 13:38–39). This is a constant refrain the apostle never tires of repeating (Rom 3:22,26; 4:3,5; 5:1; Gal 2:16). Calvinists concede that justification is received through faith because the Bible clearly says so. But in order to hold that regeneration precedes faith, they must bifurcate justification from regeneration. This results in the odd position that a person can be born again and not yet enjoy any of the other blessings of salvation— justification, eternal life, sanctification, etc.—until at a later point when that person is converted.[44]

And the Bible does not teach that only justification is contingent upon faith. It teaches that all aspects of salvation are received through the instrument of faith. We become the sons of God by faith ("for you are all sons of God through faith in Christ Jesus," Gal 3:26; cf. John 1:12).

Sometimes Scripture simply says that salvation itself is obtained by faith. Jesus told the woman who washed His feet with her tears, "Your faith has saved you" (Luke 7:50). Paul told the Philippian jailor, "Believe on the Lord Jesus, and you will be saved" (Acts 16:31). He declared, "If you confess with your mouth, 'Jesus is Lord,' and believe in your heart that God raised Him from the dead, you will be saved" (Rom 10:9; cf.

---

[44]Louis Berkhof, however, asserts that the sequence of regeneration then conversion is logical rather than necessarily temporal. "In the case of those who are regenerated after they have come to years of discretion, the two generally coincide." See L. Berkhof, *Systematic Theology* (Grand Rapids: Eerdmans, 1941), 491.

1 Cor 1:21; Eph 2:8–9). Exercising faith "results" in salvation, as he states, "With the heart one believes, resulting in righteousness, and with the mouth one confesses, resulting in salvation" (Rom 10:10). In these verses Paul does not differentiate between the various components of redemption. He plainly states that the condition to salvation is faith. As Geisler points out, the regeneration before faith view seems to be in the ironic position of denying (or at least abandoning) the key doctrine of the Reformation: salvation by faith alone—*sola fide*.[45]

The Bible teaches that the promises and blessings of the Holy Spirit are received by faith. In the Gospel of John, coming to Christ and believing on Him precede the arrival of the Spirit (John 4:10–14; 6:35; 7:37–39).[46] In Acts, Luke makes clear that it is those who repent and believe who then receive the Holy Spirit (2:38; 3:19; 5:32; 10:43–44; 11:14–17; 15:7–9). Similarly, Paul chastens the Galatian believers for not realizing they had received the promise of the Spirit by faith (Gal 3:2,5,14). He tells the Ephesians that their receiving the seal of the promised Holy Spirit was subsequent to their trusting the "word of truth, the gospel of your salvation" (Eph 1:13).

One of the strongest indications that conversion precedes regeneration is the fact that the instrument used by the Holy Spirit to bring about regeneration is the Word of God. Peter declares that believers "have been born again—not of perishable seed but of imperishable—through the living and enduring word of God" (1 Pet 1:23; cf. Jas 1:18,21). How is this accomplished? Paul explains in Rom 10:17, "So faith comes from what is heard, and what is heard comes through the message about Christ."

Jesus teaches that it is the one who "hears My word and believes" that "has passed from death to life" (i.e., that one who believes the gospel is then born again, John 5:24). Similarly, Paul teaches that resurrection from spiritual death, i.e., regeneration, is received through faith. ("You were also raised with Him through faith," Col 2:12.)

Regeneration is the act of the Holy Spirit whereby He imparts eternal life into a person, and the apostle John repeatedly declared that eternal life is received by faith. This means that eternal life (i.e., regeneration)

---

[45]N. Geisler, *Systematic Theology,* vol. 3 (Minneapolis: Bethany, 2004), 476.
[46]Toon, *Born Again,* 187.

is not prior to conversion. At this point it is appropriate to revisit what the apostle said in 1 John 5:1 ("Everyone who believes that Jesus is the Messiah has been born of God"). Does this teach that saving faith is the product of the new birth? The context provides the answer. John is not presenting the order of salvation. Rather he is distinguishing between true Christians and the breakaway heretical groups who denied the incarnation of Jesus Christ (see 1 John 2:19–23; 4:1–3; cf. 2 John 7–11).

What does John say when he is addressing salvation specifically? The message is consistently the same: "But to all who did receive Him, He gave them the right to become children of God, to those who believe in His name" (John 1:12); "The one who believes in the Son has eternal life" (John 3:36); "Anyone who hears My word and believes Him who sent Me has eternal life and will not come under judgment but has passed from death to life" (John 5:24). The list goes on (John 3:16; 3:18; 5:38,40; 6:40,47). John (and Jesus) make faith and unbelief the dividing line between being spiritually dead and being born again.

Of special note is the order of salvation in John 20:31: "But these are written so that you may believe Jesus is the Messiah, the Son of God, and *by believing you may have life in His name*" (my emphasis). Paul teaches the same sequence when he says that his salvation served as "an example to those who would believe on him for eternal life" (1 Tim 1:16). The regeneration-before-faith position requires that we see regeneration as something prior to salvation. Yet if regeneration is the beginning of our new life in Christ—eternal life—it is difficult to see how regeneration precedes conversion, since Scripture clearly teaches that we receive eternal life by faith. Unless one wants to argue that a person can be born again but yet not have eternal life, then one must acknowledge that the apostles teach that faith precedes regeneration.

At times Reformed theologians seem to contradict themselves on this point. Though Sproul Sr. advocates the regeneration-before-faith position, sometimes he seems to recognize that it is the other way around. After stating the maxim, "regeneration precedes faith," two paragraphs later he gives the following explanation of John 3:16: "What the text teaches is that everyone who believes in Christ will be saved. Whoever does A (believes) will receive B (everlasting life)."[47] Exactly. Unless Sproul Sr. wants to sever regeneration from everlasting life, he has inadvertently argued against his own view.

Fourth, the Bible teaches that God and His grace can be resisted. The doctrine of irresistible grace flies in the face of the passages that warn against resisting God's grace. The apostle Paul declares, "I do not set aside the grace of God" (Gal 2:21) and similarly exhorts the Corinthian believers, "Don't receive God's grace in vain" (2 Cor 6:1). The author of Hebrews speaks of those who have "insulted the Spirit of grace" (Heb 10:29) and urges the readers to "see to it that no one misses the grace of God" (Heb 12:15 NIV). We have a moral responsibility to not resist God, to not harden our hearts, and to not grieve the Holy Spirit (1 Sam 6:6; 2 Chr 36:12–13; Ps 95:8; Isa 1:19–20; Acts 7:51; Eph 4:30; Heb 3:8,15; 4:7; Rev 3:20).

In addition to the exhortations, the Bible also gives examples of people resisting God. God admonished Cain prior to Abel's murder, but Cain ignored Him (Gen 4:6–7). In the days of Noah, God declared, "My Spirit shall not strive with man forever" (Gen 6:3 NKJV). The Holy Spirit graciously contended with an antediluvian humanity bent on rebellion, but this gracious intercession was not without limits, as the flood demonstrated.[48] In Isaiah, God presents His case against wayward Israel in a parable in which He likens the nation to a vineyard. He asks, "What more could I have done for My vineyard than I did? Why, when I expected a yield of good grapes, did it yield worthless grapes?" (Isa 5:4). God's questions make no sense if He was withholding some type of secret, inward irresistible grace. Rather Isaiah says that Israel "rebelled, and grieved His Holy Spirit. So He became their enemy and fought against them" (Isa 63:10).

In the New Testament, Luke speaks of the Pharisees rejecting God's grace when he states that "the Pharisees and experts in the law . . . rejected

---

[47]Sproul Sr., *Chosen by God*, 72–73. John Murray also seems to argue against the regeneration-before-faith position when he states: "The faith of which we are now speaking is not the belief that we have been saved but trust in Christ in order that we may be saved." J. Murray, *Redemption: Accomplished and Applied* (Grand Rapids: Eerdmans, 1955), 109.

[48]It must be acknowledged that the proper interpretation of Gen 6:3 is a matter of debate. Some understand the verse to refer merely to the limiting of the human lifespan to 120 years. See K. A. Mathews, *Genesis 1-11:26*. New American Commentary (Nashville: B&H, 2002), 332-35.

the plan of God for themselves" (Luke 7:30; cf. Matt 21:25,32; 23:13; Mark 7:9). Stephen denounced the Jews of his day by declaring that, just as their fathers did before them, "You are always resisting the Holy Spirit!" (Acts 7:51). Similarly, the author of Hebrews exhorts his audience not to harden their hearts as Israel did in Kadesh Barnea and resist the Holy Spirit, but rather respond to God's gracious offer while the opportunity remains (Heb 3:8,15; 4:7; cf. Eph 4:30). Clearly the biblical authors considered open and public calls of God to be genuine, gracious, and in good faith.

The Bible emphasizes human choice and the graciousness of God's offer without a hint of concern about the two being in conflict, so the burden of proof is upon any theological system that infers one exists. It is one thing to say that without the Holy Spirit's enabling we cannot believe, but it is another to say the Holy Spirit necessitates we believe. Simply put, the doctrine of irresistible grace renders incomprehensible major portions of the Bible. Scripture gives too many examples of persons successfully resisting God's grace.

CALVINIST ARGUMENT #3: FAITH IS A VIRTUE

At this point, many Calvinists protest, "Even if faith is not a work and the gift of faith is resistible, still faith is a good quality in the one who believes. In other words, even if faith is not a work, it is at least a virtue. And if faith is the condition to salvation, then believers are saved because they were, in effect, more virtuous than unbelievers." This objection brings us back to the dilemma expressed at the beginning of the chapter.

Indeed, faith is a virtue. There is abundant scriptural evidence for this (Rom 12:3–6; 1 Cor 13:13; Gal 5:22–23; Heb 11:1,6). Jesus commended those who had faith and held them up as examples (Matt 8:10; 15:28; Luke 7:9). He often rewarded according to a person's faith ("Let it be done for you according to your faith!" Matt 9:29; cf. Matt 9:2; Mark 2:5) and specifically stated that one's faith made the difference ("Your faith has made you well," Matt 9:22; cf. Mark 5:34; 10:52; Luke 5:20; 7:50; 17:9). Without a doubt, it is better to believe than not to believe. So even if faith is not a meritorious work, it is certainly a morally good quality. Doesn't this imply that, even if it is just a small amount, the salvation of an individual depends on that person possessing the virtue of faith?

This is an important objection, and here is where the advantage of the overcoming grace model becomes evident over both the irresistible grace view of Calvinists and the doctrine of prevenient grace of Arminians. The only solution that I can see is to hold that God's grace is simultaneously monergistic and resistible. This way faith is entirely of God; unbelief is entirely of man.

The notion that God's work in our lives is both monergistic and resistible is not as strange as one might at first think. Paul describes his ministry by declaring, "But by God's grace I am what I am, and His grace toward me was not ineffective. However, I worked more than any of them, yet not I, but God's grace that was with me" (1 Cor 15:10). Paul makes clear that all of his service and sacrifice for Christ are manifestations of God's grace working powerfully in him. The grace of God within us gets all the credit for whatever is good, right, and praiseworthy in our lives. Our Lord tells us that "you can do nothing without Me" (John 15:5). The sanctifying work of the Holy Spirit within believers is a monergistic work ("For it is God who is working in you, enabling you both to will and to act for His good purpose," Phil 2:13; cf. 1 Chr 29:14; 2 Cor 3:5).

Yet believers can and do sometimes resist God's grace. We still dwell in a body of flesh and are susceptible to temptation. The spiritual resources to overcome any particular sin are available to every Christian (1 Cor 10:13), so if we yield to temptation we cannot transfer blame to God (Jas 1:13–16). The tension of God's grace being both monergistic and resistible is a reality all believers experience.[49]

The overcoming grace model does not embrace determinism, but it does hold to monergism. Saving faith is indeed a virtue, but it is a quality and disposition given to us by the Holy Spirit. So the Christian cannot boast because he believes. However, this grace is resistible, so the unbeliever is justly damned for his unbelief.

---

[49]The difficulty Calvinism in general and determinism in particular have with the human element in sanctification has already been noted. See the previous chapter on radical depravity.

ADVANTAGES OF THE OVERCOMING GRACE MODEL

We have made the case for the overcoming grace model: the work of God's grace in humans is monergistic and resistible. In the irresistible grace model, it is difficult not to see regeneration as a process, which is in fact the position of many Reformed theologians. By contrast, in the ambulatory model argued in this chapter, overcoming grace is understood to be the process that brings people to Christ, rather than regeneration. Scripture refers to this process as "drawing" (John 6:44), "convicting of sin" (John 16:8), and "opening the heart" (Acts 16:14). Regeneration is understood to be an event that happens in a moment—the same moment as conversion. The distinction between an effectual and ineffectual call is found in the receiver, not the call itself. This is why God's saving grace is understood to be "overcoming." The same grace that the unbeliever rejects, the elect finds irresistible. Such an approach intends to do justice to all that John 1:11–13 teaches. John states,

> [11]He came to His own [i.e., Jesus Christ was genuinely offered as Messiah to His people, the Jews]. And His own people did not receive Him [i.e., they resisted a salvation that was truly available to them]. [12]But to all who did receive Him, He gave them the right to be children of God, to those who believe in His name [i.e., all who met the condition of faith were birthed into the family of God], [13]who were born, not of blood, or of the will of the flesh, or of the will of man, but of God [i.e., yet all this is a monergistic, gracious work of God].

There are at least twelve advantages to the overcoming grace model.

First, the overcoming grace model is consistent with the biblical tension of divine sovereignty and human responsibility. Nowhere is this tension clearer than in the Gospel of John. On the one hand, John emphasizes God's sovereign work of election and drawing. Yet on the other hand, he presents Christ as the universal Savior "who takes away the sins of the world," makes repeated universal appeals, and issues universal condemnation upon unbelief. Sometimes those who focus on the texts which stress sovereignty overlook the strong universal appeals which are also in John. Jesus Christ died for the whole world (John 3:16–18). As D. A. Carson observes, "The Gospel of St. John is par excellence the Gospel of appeals, or rather one immense appeal from one end to the other (cf. 20.30f)."[50] Conversely, those who stress the invitations to "whosoever" in John sometimes go to great lengths to explain away what is said there about God's sovereign choice of His sheep. The overcoming grace model is a deliberate attempt to preserve this tension.

Often in John's Gospel, Jesus places the divine/human tension side by side. In John 5:21, our Lord declares that He gives life to whomever He pleases. Yet He in turn appeals to them "that [they] may be saved" (John 5:34) and excoriates them for their unbelief and places all responsibility on them ("And you are not willing to come to Me that you may have life," John 5:40).

Similarly, Jesus teaches that men come to faith only through the drawing of God, as when He states, "No one can come to Me unless the Father who sent Me draws him" (John 6:44; cf. 6:65; 8:47; 10:29; 15:16,19; 17:2,6,9,11–12,24; 18:9). "Draw" is a strong word, indicating God has to overcome our resistance and that the only reason a person comes to faith is because of this overcoming work. Yet He then states, "And they will all be taught by God. Everyone who has listened to and learned from the Father comes to Me" (John 6:45; i.e., all are taught by God; those who heed are saved).

After telling the unbelieving Jews, "You don't believe because you are not My sheep" (John 10:26), Jesus then appeals to the same men to believe in the miracles He had done: "This way you will know and understand that the Father is in Me and I in the Father" (John 10:38). In John's Gospel, divine sovereignty and human responsibility dwell in symbiotic union.

In certain passages in John it appears Jesus is excluding some simply because they are not elect, such as when He states, "The one who is from God listens to God's words. This is why you don't listen, because you are not from God" (John 8:47). However, it is important to remember His audience. He is speaking to Jews who are sure of their standing with God because of their ancestry. Since they are the offspring of Abraham, they reason that they are the chosen, elect. They not only reject

---

[50]D. A. Carson, *Divine Sovereignty and Human Responsibility* (Atlanta: John Knox, 1981), 168.

Jesus as Messiah, they reject any notion that they are in any spiritual peril. The crucial issue is the purpose of Jesus' statements: whether He is warning or informing. Is He informing them they are not elect, or is He warning them that they are not saved? Is He urging them to repent, or is He informing them that they are out of luck? Is He telling them they are not God's children, or is He telling them God does not want them as His children? In other words, is He warning them or is He taunting them? It is very clear that He is warning them (John 8:24) rather than merely declaring an absolute decree.

Jesus' point is not merely to teach predestination but to stress the necessity of coming to Christ. No one can claim, as the Jews who were against Jesus were claiming, that they could be in right relationship with the Father while rejecting His Son. The purpose of such language is not to express the exclusion of certain men from salvation because they were not elect but to emphasize that from beginning to end salvation is a work of God and not under human control.

The ambulatory model of overcoming grace fits the tension of the Gospel of John very well. John emphasizes that the gospel is universally provided and universally offered (John 1:29; 3:16; 4:4). The Holy Spirit graciously draws and convicts the hearts of all (John 12:21; 16:8). He stresses the requirement to exercise personal faith and the culpability of those who reject (John 3:16,18,36).

Yet John also teaches that the conversion of those who believe is the gracious result of God's drawing work (John 6:37,44,65) and designates believers as the elect (John 6:70; 15:16). Those who receive the Son are saved, but not as the result of any human effort or will (John 1:13). Salvation is a work of God from beginning to end (John 8:47; 10:29; 15:16,19; 17:2,6,11–12,24; 18:9), but those who do not believe have only themselves to blame. I do not see how one can hold to the tension set forth in the Gospel of John without embracing the overcoming grace model or something very close to it.

Second, the overcoming grace model is consistent with the gracious nature of salvation. Here I nod to my Calvinist brethren: salvation is indeed a monergistic work of God. The lost, in their natural state, do not have "free will" where it really matters (i.e., the ability to turn to God).

Paul describes lost humanity's attitude toward God and His goodness: "There is no one righteous, not even one; there is no one who understands, there is no one who seeks God" (Rom 3:10–11). All are spiritually dead (Eph 2:1), spiritually blind (2 Cor 4:4), and spiritually incapacitated (Rom 8:6–8). The apostle does not say just that the unconverted are lost, but that they lack the capacity to rightly comprehend the truth and that they have no desire or love for it. Lost humanity does not want God, godliness, or the gospel. So before anyone can be converted (i.e., repent and believe), God must graciously invade the darkness of a person's heart. God takes the initiative. Salvation is entirely a work of God.

Third, the overcoming grace model is consistent with the conditionality of salvation. Here I nod to my Arminian brethren: unbelief is the rejection of a Savior who was genuinely available. The convicting work of the Holy Spirit accompanies the preaching of the gospel and enables a response that a lost person does not intrinsically have the ability to give. This includes the ability to accept the gospel. At this point it is not a question of free will. In fact, the Bible uses a grander term than free will: it declares that the water of life is available to "whosoever will."

Fourth, the overcoming grace model is consistent with a "well-meant" offer of the gospel. Hyper-Calvinists such as David Engelsma, Herman Hoeksema, and Joseph Hussey deny that grace is offered to the nonelect. This is the hallmark of hyper-Calvinism, and that denial has been rejected by the overwhelming majority of Calvinists. Yet the dilemma remains for them: how can presenting the gospel to those from whom God withholds the ability to respond be in good faith? The overcoming grace model has no such problem, and this is a distinct advantage.

Paul told the Jews who heard him preach but refused to believe the gospel, "Since you reject it, and consider yourselves unworthy of eternal life, we now turn to the Gentiles!" (Acts 13:46). Paul understood the message to be genuinely offered to his hearers. If the word "offer" has any real meaning, then when the gospel is offered, it really is available.

Fifth, the overcoming grace model is consistent with the culpability of those who resist (Rom 2:5; 2 Thess 2:10–11). The complicating factor is that many who hear the gospel do not believe. Our Lord and the apostles repeatedly placed the blame for unbelief on the unbeliever. In the parable of the Wedding Feast, Jesus tells how the king "sent out his servants to call those who were invited to the wedding; and they were not willing to come" (Matt 22:3 NKJV). As he wept over Jerusalem, he declares, "Jerusalem, Jerusalem! The city who kills the prophets and stones those who are sent to her. How often I wanted to gather your children together, as a hen gathers her chicks under her wings, yet you were not willing!" (Matt 23:37). He further declares that the opportunity to believe was genuinely available to them (Luke 7:30).

All who hear the gospel are drawn to Christ (John 12:32). Some accept and some reject, but none are compelled to faith. Unbelievers had the same grace available as believers, and this should have resulted in their conversion also. There is no merit in believing, but there is great offense in not believing. God is just in His judgment upon their unbelief.

The mystery of exactly why one says "no" to grace remains unsolved. Evil, at a fundamental level, is irrational, and rejecting Christ is the ultimate evil (John 3:18). I can no more explain why people turn down the gospel than I can give the ultimate reason why Satan rebelled or Adam fell. The Bible gives no explanation as to why sin exists. Evil, by its very nature, seems to be an impossible conundrum.

As we stated before, the overcoming grace model puts the question in the proper slant. The question is not why some are saved, but why all are not saved. And the Bible clearly gives an answer to this. The unbeliever perishes because of his own unbelief. The ambulatory model places the mystery of sin where it should be: within the wickedness of the human heart. This is the consistent testimony of Scripture.

Sixth, the overcoming grace model is consistent with God's expression of distress and grief. The Bible presents God as expressing distress, grief, and even exasperation over unbelief, stiff-necked rebellion, and hardness of heart (Gen 6:1–3; Exod 33:3,5; 34:9; Deut 9:6,13; 10:16; 31:27; Judg 2:19; 2 Kgs 17:14; 2 Chr 30:8; 36:13; Neh 9:16; Isa 5:3–5; 46:12; 48:4; Jer 7:26; Ezek 18:30–32; 33:11; Hos 4:16; Matt 23:37; Eph 4:30; Heb 3:17).

One cannot merely label these expressions as anthropopathisms;[51] to do so is to try to explain away a significant portion of the Bible. God reveals Himself to be heartbroken at the obstinate wickedness of humanity. More specifically, He expresses regret and grief over the fact that unbelievers refuse His offers of forgiveness and grace. In turn, He also expresses anger and outrage for their continued rebellion (Deut 28:63; 2 Sam 2:25; Amos 4:6–12). The irresistible grace position renders such statements incomprehensible, while the overcoming grace model has no such problem.

Seventh, the overcoming grace position is consistent with a spectrum of responses. The ambulatory model allows for a genuine work of grace that, because of resistance, may not result in salvation. It makes faith possible without making it necessary. The fact is, both Scripture and experience demonstrate that there are some spiritual "misfires": those who were initially intrigued, attracted, or convicted by the gospel but eventually turned away (Mark 4:16–19; John 6:66–67).

Some who advocate the irresistible grace position present what could be called a "light-switch" understanding of conversion. For example, Sam Storms, in his book on election, presents a hypothetical illustration of twin brothers attending a Sunday morning worship service.[52] Initially, neither is interested, but one suddenly is moved to tears by the sermon. The other twin is bewildered by his brother's response, so he mocks and ridicules him on the way home. The first twin is elect, and at the appropriate time the spiritual lightbulb comes on via regeneration. God passes over the second twin, so he is left in spiritual blindness.[53]

The appeal of Storms's illustration is that it is simple, neat, and tidy. But in fact it is too tidy. Sometimes the contrast between two hearers is this simple and stark: one immediately responds while the other totally rejects. But this hypothetical example does not illustrate what typically occurs. Nor does the Bible present the responses typified by the twins as

---

[51] An anthropopathism is the figurative ascribing of a human emotion to God which He is thought not literally to have (e.g., a sacrifice's "pleasing aroma" to the Lord in Num 29:8; God's "fear" in Deut 32:27; God's laughter and ridicule of His enemies in Ps 2:4; His weariness with the words of His rebellious people in Mal 2:17). It is based on the principle that much of our knowledge of God is analogical.

[52] S. Storms, *Chosen for Life: The Case for Divine Election* (Wheaton: Crossway, 2007), 15–17.

[53] Ibid., 145–57.

the only two responses. Rather, their reactions represent two poles on a spectrum of responses.[54]

Storms's illustration highlights an important truth: the spiritual condition of every person is an either/or affair. One is either saved or lost, born again or spiritually dead, on the narrow road to life or on the broad way to destruction. And in the great day of judgment, there will be only two types of persons standing before God: the redeemed and the rejected, the sheep and the goats. But as an explanation or even a description of the work of the Word and the Spirit upon the hearers of the gospel, the light-switch approach is an oversimplification.

The Bible presents people as reacting to the gospel in a variety of ways. The parable of the Sower (Matt 13:1–8) teaches that some will dismiss the gospel out of hand, some will make an insincere profession, others will make an incomplete commitment, and still others will genuinely receive the Word. Jesus warned more than once about false professions in His preaching (Matt 7:21–23) and in parables such as the stories of the wheat and the tares (Matt 13:24–30) and the ten virgins (Matt 25:1–12). The motivations for making a counterfeit profession are complex and difficult to understand, and they do not fit easily in the irresistible grace paradigm. In fact, Calvin and Beza argued that the Holy Spirit gave a false, temporary faith to some reprobates in order to make their damnation even more severe.[55] We will cover these matters more thoroughly in the chapter on assurance of salvation, but for now let it be noted that the irresistible grace position sometimes leads to the conclusion that God is the Author even of false professions of faith. The overcoming grace model does not necessitate such conclusions and allows for a litany of responses.

And a litany of responses is what we find in Scripture. The book of Acts presents the entire gamut of reactions to the message of Christ. Many gladly receive the good news (2:41; 4:4). Some make an incomplete conversion (8:13,20–23). Others, like Saul and the Philippian jailor, first exhibit great hostility and then are dramatically converted (9:1–9;

---

[54]To his credit, Storms cautions that the mystery of salvation cannot be reduced to "a mechanical sequence" akin to a mathematical formula. Ibid., 145.

[55]See Theodore Beza, *A Little Book of Christian Questions and Responses,* Q. 209 (Allison Park, PA: Pickwick Publications, 1986), 96-97.

16:30–34). Some resist while others gladly respond (13:45–52). Some, such as the Ethiopian eunuch and Lydia, receive the gospel quickly (8:36–38; 16:14), while others, such as Sergius Paulus, take a while to be convinced (13:6–12). Felix is moved by the gospel to the point he "trembles" with fear, yet he eventually loses interest (24:24–26). Festus dismisses the message as madness (26:24), while Agrippa replies to Paul's appeal, "You almost persuade me to become a Christian" (26:28 NKJV).[56] Acts presents a remarkable array of responses to the gospel.

Compared to the irresistible grace position the overcoming grace model is messy. But the complex variety of responses presented by the Bible and the history of evangelism is also untidy. Some respond immediately—either in faith or in derision. Others wrestle terribly, with some being birthed into the kingdom while others tragically turn away. For years I was one of those whose knuckles turned white from holding on to the back of the pew in front of me, resisting the appeal to respond. I thank God He continued to call. The simplicity of the Calvinist paradigm of irresistible grace is its greatest attraction—and its flaw. It simply does not fit the testimony of Scripture or what we witness occurring in evangelistic work. The overcoming grace model posits that God's convicting but resistible grace works mightily in every hearer, and therefore this model better accounts for the wide range of responses.

Eighth, the overcoming grace model is consistent with the limited, temporary nature of the call. There is no reason to believe that the opportunity for any particular person to be saved is open-ended or indefinite. God warns that His Spirit deals with men only for a period of time (Gen 6:3). Isaiah exhorts Israel to "seek the LORD while He may be found; call to Him while He is near" (Isa 55:6), and Paul urges, "Look, now is the acceptable time; now is the day of salvation" (2 Cor 6:2). The overcoming grace model argues that the window of opportunity for salvation is real, but temporary. Some are gloriously saved on their deathbed (and for that we praise God), but none should presume that God will continue to deal graciously with them until their final hours.

---

[56]Just how sincere Agrippa is when he makes this statement (or whether the statement is actually a sarcastic question) is a matter of debate. See J. A. Fitzmyer, *The Acts of the Apostles,* Anchor Bible (N.Y.: Doubleday, 1998), 764–65.

The author of the book of Hebrews uses the Kadesh Barnea incident (Numbers 14) to build a sustained case that grace must be responded to while it is available. The children of Israel refused to enter the promised land, so God sentenced them to forty years of wandering. Even though they later feigned repentance, it was too late (Num 14:39–45). The writer of Hebrews urges not to "harden your hearts" (Heb 3:8; cf. Ps 95:8) so that we do not become like them. We must not "insult the Spirit of grace" (10:29) and "see to it that no one misses the grace of God" (12:15 NIV).

Again a word of personal testimony is in order here. I was converted under the ministry of evangelist Clifford Rice, who is now with the Lord. The night I was saved he preached a message entitled, "Too Late!" He preached on the drowning of the Egyptian army in the Red Sea in which the text states, "And He [the Lord] took off their chariot wheels" (Exod 14:25 NKJV). His point was that one cannot presume that God's grace will always be available. In fact, once God moves in judgment, the opportunity for redemption is past. As someone who had been resisting and delaying, intending to eventually come to Christ, I found his warning compelling.

The fact is that the gospel does not leave the hearer unchanged. A decision is required, and the wrong choice has a terrible effect on the unbeliever. The person who does not listen but remains disobedient is compelled to go the way of judgment. Those who will not believe eventually cannot believe, which leads to our next point.

Ninth, the overcoming grace model is consistent with the phenomena of the hardening of the unbeliever. At times the Bible speaks of God rendering some persons incapable of understanding spiritual truth. The Lord instructs Isaiah, "Say to these people: Keep listening, but do not understand; keep looking, but do not perceive. Dull the minds of these people; deafen their ears and blind their eyes; otherwise they might see with their eyes and hear with their ears, understand with their minds, turn back, and be healed" (Isa 6:9–10; cf. Jer 5:21; 6:10). This passage figures prominently in the New Testament and is cited often as a prophecy of the spiritual condition that Israel would display during the first coming of Jesus (Matt 13:13–15; Mark 4:12; Luke 8:10; John 12:37–40; Acts

28:25–27). Other passages speak of God causing some to be unable to respond to the truth, such as when God is said to harden Pharaoh's heart (Exod 4:21; 7:3; 9:12; 10:1,20,27; 11:10; 14:4,8,17). Without a doubt, God afflicts certain ones with spiritual blindness and inability. What are we to make of this?

First, the act of hardening is always presented as an act of judgment. For instance, in a particularly terrifying passage, Paul speaks of those who will follow the "lawless one": "They perish because they did not accept the love of the truth in order to be saved. For this reason God sends them a strong delusion so that they will believe what is false, so that all will be condemned—those who did not believe the truth but enjoyed unrighteousness" (2 Thess 2:10b–12). God eventually deals with sin and sinners, and when He does so He acts as forcefully and coercively as He sees fit. The time of free choice is over when God moves in judgment. No one will attend the Great White Throne voluntarily.

Second, the act of hardening is always in response to prior rejections of offers of grace. For example, context makes this clear in the 2 Thessalonians passage of the previous paragraph. God sends them strong delusions "because they did not accept the love of the truth" and because they "did not believe the truth but enjoyed unrighteousness" (vv. 10,12). When the Isaiah passage which speaks of God closing Israel's ears and eyes (Isa 6:9–10) is viewed in the context of the many times Isaiah presents God as pleading with Israel (Isa 1:16–19; 43:25–26; 44:22; 55:6–7), it becomes apparent that Israel had numerous opportunities to repent before God removed the ability.

The New Testament repeats this principle and expands it. Jesus warned, "Pay attention to what you hear. By the measure you use, it will be measured and added to you. For to the one who has, it will be given, and from the one who does not have, even what he has will be taken away" (Mark 4:24–25). In other words, those who respond are given additional light, while those who reject are further hardened.

Third, God's hardening of the heart always occurs in the context of self-hardening. The Exodus account speaks as often of Pharaoh hardening his heart as often as it does of God hardening his heart. Indeed, rather than God simply hardening the reprobate, the Bible presents God as the

One who warns against turning one's heart into stone (Ps 95:8; Heb 3:8, "Do not harden your hearts"). Similarly, Paul teaches that if someone is hardened against God it is because of his own unbelief (Rom 11:20; cf. Rom 10:3; 11:7,25). God hardens the sinner's heart passively (i.e., God ceases His striving, restraining work), and the unbeliever willingly descends into spiritual imperviousness.

God's rendering some unbelievers incapable of responding implies they previously had the ability to do so. When the divine judgment of hardening is viewed through the lens of determinism, it is barely distinguishable from fatalism. The Bible does not simply portray God as the ultimate cause of spiritual inability. Rather, it presents Him as the sovereign Judge who curses spiritual hard-heartedness by rendering such dispositions permanent.

Tenth, the overcoming grace model is consistent with the soft libertarian view of human choice. The soft libertarian model of human choice is spelled out in the previous chapter on radical depravity. In this view, fallen humanity does not have the ability to turn to God on its own. A lost person has the ability to choose within the parameters of his character, but those parameters do not include the ability to please, trust, or obey God. Grace must first invade the sin-darkened blindness of every lost person. God must take the initiative.

Eleventh, the overcoming grace position is consistent with the Molinist view of election. Sufficient grace is effective for the elect. This is why certain texts, such as Rom 8:29, speak of the effectual nature of God's call. In the Molinist paradigm, God knows in what possible world or scenario one person would accept the gospel and another person would reject it. We do not claim to know why God has ordained this particular world, but we can be sure His decision was consistent with His benevolent and wise nature. But when He used His exhaustive foreknowledge to choose this world, He actively ordained the salvation of those who believe. Therefore, Molinists can affirm statements such as, "Everyone the Father gives Me will come to Me" (John 6:37). We will address the matter of election in the next chapter.

Twelfth, the overcoming grace model is consistent with what Calvinists also want to affirm: salvation is all of divine grace; damnation is all of man. Yet I believe that the ambulatory model preserves this tension in a way proponents of the irresistible grace model want to do but cannot. In short, the overcoming grace position argues that the call of the Holy Spirit through the gospel is effectual in those for whom it was intended (i.e., the elect), but this same call was sincerely offered to every hearer in good faith. Salvation is genuinely available to those who reject Jesus Christ. They have no one to blame but themselves. Salvation is all of God; damnation is all of man. As Balthasar Hubmaier the Anabaptist martyr put it: "Whoever is not persuaded by this answer, namely, that the mercy of God is the cause of our salvation and our malice to blame for our damnation, must ask God himself."[57]

---

[57]B. Hubmaier, "Freedom of the Will, II" in *Balthasar Hubmaier: Theologian of Anabaptism* (Scottdale, PA: Herald, 1989), 469.

CHAPTER 5

RO**S**ES

IS FOR SOVEREIGN ELECTION

*Do you believe that God created man and arbitrarily, sover-
eignly—it is the same thing—created that man, with no other
intention, than that of damning him? Made him, and yet, for no
other reason than that of destroying him forever? Well, if you can
believe it, I pity you, that is all I can say: you deserve pity, that you
should think so meanly of God, whose mercy endureth forever.*
                                                            —C. H. Spurgeon[1]

SOUTHEASTERN BAPTIST THEOLOGICAL SEMINARY, where I
teach, has a confession of faith called the Abstract of Principles.
Written originally for Southern Seminary by Basil Manly Jr., article four of the Abstract states, "God from eternity decrees or permits
all things that come to pass and perpetually upholds, directs and governs
all creatures and all events; yet so as not in any wise to be author or ap-
prover of sin nor to destroy the free will and responsibility of intelligent
creatures."

The article seems self-contradictory. It declares that God's decisions oversee all things, yet at the same time God only *permits* evil,
He is not "in any wise" the origin of sin, and His choices do not negate
human free will. One model of divine sovereignty and human responsibility that attempts to reconcile all the declarations of the above article
is called Molinism. This chapter presents the Molinist understanding of
election and argues that it provides an alternative for the believer who is
convinced that election is a sovereign and gracious choice of God but is
unconvinced that this entails accepting the five points of Calvinism.

---

[1] C. H. Spurgeon, "Jacob and Esau," *The New Park Street Pulpit* (Pasadena: Pilgrim Pub., [1859]
1981), 118. Spurgeon was a Calvinist and made these statements against supralapsarianism. During his
years of ministry he opposed hyper-Calvinism as strenuously as he did Arminianism. See I. H. Murray,
Spurgeon v. Hyper-Calvinism: The Battle for Gospel Preaching (Edinburgh: Banner of Truth, 1994).

TWO ESSENTIAL DOCTRINES: SOVEREIGNTY AND PERMISSION

The God of the Bible created the world out of nothing—*creatio ex nihilo*—and this truth entails two corollaries: sovereignty and permission. God's sovereignty is His lordship over creation. Divine sovereignty means that God rules and, yes, controls all things.

In his crafting of the *Abstract of Principles*, Manly was careful to include the concept of permission. Permission is the decision by God to allow something other than Himself to exist. Mere existence seems to be what God gave to most of creation because most of this immense universe consists simply of physical materials that obey natural laws. He gave a level of freedom, within limits, to certain agents—namely angels and humans. God did not grant us absolute independence or complete autonomy. Using the word *permission* highlights the point that our freedom is a derived freedom. He gave us the ability to choose, and with this ability came the moral responsibility for those choices. The concept of permission means that though God controls all things He does not cause all things.[2] How much freedom did He permit us? Enough freedom to rebel.

Sovereignty and Permission as They Relate to Predestination

The difficult goal before us is to achieve a balanced understanding of both sovereignty and permission, particularly as it pertains to predestination. Those who emphasize sovereignty tend to be Calvinists; those who emphasize permission tend to be Arminians. Extremes exist beyond both sides of the boundaries of Christian doctrine. If one wants to see divine sovereignty emphasized to the point of fatalism, he needs look no further than Islam. The world *Islam* means "submit," and the goal of the devout Muslim is to submit to the irresistible will of Allah.

Opposite of Islam at the other end of the spectrum is process theology. In process thought God is changing and evolving along with the world and needs the world as much as it needs Him. According to the

---

[2]Of course, God is the ultimate cause of all that exists. I use "cause" in this instance in the immediate sense that God does not directly cause anything wicked. This chapter argues that, between God and the sinfulness of this world, morally responsible free agents exist. Their choices are the cause of evil, including the evil of rejecting Christ and His salvation.

process theologian, evil happens because God is not able to stop it, and the world literally is out of control. Located between the extremes of Islam and process theology is the biblical truth that God sovereignly rules over creatures that He permitted to have a relative amount of freedom.

The Similarities of Infralapsarian Calvinism and Molinism

Within orthodox Christian beliefs two approaches consciously attempt to do justice to the twin biblical doctrines of divine sovereignty and divine permission by simultaneously affirming both. They are infralapsarian Calvinism and Molinism. Both affirm that God's sovereignty is meticulous and overarching. Both affirm the concept of permission and agree that God did not cause the fall, nor is He the cause of evil, but He permits sin. The real problem is, as always, the problem of evil. As it relates to the issue of election, the question is how humans came to be viewed in the eternal mind of God as sinners in the first place. The debate concerning predestination is over the role that permission plays in God's decrees.

Few Christians have a problem with the doctrine of election per se. The Scriptures teach, and our experience confirms, that if God had not first chosen us we would not have chosen Him (John 15:16). According to Paul, God chose us "in Him [Christ], before the foundation of the world" (Eph 1:4), and Peter identifies believers as those who are "chosen [Gk. *eklektos*] according to the foreknowledge of God the Father and set apart by the Spirit for obedience and for sprinkling with the blood of Jesus Christ" (1 Pet 1:1b–2). Election is the clear teaching of Scripture (cf. Rom 8:29).

The question of the reprobate poses a problem. Reprobation is God's decision to reject or pass over certain ones. If God rejects the reprobate because of his sin and unbelief, then reprobation is based on God's justice, and His decision poses no moral dilemma. But it would also mean that some aspects of God's decree were conditional rather than unconditional and that in certain ways the free choices of morally responsible creatures affected the eternal decisions of God.

Some Calvinists (following their namesake, John Calvin) cannot accept that there is any conditionality in God's decrees, so they bite the bullet and dismiss permission altogether.[3] They embrace a double predestination in which God chose some and rejected others and then subsequently decreed the fall in order to bring it about. As we saw in chapter 2, those who hold this position are called supralapsarians because they understand the decree of election and reprobation as occurring logically prior (*supra*) to the decree to allow the fall (*lapsus*), hence the word *supralapsarianism.*

Most Calvinists blanch at this approach. Reformed theology generally teaches that God first decreed to permit the fall and then from fallen humanity chose certain ones to salvation for reasons known only to Him. This approach is called infralapsarianism (*infra* meaning "after") because it views God's electing choice as occurring logically after He decided to permit the fall.

The crucial concept to the infralapsarian Calvinist model is the notion of permission. God did not cause the fall; He allowed it. God does not predestine the reprobate to hell; He permits the unbeliever to go his own way. Permission is problematic for the Calvinist—particularly to those who hold to determinism—because permission entails conditionality, contingency, and viewing humans as in some sense the origin of their own respective choices. As we noted in the chapter on radical depravity, Calvinists such as John Feinberg define God's sovereignty in terms of causal determinism, and this leaves little room for a logically consistent understanding of permission.[4] I am arguing that what Calvinists want to achieve in infralapsarianism, Molinism actually accomplishes. Molinism combines a high view of sovereignty with a robust understanding of permission.

As we will see, one feature that distinguishes Molinism from Arminianism is the way it understands God's foreknowledge. Arminianism solves the problem of reprobation by presenting God's decision concerning individuals as something entirely passive. God decrees to elect the church as a

---

[3]Some supralapsarians speak of God's permission, but they generally redefine it in a way that is not acceptable even to infralapsarians.

[4]J. Feinberg, *No One Else Like Him* (Wheaton: Crossway, 2001), 637: "So, an act is free, though causally determined, if it is what the agent wanted to do."

corporate body, and those individuals who choose Christ are then viewed as the elect, while those who reject Him are reprobate. In this respect Arminians view God's decree as the mere ratification of human choices.[5] But the Bible presents God's electing decision as something much more active and decisive. Unlike Arminianism, Molinism describes God as using His foreknowledge in a sovereign, unconditional manner.

The Two Calvinistic Approaches to Election Compared with Molinism		
Supralapsarianism	**Infralapsarianism**	**Molinism**
God *ordains* the salvation of the elect and the damnation of the reprobate *in an equal manner*.	God *ordains* the salvation of the elect but only *permits* the damnation of the reprobate.	God *ordains* the salvation of the elect but only *permits* the damnation of the reprobate.
The concept of permission is denied.	Admits to an inconsistent and incoherent view of permission.	Able to maintain a consistent view of permission.

CALVIN'S SUPRALAPSARIANISM: THE CONCEPT OF PERMISSION REJECTED

Calvin approached the issue of predestination with the premise that "the will of God is the chief and principal cause of all things,"[6] an assumption that left little or no room for permission. Some try to argue that Calvin's successor, Theodore Beza, transformed Calvin's teaching on election into supralapsarianism; but Calvin's work on the subject, a book entitled *Concerning the Eternal Predestination of God*, reveals that Calvin held to double predestination just as firmly as his protégée.[7]

---

[5]See R. Shank, *Elect in the Son* (Minneapolis: Bethany House, 1989), 45–55.

[6]J. Calvin, *Concerning the Eternal Predestination of God,* trans. J. K. S. Reid (Louisville: Westminster John Knox, [1552] 1961), 177.

[7]In addition, J. V. Fesko sets the teachings of Calvin and Beza on reprobation side by side and demonstrates the two men were in agreement on this point. See J. V. Fesko, *Diversity within the Reformed*

In supralapsarianism God's decision to elect and to reprobate is primary. Essential to understanding supralapsarianism is the distinction it makes between reprobation and damnation.[8] Reprobation is God's rejection of an individual; damnation is God's judgment upon that person for his sins. In this paradigm God does not reject the reprobate because he is a sinner; it is the other way around. The reprobate becomes a sinner because God rejected him. God rejected certain ones and then decreed the fall in order to actualize His disfavor toward them. Calvin made this clear when he declared that "the highest cause" of reprobation is not sin but "the bare and simple pleasure of God."[9]

If God's decree of double predestination is primary, then its components of election and reprobation have equal ultimacy, a point affirmed repeatedly by modern supralapsarians such as Cornelius Van Til, Herman Hoeksema, and more recently Robert Reymond.[10] God's relationship to both classes of individuals is symmetric. He rejected the reprobate in the same way He chose the elect.[11]

As Bruce Ware, an infralapsarian Calvinist, points out, grace plays no part in the supralapsarian understanding of the initial double decree.[12] This is because when God decided whom He would choose and whom He would reject, humans were not sinners in need of grace or deserving of judgment. Grace did not logically enter the picture until after God determined to rescue His chosen from the fall. This is why some supralapsarians such as David Engelsma do not hesitate to speak of God's attitude toward the nonelect as one of eternal hatred.[13] In supralapsarianism, sovereign grace gives way to mere sovereignty.

Tradition: Supra- and Infralapsarianism in Calvin, Dort, and Westminster (Greenville, SC: Reformed Academic, 2001), 138–50.

[8]See Calvin, *Concerning the Eternal Predestination of God,* 121; C. Van Til, *The Defense of the Faith* (Philadelphia: P&R, 1955), 414–15.

[9]Calvin, *Concerning the Eternal Predestination of God*, 120–21. See also id., *The Epistles of Paul the Apostle to the Romans and to the Thessalonians* (Grand Rapids: Eerdmans, 1960), 190–219.

[10]Van Til, *The Defense of the Faith*, 413; H. Hoeksema, *Reformed Dogmatics* (Grand Rapids: Reformed Free Publishing, 1966), 161; and R. Reymond, "A Consistent Supralapsarian Perspective on Election," in *Perspectives on Election: Five Views*, ed. C. O. Brand (Nashville: B&H, 2006), 153.

[11]"For first there is certainly a mutual relation between the elect and the reprobate, so that the election spoken of here cannot stand, unless we confess that God separated out from others certain men as seemed good to Him." Calvin, *Concerning the Eternal Predestination of God*, 68–72.

[12]B. A. Ware, "Divine Election to Salvation," in Brand, *Perspectives on Election: Five Views*, 56.

[13]"Reprobation is the exact, explicit denial that God loves all men, desires to save all men, and conditionally offers them salvation. Reprobation asserts that God eternally hates some men; has immutably

Calvin had no room for permission. Calvin lampooned the notion when he stated,

> It is easy to conclude how foolish and frail is the support of divine justice by the suggestion that evils come to be not by His will, but merely by His permission. Of course, so far as they are evils. . . . I admit they are not pleasing to God. But it is quite a frivolous refuge to say that God otiosely permits them, when Scripture shows Him not only willing but the author of them.[14]

So Calvin makes the breathtaking claim that God is the very "author" of sin, an assertion that subsequent Calvinists reject.

INFRALAPSARIANISM: THE ATTEMPT TO BLEND CALVINISM AND PERMISSION

Even though Calvin and Beza both advocated supralapsarianism, no major Reformed confession or creed followed their lead. The reason is obvious: supralapsarianism places the origin of sin at God's feet; and as the Canons of Dort declare, the notion that God is the author of sin in any way "at all" is "a blasphemous thought."[15] The Westminster Confession makes a similar declaration.[16]

In Calvin's day a physician in Geneva by the name of Bolsec objected to Calvin's teaching on predestination on the grounds that it impugned the character of God. Bolsec was arrested, convicted, and eventually banished from Geneva; and Calvin sought support from Reformers in other Swiss cities for his supralapsarian position. He seemed to have been genuinely surprised when Reformers such as Heinrich Bullinger disagreed with him and argued instead for infralapsarianism.[17] In the subsequent debates between the infralapsarian and supralapsarian parties, the creeds and confessions reveal that the Reformed churches universally chose Bullinger over Calvin. The great preacher Charles Spurgeon expressed

---

decreed their damnation; and has determined to withhold from them Christ, grace, faith, and salvation." D. Engelsma, *Hyper-Calvinism and the Call of the Gospel* (Grand Rapids: Reformed Free Publishing, 1994), 58.

[14]Calvin, *Concerning the Eternal Predestination of God*, 176.

[15]Canons of Dort, Art. 15.

[16]Westminster Confession, 3.1.

[17]Fesko, *Diversity with the Reformed Tradition*, 135–38.

the revulsion most modern Calvinists feel toward supralapsarianism when he asked and then declared, "Do you believe that God created man and arbitrarily, sovereignly—it is the same thing—created that man, with no other intention, than that of damning him? Made him, and yet, for no other reason than that of destroying him forever? Well, if you can believe it, I pity you, that is all I can say: you deserve pity, that you should think so meanly of God, whose mercy endureth forever."[18]

Infralapsarianism refuses to draw out the logical implications of double predestination. The infralapsarian system argues that in some aspects God's sovereign decree is conditional. In addition, this model also argues that in the process of bringing the decree to fruition, some aspects of God's relationship to events—particularly to evil and sinful events—are permissive.

Bruce Ware, arguing for infralapsarianism, declared,

> It seems to me, that the strain in Calvinism that has been reluctant
> to embrace the "permissive will of God" simply rejects one of
> the very conceptual tools necessary to account for God's moral
> innocence in regard to evil. Surely more is needed than just this
> manner of divine activity. But I don't see how we can proceed if
> God's sovereign dealings in matters of good and evil are, in fact,
> symmetrical.[19]

In other words, in order to protect God from the accusation of being the author of evil, we must embrace the notion of permission.

Louis Berkhof concurred with Ware. He pointed out that when the Bible presents God's rejecting a man such as King Saul or a people such as unbelieving Israel, His rejection of them was predicated on their prior rejection of Him.[20] Therefore, election is unconditional but reprobation is conditional. God actively ordains the salvation of the elect, but He only permits the damnation of the reprobate.

Infralapsarianism perceives God to have an asymmetrical relationship with election and reprobation.[21] God first allows all of humanity to fall. Then, viewing all of humanity as justly condemned in their sins,

---

[18]Spurgeon, "Jacob and Esau," 118.
[19]Ware, *God's Greater Glory*, 26.
[20]L. Berkhof, *Systematic Theology*, 2nd ed. (Grand Rapids: Eerdmans, 1996), 105–17.
[21]Ware, "Divine Election to Salvation," 54–55.

God ordains unconditionally a certain number: these are the elect. God permits humanity to fall; He does not cause them to fall. Infralapsarianism incorporates the historical into the eternal decree. Even supralapsarian Cornelius Van Til stated, "From eternity God rejected men because of the sin that they would do as historical beings."[22] The reprobation decreed in eternity was conditioned by what would occur in time.

Problems with the Infralapsarian Position

Infralapsarianism hinges on the concept of permission, but reconciling permission with the traditional Reformed view of sovereignty is difficult. Calvin declared that "the will of God is the chief and principal cause of all things."[23] If all events are causally determined, what room is there for permission? Some infralapsarian Reformers speak of an "efficacious permission" or a "determinative permission." For example, Jerome Zanchius, one of the first advocates of infralapsarianism, declared that "God permissively hardens the reprobate with an efficacious permission."[24] Seeing the term "efficacious permission" as something other than an oxymoron is a challenge.

To genuinely embrace the concept of permission would require the infralapsarian to abandon some of the key tenets of Reformed theology. Berkhof recognized this when he warned, "Infralapsarianism really wants to explain reprobation as an act of God's justice. It is inclined to deny either explicitly or implicitly that it is an act of the mere good pleasure of God. This really makes the decree of reprobation a conditional decree and leads into the Arminian fold."[25] Infralapsarians have a choice. If the decree to reprobation is conditional, then it is not according to God's mere good pleasure. If it is unconditional, then it is not according to God's permission. Infralapsarianism wants to teach that God damns the reprobate in response to their sins, but this would abandon the classic Reformed view of God's sovereignty, which is why Calvin rejected the concept of permission out of hand.

---

[22]Van Til, *The Defense of the Faith*, 408.
[23]Calvin, *Concerning the Eternal Predestination of God*, 177.
[24]See P. K. Jewett, *Election and Predestination* (Grand Rapids: Eerdmans, 1985), 83–97.
[25]Berkhof, *Systematic Theology*, 123.

Second, as many Calvinists concede, the infralapsarian system is rationally inconsistent. Paul Jewett stated that a rational fallacy lies at the heart of the infralapsarian position.[26] He likens infralapsarianism to a pendulum that swings back and forth from the mere foreknowledge position of the Arminians to the pure foreordination position of the supralapsarians. "And so in the end, it seems, there is no consistent position between a mere foreknowledge of the fall, which is Arminianism, and a foreordination of the fall, which (by implication at least) is supralapsarian. For this reason the pendulum of the infralapsarian argument swings now to one side, now to the other."[27]

Third, the concept of permission as presented in the infralapsarian system doesn't solve anything if reprobation is still the result of "God's good pleasure." The Canons of the Synod of Dort state, "Not all, but some only, are elected, while others are passed by in the eternal decree; whom God, out of His sovereign good pleasure, has decreed to leave in the common misery."[28] So even in the infralapsarian system presented by the Synod of Dort, reprobation is not the result of sin but the good pleasure of God.

Supralapsarians like David Engelsma criticize infralapsarianism for its incoherence:

> If reprobation is the decree not to give a man faith, it is patently false to say that unbelief is the cause of reprobation. That would be the same as to say that my decision not to give a beggar a quarter is due to the beggar's not having a quarter. That reprobation is an unconditional decree is also plain from the fact that if unbelief were the cause of reprobation, all men would have been reprobated, and would not have been elected, for all men are equally unbelieving and disobedient.[29]

Engelsma is pointing out that if sin is the basis for reprobation, then no one can be elect since all are sinners.

In the final analysis infralapsarianism teaches that reprobation is as much a part of God's decrees as is election. Infralapsarianism and

---

[26]Jewett, *Election and Predestination*, 83–97.
[27]Ibid., 96.
[28]Canons of Dort, Article 15.
[29]Engelsma, *Hyper-Calvinism and the Call of the Gospel*, 57–58.

supralapsarianism are simply nuances of the same approach as long as both begin with God's eternal decrees and reject the notion that God would (or even could) grant any type of libertarian choice to responsible creatures.

Conclusions among Calvinists Concerning Infralapsarianism

Many supra-Calvinists dismiss the infra- position as incipient Arminianism (one cannot help but smile at Robert Reymond's accusing John Gerstner of being an Arminian),[30] and a number of infralapsarians, such as Louis Berkhof, concede the point.[31] Some Calvinists despair of the enterprise completely. G. C. Berkouwer called the exploration of the decrees a case of "theological trespassing." John Feinberg concluded that "the whole discussion is misguided" and that "this question should not have been asked." John Frame advocated agnosticism.[32] The verdicts of Paul Jewett and Tom Schreiner are in unison. Jewett stated, "In any case, when all is said and done, the problem of reprobation remains unresolved and, it would appear, unresolvable," while Schreiner concluded, "The scandal of the Calvinist system is that ultimately the logical problems posed cannot be fully resolved."[33]

At this point many infralapsarian Calvinists appeal to mystery, but what we are dealing with is not a mystery but a contradiction. An epistemic paradox and a logical paradox are different.[34] An epistemic paradox results from insufficient information, but a logical paradox indicates an error either in one's starting assumptions or his reasoning processes. The decretal Calvinist cannot accept his own conclusions. This means that something is wrong somewhere.

This situation is not like contemplating the Trinity or the incarnation, where one encounters transcendent truths in which he can go no

---

[30]Reymond, "A Consistent Supralapsarian Perspective on Election," 170–71; also Hoeksema, *Reformed Dogmatics*, 158; Van Til, *Defense of the Faith*, 415–16.

[31]Berkhof, *Systematic Theology*, 118, 121–24.

[32]G. C. Berkouwer, *Divine Election* (Grand Rapids: Eerdmans, 1960), 254; Feinberg, *No One Else Like Him*, 533; J. Frame, *The Doctrine of God* (Phillipsburg, NJ: P&R, 2002), 337.

[33]Jewett, *Election and Predestination*, 97; T. R. Schreiner, "Does Scripture Teach Prevenient Grace in the Wesleyan Sense?" in *The Grace of God, the Bondage of the Will*, vol 2, ed. T. R. Schreiner and B. A. Ware (Grand Rapids: Baker, 1995), 381.

[34]D. Ciocchi, "Reconciling Divine Sovereignty and Human Freedom," *JETS* 37:3 (1994): 397.

further. The dilemma for the Calvinist is that he cannot take his starting assumptions to their logical conclusions. As noted in the chapter on
radical depravity, John Gerstner warned his fellow Calvinists that in its
formulation of the relationship of God's decree to sin, Reformed theology "hovers" over "the abyss of blasphemy."[35] To their credit, Calvinists
by and large do not take the plunge. All these problems indicate that it is
questionable whether one should use the doctrine of election as a control
belief when considering issues such as the extent of the atonement.

MOLINISM: SIMULTANEOUSLY AFFIRMING
BOTH SOVEREIGNTY AND PERMISSION

Let's go back to our two control beliefs. It may not make the Arminian happy, but let's affirm that God sovereignly controls all things.[36] The
Calvinist may be displeased, but let's understand *permission* the way the
dictionary defines it: "permission is the giving of an opportunity or a possibility to another." This is the way permission is normally understood.
Permission entails that God has granted at least some type of libertarian
choice to the moral causal agents He created.[37]

Molinism simultaneously affirms meticulous, divine sovereignty
and genuine human freedom. How does it do this? In short, Molinism
argues that God is able to exercise His sovereignty primarily by His omniscience. In this way God controls all things but is not the determinative
cause of all things. As we saw in chapter 1, the distinctive feature to Molinism is its contention that God's knowledge of all things can be understood in three logical layers or moments. Molinism is particularly noted

---

[35]J. Gerstner, "Augustine, Luther, Calvin and Edwards on the Bondage of the Will," in *The Grace of God, the Bondage of the Will, Vol 2*, 279–94.

[36]Flint, *Divine Providence*, 12–21; Olson stated that Molinism's affirmation of God's control of all things is the reason most Arminians reject it. Olson, *Arminian Theology*, 194–99.

[37]We have been arguing for what could be called "soft libertarianism." Soft libertarianism holds to agent causation and argues that the ultimate responsibility for a person's decisions rests on that indi-vidual, which indicates in a profound way that he is in some way the origin of his choices. Two excellent defenses of libertarianism are R. Kane, *The Significance of Free Will* (Oxford: Oxford University Press, 1998) and T. O'Connor, *Persons and Causes: The Metaphysics of Free Will* (Oxford: Oxford University Press, 2000). It may come as a surprise to some Calvinists that libertarians by and large do not view free will as "the absolute ability to choose the contrary" or as "the freedom of indifference." See chapter 3 for further discussion.

for its view that God can infallibly assure the choices of free creatures by using His middle knowledge.

The Three Moments in Molinism Applied to Election

Decretal theology (i.e., supra- and infralapsarianism) attempts to discern the logical order of God's decrees. Molinism, on the other hand, posits that there is only one decree (a point that has scriptural support and that many Reformed scholars recognize)[38] but attempts to discern the logical order of God's knowledge. Rather than attempting to explore the "layers" of God's decree, Molinism explores the "layers" of God's omniscience. Decretal Calvinism perceives logical moments in God's *will*; Molinism perceives logical moments in God's *knowledge*.[39]

Discerning moments in God's knowledge is not unique to Molinism. Reformed theologians generally agree with Molinists that God's knowledge can be understood in terms of moments or aspects. For example, Louis Berkhof recognizes two moments of divine omniscience: God's natural knowledge and His free knowledge.[40] By His nature, God knows all things, so this aspect of His knowledge is labeled natural knowledge. This natural knowledge contains all truths that are necessarily true in the actual world (for example, "a triangle is a three-sided object" or "God cannot die") and all necessary truths in all possible worlds (for example, "what the world would be like if you or I had never been born"). So God's natural knowledge contains all necessary truths.

When we consider God's natural knowledge of possible or hypothetical truths, things get a little complicated. Remember that a possible state of affairs, i.e., something that is hypothetically true, is called a *counterfactual*, a state of affairs that does not obtain. A counterfactual is a statement that has truth content but is contrary to fact.[41] The Bible recognizes counterfactuals, and biblical writers used them often. For example, Paul said that "if Christ has not been raised . . . [then we] are still in [our] sins" (1 Cor 15:17). That is a counterfactual state of affairs

---

[38]Berkhof, *Systematic Theology*, 102; Feinberg, *No One Else Like Him*, 533–36.

[39]These moments are logical moments, not chronological moments. Nothing temporal is implied with the use of the word *moment*.

[40]Berkhof, *Systematic Theology*, 102; also Hoeksema, *Reformed Dogmatics*, 157.

[41]Or, more precisely, a counterfactual is a proposition contained within a statement.

that gloriously does not obtain.[42] Molinists label these complex scenarios made up of counterfactuals as *possible worlds*. Just contemplating the notion that God knows not only all actual truths but also all possible truths staggers our finite minds, but accomplishing this presents no burden to our omniscient God.

As stated earlier, Berkhof recognized a second moment in God's knowledge—His free knowledge. He defined God's free knowledge as "the knowledge of everything about this particular world." Out of all the possible worlds He could have created, God freely chose this one. This world is the product of God's free choice, which is why His knowledge of it is called His free knowledge.

Reformed theologians (such as Berkhof) acknowledge that God's knowledge has at least two moments: His natural knowledge and His free knowledge. Molinists would also agree with Berkhof's assertion that "the decree of God bears the closest relation to the divine knowledge."[43] That is, God brings about His sovereign will primarily by using His omniscience. What about all the possible choices of genuinely free creatures? Where are these counterfactuals located in the realm of God's knowledge? Here is where the Molinist's concept of middle knowledge enters the picture.

As Thomas Flint explained, God's knowledge of counterfactuals of creaturely freedom should be distinguished from His natural knowledge because counterfactuals are contingencies that would occur due to the choices of free creatures. Nor can these counterfactuals belong to God's free knowledge since they are only hypothetical and not actual. Molinists argue that God possesses a third type of knowledge, located "between" God's natural knowledge and His free knowledge (hence the label *middle knowledge*).[44] The divine natural knowledge is populated with truths that are true due to God's nature, and God's free knowledge is populated with that which is true due to God's will, but middle knowledge is of truths in which the decisions of free creatures are the truth makers (even though

---

[42]Some other scriptural examples of counterfactuals are found in 1 Sam 23:6–10; Jer 38:17–18; and 1 Cor 2:8. Jesus often made use of counterfactual knowledge as seen in Matt 11:23; 17:27; 26:24; John 15:22,24; 18:36; and 21:6, to list a few.

[43]Berkhof, *Systematic Theology*, 102.

[44]Flint, *Divine Providence*, 42–43.

God knows these decisions innately).[45] This is what a robust concept of permission entails.

Armed with these three conceptual tools, Molinism argues that God accomplishes His sovereign will via His omniscience. First, God knows everything that *could* happen. This first moment is His *natural knowledge*, where God knows everything due to His omniscient nature. Second, from the set of infinite possibilities, God also knows which scenarios *would* result in persons freely responding in the way He desires. This crucial moment of knowledge is between the first and third moment, hence the term *middle knowledge*. From the repertoire of available options provided by His middle knowledge, God freely and sovereignly chooses which one He will bring to pass. This results in God's third moment of knowledge, which is His foreknowledge of what certainly *will* occur.[46] The third moment is God's *free knowledge* because it is determined by His free and sovereign choice.

By utilizing these three phases of knowledge, God predestines all events, yet not in such a way that violates genuine human freedom and choice. God meticulously "sets the table" so that humans freely choose what He had predetermined. Remember the example of Simon Peter's denial of the Lord. The Lord predicted Peter would deny Him and by use of middle knowledge ordained the scenario with infallible certainty that Peter would do so. However, God did not make or cause Peter to do as he did.

The Advantages of the Molinist Approach

The Molinist approach has a number of advantages over both Calvinism and Arminianism. First, *Molinism affirms God's genuine desire for all to be saved in a way that is problematic for Calvinism.* God has a universal salvific will even though not all, maybe not even most, will repent and believe the gospel. We saw in chapter 3 that Calvinists have struggled with this question. Most have either denied God's desire for all

---

[45]Ibid., 46–50.

[46]Remember, the verbs *could, would,* and *will* highlight the distinctions in the moments of God's knowledge. From knowledge of what *could* happen (first moment), God knows which ones *would* bring about His desired result (second moment), and He chooses one possibility which means He knows it *will* come about (third moment).

to be saved, or else they claimed that God has a secret will which trumps His revealed will.

Molinism fits well with the biblical teaching that God universally loves the world (John 3:16) and yet Christ has a particular love for the Church (Eph 5:25). William Lane Craig suggests that God "chose a world having an optimal balance between the number of the saved and the number of the damned."[47] In other words, God has created a world with a maximal ratio of the number of saved to those lost. The Bible teaches that God genuinely desires all to be saved, and even though many perish, still His will is done. Molinism better addresses this apparent paradox.

An illustration may be helpful here. Before the Normandy invasion General Dwight Eisenhower was told by many of his advisors that casualties might exceed 70 percent. The actual human toll was terrible, but thankfully not that high. Eisenhower gave the order for the invasion to proceed, but he would have been quick to tell you he genuinely desired that none of his men should perish. Molinism understands God's will for all to be saved to operate in a similar fashion, though we recognize all analogies break down eventually.

To try to explain the Calvinist view of God's salvific will, John Piper and Bruce Ware also used illustrations of leaders—George Washington and Winston Churchill, respectively—who are forced to make similarly difficult decisions.[48] Their illustrations work against their position because a key component of the Calvinist doctrine of election is that the reprobate is passed over because of "God's good pleasure." Molinism better fits the biblical description of the two wills of God (or the two aspects of God's will)—His antecedent and consequent wills. The Molinist can affirm without qualification that God is "not wanting any to perish but all to come to repentance" (2 Pet 3:9).

Second, *Molinism provides a better model for understanding how simultaneously God's decree of election is unconditional while His*

---

[47]W. L. Craig, "'No Other Name:' A Middle Knowledge Perspective on the Exclusivity of Salvation through Christ," *Faith and Philosophy* 6:2 (April 1989): 185.

[48]J. Piper, "Are There Two Wills in God? Divine Election and God's Desire for All to Be Saved," in *The Grace of God, the Bondage of the Will,* vol. 1, 122–24; and Bruce Ware, "Divine Election to Salvation," 33–34.

rejection of the unbeliever is conditional. God's omniscient foreknowledge is the Achilles' heel for most Arminian presentations of election. If
God has exhaustive knowledge of all future events, then conditional election does not really remove the unconditional nature of God's decisions.
If God knows that a certain man will freely accept the gospel while that
man's brother freely will not, and yet God decides to create both of them
anyway, then this is a mysterious, sovereign, and unconditional determi-
nation on the part of God.[49]

Some Arminians recognize this dilemma and opt for open theism
instead. In open theism, God does not know how an individual will respond to the gospel. He creates a person and hopes for the best. The open
theist sees God as an actuary working the odds, and it understands God's
sovereignty as an exercise in risk management.

Molinism provides a much better answer. Why does the reprobate
exist? Because of God's sovereign will. Why is he reprobated? Because
of his own unbelief. When God made the sovereign choice to bring this
particular world into existence, He rendered certain but did not cause the
destruction of certain ones who would reject God's overtures of grace.
According to Molinism, our free choice determines how we would
respond in any given setting, but God decides the setting in which we
actually find ourselves. As Craig stated, "It is up to God whether we
find ourselves in a world in which we are predestined, but it is up to us
whether we are predestined in the world in which we find ourselves."[50]

In other words, the Molinist paradigm explains how it is possible
for there to be a decree of election without a corresponding decree of
reprobation, which is in fact the biblical witness. One of the strongest
motivations for the infralapsarian position is the conviction that God did
not ordain the reprobate to hell in the same way He ordained the elect
to salvation. The Molinist model presents an asymmetric relationship
between God and the two classes of people, the elect and the reprobate,

---

[49]In a helpful chapter entitled "*Scientia Media* According to Molina, not Arminius," Kirk
MacGregor delineates the differences between Molina's and Arminius's approach to middle knowledge.
See K. R. MacGregor, *A Molinist-Anabaptist Systematic Theology* (Lanham, MD: Univ. Press of Amer.,
2007), 63–86.
[50]See Craig, "No Other Name," 172–88.

in a manner that infralapsarianism cannot. This is a great advantage to Molinism.

The third point is the converse to the previous one: *in the Molinist system, unlike Arminianism, God is the author of salvation who actively elects certain ones.* In Arminianism God employs only a passive foreknowledge (in open theism God elects no individuals at all). Molinists contend that God uses His exhaustive foreknowledge in an active, sovereign way. God determines the world in which we live. Whether I exist at all, have the opportunity to respond to the gospel, or am placed in a setting where I would be graciously enabled to believe are sovereign decisions made by Him. The Molinist affirms that the elect are saved by God's good pleasure. The distinctive difference between Calvinism and Molinism is that Calvinism sees God accomplishing His will through His omnipotent power while Molinism understands God's using His omniscient knowledge.

The fourth point expands the third point: *Molinism has a more robust and scriptural understanding of the role God's foreknowledge plays in election than does either Calvinism or Arminianism.* The Bible repeatedly states that "those He foreknew he also predestined" (Rom 8:29) and that the saints are "chosen according to the foreknowledge of God the Father" (1 Pet 1:2). Calvinists generally claim that in these instances God's foreknowledge should be understood as His "forelove." This seems to be a case of special pleading. Arminians contend that what is foreknown by God is merely the believer's faith. Molinism rejects both explanations.

In the Calvinist understanding of foreknowledge and predetermination, the future is the product of the will of God. The Calvinist view clearly presents God as sovereign, but He also appears to be the cause of sin. In the Arminian formulation God looks forward into a future made by the decisions of free creatures and then makes His plans accordingly. The Arminian model emphasizes that God is a loving Father, but unfortunately His will has nothing to do with much that happens.

By contrast Molinism contends that God actively uses His foreknowledge. Among the many possibilities populated by the choices of free creatures, God freely and sovereignly decided which world to bring into existence. This view fits well with the biblical simultaneous affirmation of both foreknowledge and predetermination (Acts 2:23). Some Calvinists such as J. I. Packer and D. A. Carson affirm both, but they call their view the antinomy or paradox position because they know it cannot be reconciled with either the supra- or infralapsarian models.[51] Molinism is the one position that can confidently affirm both with logical consistency.

In his book *Hyper-Calvinism and the Call of the Gospel*, supralapsarian Calvinist David Engelsma denies that the gospel is offered to everyone who hears it. He contends that no one who adheres to five-point Calvinism and to reprobation according to God's inscrutable decree can consistently hold to a "well-meant offer." He claims that his position is not hyper-Calvinism but consistent Calvinism. I believe Engelsma is in fact a hyper-Calvinist, but his argument highlights the problem Reformed theology has with affirming that the gospel is presented to every hearer in good faith. By contrast, Molinism has no difficulty in holding that the offer of the gospel is sincere and well meant. This is another decided advantage to the Molinist view.

Fifth, *Molinism provides a better model for understanding the biblical tension between divine sovereignty and human responsibility*. With both the Calvinist and Arminian scenarios, at times one gets the distinct impression that whole classes of passages are being shoehorned in order to fit the respective theological systems or that some passages are not interpreted so much as they are explained away. By contrast, when the Molinist assembles his theological paradigm, fewer biblical spare parts are left over.

For example, consider Jesus' condemnation of the cities of Chorazin, Bethsaida, and Capernaum for failing to repent, and then His subsequent prayer and invitation (Matt 11:20–28). In this way, our Lord brings human responsibility immediately alongside divine sovereignty, a coupling that occurs throughout Scripture.[52] Jesus first denounces the unrepentant:

---

[51]J. I. Packer, *Evangelism and the Sovereignty of God* (Downers Grove: InterVarsity, 1961); and D. A. Carson, *Divine Sovereignty and Human Responsibility* (Atlanta: John Knox, 1981).

[52]E.g., Gen 50:20; Isa 10:5–19; Acts 2:23; 3:17–21; 4:24–28; 13:48–14:1.

> "Woe to you, Chorazin! Woe to you, Bethsaida! For if the mira-
> cles that were done in you had been done in Tyre and Sidon, they
> would have repented in sackcloth and ashes long ago! . . . And
> you, Capernaum, will you be exalted to heaven? You will go
> down to Hades. For if the miracles that were done in you had
> been done in Sodom, it would have remained until today." (vv.
> 21,23)

Jesus places the blame at their feet. They should have responded but they
did not.

But in a turnabout that affirms the unimpeded sovereignty of God,
Jesus then praises the Father:

> At that time Jesus said, "I praise You, Father, Lord of heaven and
> earth, because You have hidden these things from the wise and
> learned and revealed them to infants. Yes, Father, because this
> was Your good pleasure." (vv. 25–26)

By so praying, Jesus reveals that God's sovereign will is still being accomplished. Despite appearances to the contrary, God was in complete
control.

Arminians tend to focus on vv. 20–24 with its emphasis on human
responsibility, while Calvinists give prominence to the stress on divine
sovereignty in vv. 25–26. But how can Jesus' warning and prayer both
be true? And if God's will is somehow being done through their unbelief,
how can Jesus conclude with an invitation to "Come to Me, all of you
who are weary and burdened, and I will give you rest" (v. 28)? How can
His offer be sincere?

Molinists point to Jesus' use of counterfactual knowledge to find a
solution. Jesus highlights the guilt of the surrounding cities by contrast-
ing their opportunity with that of some of the most evil cities of the Old
Testament. Jesus knows how His message would have been received by
the wicked inhabitants of Tyre, Sidon, or even Sodom, and He expresses
this knowledge counterfactually. *If* they had had the opportunity that Israel had received, *then* they would have repented (vv. 21,23). Jesus indicates counterfactual knowledge of the choices they would have made had
they been given the chance.

One might ask at this point why the citizens of Sodom, Tyre, and Sidon were not given the same opportunity the inhabitants of the Galilee region were given. Jesus teaches us that God's good and sovereign plan (His "good pleasure") necessitated otherwise (vv. 25–27). Think again of Eisenhower's order for the invasion of Normandy, for the analogy applies here also. God desires the salvation of all and is accomplishing the work of redemption in a maximal way, but this does not guarantee nor require that everyone have an optimal opportunity. Besides, Jesus clearly indicates that the responsibility for unbelief rests on the unbeliever, regardless of the level of opportunity, because he could have repented.

Molinism argues that, as the text indicates, God used his middle knowledge to accomplish His will despite (and even through) the unbelief of Israel. Since Molinism affirms the reality of both human agency (vv. 20–24) and divine agency (vv. 25–27), it holds that God is meticulously achieving His will and that Jesus' offer is in good faith when He invites all freely to come to Him. Like so many other passages, Matt 11:20–28 simultaneously teaches human choice and divine sovereignty. Molinism is in the unique position of not having to bludgeon one truth into submission for the sake of the other.

The biblical text which directly addresses God's use of Israel's unbelief is Romans 9, where we find that, once again, Molinism fits well.[53] The main issue addressed by Paul in that chapter is whether or not God's plans had failed (v. 6, "But it is not as though the word of God has failed"). The Messiah came to the people of Israel, but they rejected Him. Even after the day of Pentecost, the offer to receive Jesus as Lord and Christ was made to the wayward nation. After the healing of the lame man at the Gate Beautiful, Simon Peter proclaimed, "Therefore repent and turn back, that your sins may be wiped out so that seasons of refreshing may come from the presence of the Lord, and He may send Jesus, who has been appointed Messiah for you" (Acts 3:19–20). Remarkably, the apostle promised Israel that it still was not too late to receive its King.

---

[53]The difference between Molina's handling of Romans 9 and Arminius's approach is striking. Arminius interpreted the chapter in corporate terms entirely, while Molina understood Paul to be speaking also of individuals. See MacGregor, *A Molinist-Anabaptist Systematic Theology*, 64–70.

In light of such offers and their subsequent rejection, there are questions that have to be answered: Did God's mission to Israel fail? Was God's present work among the Gentiles plan B, an alternative scheme, a fallback plan? Was the Church a consolation prize? In Romans 9, Paul declares that God's sovereign intention all along was to work through Israel's rebellion. Rather than being thwarted, God's plan that His Son would die for the sins of the world gloriously succeeded.

Paul expresses his grief over Israel's unbelief and spiritual condition ("I have intense sorrow . . . [for] my brothers, my countrymen . . . ," 9:2–3), and he prayed that his kinsmen might be saved ("[My] prayer . . . concerning them is for their salvation!" 10:1). However, he points out that being an offspring of Abraham was never an automatic guarantee of salvation, as Ishmael and Esau illustrate ("Neither are they all children because they are Abraham's descendants," v. 9:7). Paul uses the examples of Pharaoh and Israel in the wilderness to assert that God has the sovereign right to show mercy whenever and however He sees best ("I will show mercy to whom I will show mercy," v. 15).

At this point a hypothetical objector protests that if what Paul is saying is true, then Israel cannot be blamed for its sin because it is impossible to resist God. Paul retorts that a man has no more right to talk back to God than clay has the ability to resist the potter ("But who are you, a mere man, to talk back to God?" v. 20). Then Paul asks two provocative questions:

> And what if God, desiring to display His wrath and to make His power known, endured with much patience objects of wrath ready for destruction? And what if He did this to make known the riches of His glory on objects of mercy that He prepared beforehand for glory—on us, the ones He also called, not only from the Jews but also from the Gentiles? (vv. 22–24)

In other words, what if God chooses to use certain wicked persons to accomplish His glorious and greater purpose?

The point Paul seems to be making is this: though God desires the salvation of all, and though the offer of salvation and redemption was genuinely offered to Israel, God has actualized a world in which Israel would certainly rebel. (Remember the distinction between certainty and necessity made in chap. 1.) Of all the feasible worlds available, God actualized this world—a world in which unbelieving Israel (the "objects of wrath") would be used by God to accomplish an immensely greater and more glorious salvation for the Church (the "objects of mercy"). It is crucial to note that when Paul says the objects of mercy were "prepared beforehand," he uses an active participle (v. 23). But he uses a middle/passive participle when he describes the objects of wrath as "ready for destruction" (v. 22). In other words, God actively elected the saved but passively allows the ruin of the lost. Then Paul asserts that, rather than indicating a failure in God's plan, Israel's apostasy and God's choice of the Gentiles was prophesied by both Hosea and Isaiah (vv. 25–29; cf. Hosea 1:10; 2:23; Isa 1:9; 10:22–23).

What Paul declares next is jarring. Drawing the section to a close, he asks what we should conclude. Answering his own question, he states that the Jews did not attain salvation because of their own unbelief ("Why is that? Because they did not pursue it by faith," v. 32)! If Paul merely wanted to teach double predestination, then he would have given a different conclusion. Rather than point to God's sovereign purposes, the apostle places the blame solely and completely on Israel. The way Paul juxtaposes God's unstoppable divine will with genuine human participation is breathtaking. Molinism is in the unique position of being able to affirm both.

To illustrate the Molinist understanding of the interaction between divine foreknowledge and predetermination in Romans 9, let's revisit again the D-Day analogy and expand it. Imagine that Dwight Eisenhower was an infinitely brilliant general, to the point he knew beforehand precisely how many casualties would be incurred. But beyond that, he even knew exactly who would survive the Normandy invasion and who would not. Now suppose the general knows that if Joe puts in at Omaha Beach he will live, but if Joe lands at Utah Beach he will be a fatality. But Eisenhower also knows that Joe arriving at Utah rather than Omaha will result in the overall fatalities being much lower. The general could choose the option that will be more beneficial for the invasion force as a whole but not for Joe in particular. (Christ's statement concerning Judas comes to mind, "It would have been better for that man if he had not been born," Matt 26:24).[54]

At an important point the D-Day analogy breaks down, but it does so in a way that actually is in favor of Molinism. Many of the D-Day casualties had little or no say in the matter. Joe may simply be in the wrong place at the wrong time when the mortar or bullet arrives. However, in the Molinist paradigm, every person who dies unsaved has the sufficient ability and opportunity to respond to God's graces. This is why the lost will not be able to accuse God of running a cosmic "sting operation" in which they were entrapped (hence Paul's rebuke to the objector in Rom 9:19–20).

Sixth, *Molinism places mystery where it should be located, i.e., in God's infinite attributes rather than in His character.* Critics of Molinism, particularly open theists, contend that Molinism fails to give an adequate explanation of how God infallibly knows what choices free creatures are going to make. This is generally known as "the grounding objection" because it questions whether Molinism provides any grounds or basis for God's middle knowledge.

Molinists generally reply by arguing that God innately knows all things by virtue of His omniscience and that for God to have infallible knowledge of all things is simply in His nature. The Molinist advocate affirms but may not be able to explain to everyone's satisfaction that God has exhaustive foreknowledge of what creatures with libertarian freedom will do.[55]

If Molinists have to appeal to mystery at this point, they do so at a better and more reasonable point. I'd rather have the Molinist difficulty of not being able to explain how God's omniscience operates than the Calvinist difficulty of explaining how God is not the author of sin. In other words, Molinism's difficulties are with God's infinite attributes rather than His holy and righteous character. Implicit in the grounding objection is the denial that God has the ability to create creatures

---

[54]It must be noted that I am not appealing to the "transworld depravity" argument made by some Molinists. This argument posits that the only lost persons God creates are those who would have been lost in all possible worlds. This position seems to go against Matt 11:20–28 and 26:24.

[55]For a response to the grounding objection, see W. L. Craig, "Middle Knowledge, Truth-Makers, and the 'Grounding Objection'," *Faith and Philosophy* 18:3 (2001): 337–52.

with libertarian freedom (of the morally significant kind). This places a surprising constraint on the scope of God's sovereignty. The Molinist embraces a richer conception of God's sovereignty since God exercises meticulous providence despite the existence of free creatures![56]

One of the things we understand least about God is how His infinite attributes operate—His omniscience, omnipotence, and omnipresence. Why place the mystery of reprobation in God's character? Molinists do not claim to know God's purposes exhaustively, but among the things most clearly revealed about God are His holiness, righteousness, and goodness. Would we not rather place the mystery within the transcendent, infinite, inexhaustible omniscience of God than the revealed character and purposes of God?

Seventh, *Molinism has a valid concept of permission that does not have to resort to special pleading.* In infralapsarian Calvinism, what exactly does *permission* mean? Not much. Many within Reformed theology acknowledge that the language of permission is used merely to make Calvinism seem to be less harsh. John Frame stated, "Evidently, the Reformed use *permit* mainly as a more delicate term than cause."[57] Berkhof concurred, saying that infralapsarians speak of a permissive decree because it sounds "more . . . tender."[58] This opens Reformed theology to the accusation of using the term in a misleading manner because, as Frame pointed out, in the final analysis Calvinism sees permission as just another "form of ordination, a form of causation."[59] In Molinism, *permit* means "permit."

One of the interesting developments in recent days is the appearance of "middle knowledge Calvinism." Bruce Ware, John Frame, and Terrance Tiessen are among the Reformed theologians who are trying to incorporate the insights of Molinism into infralapsarian Calvinism.[60] They do so for the express purpose of using the concept of permission in a quasi-Molinist manner because they recognize the problems with the Calvinist

---

[56]I want to thank Doug Geivett for his insights and help with this paragraph.

[57]Frame, *The Doctrine of God*, 178.

[58]Berkhof, *Systematic Theology*, 124.

[59]Frame, *The Doctrine of God*, 178.

[60]For example, see T. Tiessen, "Why Calvinists Should Believe in Divine Middle Knowledge, although They Reject Molinism," *WTJ* 69 (2007): 345–66.

formulation of the decrees. However, the concept of middle knowledge is superfluous in any system that holds to causal determinism.

Sometimes Molinism is described as inconsistent Calvinism, but one could argue that it is the other way around. Perhaps infralapsarian Calvinism is inconsistent Molinism. To my infralapsarian brothers, I say, in regard to the concept of permission, Molinists have simply taken the steps you want to take or at least you want to appear to have taken. If you wish to be consistent, you have a choice: either supralapsarianism or Molinism.

CONCLUSION

I am thankful for the contributions that Calvinists make in the evangelical community. They are right to call evangelicals away from pragmatic methodologies and reaffirm that salvation is a sovereign work of God. However, the decretal approach to election taken by Calvinism seems to create more problems than it solves.

Molinism does not provide an explanation as to why God created a world in which it was possible for sin to enter, but it is not necessary to do so. Molinism is a defense, not a theodicy. A theodicy is an attempt to explain *why* God ordained the world He did. A defense is much more modest, simply attempting to demonstrate that it is *logically consistent* to believe that a good and sovereign God can purpose to create a world like ours. Molinism accomplishes this.

If we are going to do justice to the doctrine of God, we must affirm both God's sovereignty and His permission. Molinism presents a forceful affirmation of both.

CHAPTER 6

ROS**E**S

IS FOR ETERNAL LIFE

Blessed assurance, Jesus is mine!
Oh, what a foretaste of glory divine!

—Fanny Crosby

T A SYMPOSIUM honoring Dale Moody, I. Howard Marshall recited the old saw that Arminians know they are saved but are afraid they cannot keep it, while Calvinists know they cannot lose their salvation but are afraid they do not have it.[1] Aside from being witty, this highlights the two components of the question about assurance. First, is it possible to know absolutely or even confidently that one is saved, and second, is it possible for those who currently believe they are saved to have assurance that they will remain in a state of grace until the day of redemption? It is more than just a little ironic that though they travel different routes, many Arminians and Calvinists arrive basically at the same answer—assurance is based on evidence of sanctification.[2] Michael Eaton points to the nineteenth-century preacher Asahel Nettleton as a good example of this odd state of affairs when he quotes Nettleton: "The most that I have ventured to say respecting myself is, that I think it possible I may get to heaven."[3] Words perhaps expected from an Arminian, but Nettleton was a Calvinist.

Paul gives the two aspects of assurance of salvation when he states, "For I know whom I have believed, and am persuaded that he is able to

---

[1] See I. H. Marshall, *Kept by the Power of God: A Study of Perseverance and Falling Away,* 3rd ed. (London: Paternoster, 1995), 267.

[2] Both Marshall and D. A. Carson make this observation. See D. A. Carson, "Reflections on Christian Assurance," *Westminster Theological Journal* 54 (1992), 21. Carson states, "Thus at their worst, the two approaches meet in strange and sad ways."

[3] Cited by M. Eaton, *No Condemnation: A New Theology of Assurance* (Downers Grove: InterVarsity, 1995), 3.

keep that which I have committed unto him against that day" (2 Tim 1:12 KJV). The apostle affirms that (1) a person can know with certainty he is presently saved ("For I know whom I have believed"), and that (2) he can know with certainty he will remain saved ("and am persuaded that he is able to keep that which I have committed unto him against that day").[4] This chapter argues that the basis of assurance is the same as the basis for salvation itself: Jesus Christ—who He is, what He has done, and what He has promised. In other words, assurance is found in our justification in Christ rather than in our sanctification.

The doctrine of *forensic justification* is crucial for assurance of salvation. "Forensic" means that justification is the legal act where God *declares* a sinner righteous through Jesus Christ. This is in contrast to *sanctification*, which is the lifelong work of grace whereby God *makes* a sinner righteous. It is this distinction between justification and sanctification that liberated Martin Luther from the bondage of attempting to merit salvation. Luther tells of meditating on Rom 1:17 ("For in it God's righteousness is revealed from faith to faith, just as it is written: The righteous will live by faith") and coming to the realization that God's righteousness was a gift given to sinners rather than a standard that sinners must meet.

> There I began to understand that the righteousness of God is that by which the righteous lives by a gift of God, namely by faith. And this is the meaning: the righteousness of God is revealed by the gospel, namely, the passive righteousness with which merciful God justifies us by faith. . . . Here I felt that I was altogether born again and had entered paradise itself through open gates. There a totally other face of the entire Scripture showed itself to me.[5]

Like Luther, I argue that a person finds assurance when he trusts the justifying work of Christ alone. I also contend that the gift of faith remains (i.e., perseveres), and it inevitably manifests itself in the life of a believer. However, the level of manifestation varies from saint to saint.

---

[4]For a defense of this view of *tēn parathēkē mou,* lit. "my deposit," in 2 Tim 1:12 see W. D. Mounce, *Pastoral Epistles,* Word Biblical Commentary (Nashville: Thomas Nelson, 2000), 487–88; G. W. Knight III, *The Pastoral Epistles,* New International Greek Testament Commentary (Grand Rapids: Eerdmans, 1992), 378–80.

[5]M. Luther, "Preface to Latin Writings," in *Luther's Works,* vol. 34 (Philadelphia: Muhlenberg, [1545]1960), 337.

Abraham and Lot were both justified (2 Pet 2:7–8), but they evidenced
it very differently.

Recently, Reformed scholars Thomas Schreiner and Ardel Caneday
presented an updated version of the position set forth earlier by Louis
Berkhof and G. C. Berkouwer. They attempted to reconcile the biblical
passages that affirm unconditional election with passages that warn of
divine judgment (particularly the five warning passages in the book of
Hebrews) by positing that, in Schreiner's words, "adhering to the warnings is the means by which salvation is obtained on the final day."[6] The
believer's salvation is not merely manifested by perseverance, but rather,
eschatologically speaking, a believer actually is saved by perseverance
(i.e., in the faith). However, Schreiner and Caneday deny that the elect
will apostatize, claiming that the warning passages are a "crucial" means
by which God has chosen to preserve the elect.

Schreiner and Caneday call their position the "Means-of-Salvation"
view. Though they affirm salvation by grace through faith alone, at times
they use language that seems to meld Arminian and Calvinist soteriology.[7] For example, on the one hand they define perseverance as a persistent and abiding faith, but on the other hand they speak of obtaining final
salvation through persevering obedience. Most who hold to eternal security also affirm that saving faith produces the evidence of a godly life.
Schreiner and Caneday go beyond that. Based especially on 1 Tim 2:15
and 4:16, they state, "Persevering in godly behavior and sound teaching
are necessary to obtain salvation..." and believers "must practice godly
behavior to receive it [i.e., final salvation]."[8] One cannot help but appre-
ciate their attempts to take the warning passages seriously. For this reason at least, I must confess some sympathies for their position. However,

---

[6]T. R. Schreiner, "Perseverance and Assurance: A Survey and a Proposal," *The Southern Baptist
Journal of Theology* 2:1 (1998): 53. See T. R. Schreiner and A. B. Caneday, *The Race Set Before Us: A
Biblical Theology of Perseverance and Assurance* (Downers Grove: InterVarsity, 2001); G. C. Berkou-
wer, *Faith and Perseverance* (Grand Rapids: Eerdmans, 1958), 88–124; L. Berkhof, *Systematic Theol-
ogy,* rev. ed. (Grand Rapids: Eerdmans, 1996), 548. John Piper takes a similar position in *Future Grace*
(Sisters, OR: Multnomah, 1995), 231–59.

[7]John Mark Hicks claims that since both Arminians and Calvinists affirm that perseverance is necessary to obtain final salvation, then—despite appearances—both positions concerning the conditions to
salvation are essentially the same. He concludes that a truce, or at least the calling of a draw, is in order.
See J. M. Hicks, "Election and Security: An Impossible Impasse?" (Paper presented at the annual meeting of the Evangelical Theological Society, Colorado Springs, CO, 14–16 Nov. 2001), 12–17.

[8]Schreiner and Caneday, *The Race Set Before Us,* 51.

some critics, such as Roy Zuck, charge that their view "comes danger-ously close to salvation by works, and it fails to give absolute unqualified assurance of salvation for any believer."[9] His charge is not entirely base-less, and some of Schreiner and Caneday's arguments are less than clear, although they affirm that "because God is the one who enables those who persevere," their view "cannot be labeled works-righteousness."[10]

First, we will briefly survey the answers that have been proposed to our two questions regarding assurance of salvation and eternal secu-rity. Second, additional attention will be given to the Means-of-Salvation position of Schreiner and Caneday, which is sure to be the topic of con-tinuing discussion in evangelical circles. Third, I will argue that, though Schreiner and Caneday have made a positive contribution to the discus-sion about assurance, a variation of the Evidence-of-Genuineness posi-tion best explains the tension between the biblical texts that assure and those that admonish.

COMPONENT # 1: PRESENT CERTAINTY
HOW DO WE KNOW WE ARE GENUINELY SAVED?

Three schools of thought have provided three different answers to the question of how an individual believer knows if he or she is genu-inely saved. The first view, held by the Roman Catholic Church, regards the claim of assurance of salvation to be a demonstration of spiritual arrogance. Roman Catholic soteriology does not separate sanctification from justification and therefore does not present assurance as something currently available. The second view is that of the Reformers. Flying the banner of *sola fide*, they trumpeted a certainty to salvation that made saving faith and assurance virtual synonyms. The post-Reformation Cal-vinists and Puritans held to a third view which saw assurance as a grace given subsequent to conversion and discerned by careful self-examina-tion. The second and third answers still predominate in evangelicalism today.

---

[9]R. B. Zuck, "Review of *The Race Set Before Us*," *Bibliotheca Sacra* 160 (April-June 2003): 241-42.

[10]Schreiner and Caneday, *The Race Set Before Us,* 16–17.

The Roman Catholic View: Assurance Is Not Possible

If salvation is a lifetime process that may or may not be success-fully completed, then assurance of salvation is not possible. Following Augustine, official Catholic doctrine views justification as a process that occurs within the individual Christian over the course of his lifetime and perhaps even continues after death. No one can know for sure how far along he is on the journey of faith or if he will continue the difficult task of walking in the Way. Seen from this light, the Reformed doctrine of justification by faith alone seems to present a truncated soteriology. The Council of Trent condemned all who claim to have assurance of salva-tion, declaring, "If any one saith, that a man, who is born again and justi-fied, is bound of faith to believe that he is assuredly in the number of the predestinate; let him be anathema."[11] The Tridentine Council reasoned that since only the elect will persevere, and since only God knows who is and who is not elect, then special revelation would be required for someone to have assurance of salvation.[12] Calvin responded by declaring that the Word of God was all the special revelation the elect needed to have assurance.[13]

The Reformers: Assurance Is the Essence of Faith

So how do we know if we are saved? The answer of the Reformation was that this knowledge is a part of salvation itself. Calvin defined faith as "a firm and certain knowledge of God's benevolence toward us, founded upon the truth of the freely given promise in Christ, both revealed to our minds and sealed upon our hearts through the Holy Spirit."[14] The very nature of conversion and regeneration insures that the believer will know when he has believed. Anyone can know whether or not he has

---

[11]"Canons Concerning Justification," canon 15 (DS 1565) in *The Teaching of the Catholic Church*, ed. K. Rahner (Cork: Mercer, 1966), 400.

[12]Ibid., canon 16 (DS 1566). For a Catholic discussion of the Council's view on assurance see A. Dulles, *The Assurance of Things Hoped For* (New York: Oxford University Press, 1994), 48–50.

[13]J. Calvin, "Acts of the Council of Trent with the Antidote," in *Selected Works of John Calvin,* vol. 3 (Grand Rapids: Baker, 1983), 155. Calvin asks, "What else, good Sirs, is a certain knowledge of our predestination than that testimony of adoption which Scripture makes common to all the godly?"

[14]J. Calvin, *Institutes of the Christian Religion* (Philadelphia: Westminster, 1960), 551.

believed in Jesus Christ, and all who believe in Him are saved. Therefore, assurance is of the essence of saving faith.[15]

Having certain knowledge at the time of conversion does not exclude the possibility that a believer may have doubts after his salvation, nor does it mean that only those with absolute certainty are saved. Luther stated,

> Even if I am feeble in faith, I still have the same treasure and the same Christ that others have. There is no difference; through faith in him (not works) we are all perfect. It is just as if two people have a hundred gulden—one may carry his in a paper bag, the other store and bar his in an iron chest; but they both have the treasure whole and complete. So with Christ. It is the self-same Christ we possess whether you or I believe in him with a strong or weak faith. And in him we have all, whether we hold it with a strong or weak faith.[16]

Both Luther and Calvin realized that many genuine believers have subsequent doubts. Nevertheless, this view does contend that when a person is saved, he knows it, and this core conviction, though buffeted, will never die.

However, certain doctrines advocated by the Reformers for the purpose of establishing assurance often produced the opposite effect. The doctrines of the absolute decree of election and reprobation made within the hidden will of God, limited atonement, and temporary faith created a tension in later Calvinist theology and made assurance of salvation very difficult to obtain. This difficulty manifests itself particularly in the theology and practice of the Puritans.

The Puritans: Assurance Is Logically Deduced

A number of significant Puritans struggled terribly with assurance of salvation. It is intensely debated whether these struggles were the result of their departure from the teachings of Calvin or if they simply took

---

[15]Heb 11:1, "Now faith is being sure of what we hope for and certain of what we do not see" (NIV). Both Zane Hodges and Thomas Schreiner hold that assurance is the essence of saving faith. When we get to the "Once-Saved-Always-Saved" section it will become evident that Hodges and Schreiner generally disagree more than they agree.

[16]Cited by R. Olmsted, "Staking All on Faith's Object: The Art of Christian Assurance According to Martin Luther and Karl Barth," *Pro Ecclesia* 10/2 (2001): 138.

Calvin's theology to its logical conclusion. R. T. Kendall and Charles Bell argue that Calvin held to a doctrine of unlimited atonement and to a Christocentric doctrine of assurance. Their thesis is that later Calvinism, beginning with Theodore Beza, departed from Calvin by adhering to a doctrine of limited atonement and to a doctrine of assurance that begins with the absolute decree of the hidden God as its starting point.[17] Others have responded that the confusion begins with Calvin himself, and that his followers' works simply highlighted his confusion.[18] Either way, it is a historical fact that much of the Puritans' life was defined by their search for assurance. This concern about assurance would mystify the average Evangelical today.

Post-Reformation Calvinists stressed the doctrines of double predestination and limited atonement to emphasize that the believer's salvation is completely by grace and is as secure as the nature and character of God Himself. But the doctrine of limited atonement implies that the anxious inquirer cannot presume that Christ died for him; Christ died for an individual if and only if that person is one of the elect. How does one know if he is elected? The electing decree is part of the hidden will of God, so the only way a person knows that he is elect is if he truly believes in Jesus Christ for salvation. But how does one know whether his faith is genuine or if he is deceived? A genuine faith manifests itself by persevering in doing good works. In the final analysis, the basis of assurance in post-Reformation theology is sanctification, not justification.

The doctrine of temporary faith, a notion first formulated by Calvin but later developed by Beza and William Perkins, further intensified the

---

[17]R. T. Kendall, *Calvin and English Calvinism to 1649* (New York: Oxford University Press, 1979); and C. Bell, *Calvin and Scottish Theology: The Doctrine of Assurance* (Edinburgh: The Handsel Press, 1985).

[18]Zachman and Thomas argue that the trouble begins with the inconsistencies of Calvin's formulation of the doctrine of assurance and that the later Calvinists are closer to Calvin than Kendall or Bell want to admit. Thorson concludes that "Calvin is not just complex, but inconsistent." See R. Zachman, *The Assurance of Faith: Conscience in the Theology of Martin Luther and John Calvin* (Minneapolis: Fortress, 1993); G. M. Thomas, *The Extent of the Atonement: A Dilemma for Reformed Theology from Calvin to the Consensus (1536–1675)* (Carlisle: Paternoster, 1997); and S. Thorson, "Tensions in Calvin's View of Faith: Unexamined Assumptions in R. T. Kendall's *Calvin and English Calvinism to 1649,*" *Journal of the Evangelical Theological Society* 37.3 (1994): 423. Beeke and Hawkes defend the Puritan approach to assurance, calling it a thoroughly Trinitarian model and "especially elegant." See J. Beeke, *The Quest for Full Assurance: The Legacy of Calvin and His Successors* (Edinburgh: Banner of Truth, 1999); and R. M. Hawkes, "The Logic of Assurance in English Puritan Theology," *Westminster Theological Journal* 52 (1990): 260.

problem of assurance in Calvinist and Puritan theology. According to them, God gives to the reprobate, whom He never intended to save in the first place, a "taste" of his grace. Based on passages such as Matt 7:21–23; Heb 6:4–6, and the parable of the Sower, Beza and Perkins attribute this false, temporary faith to an ineffectual work of the Holy Spirit. Perkins propounds a system in which the reprobate might experience five degrees of ineffectual calling that to him is indistinguishable from a genuine conversion experience. Those who profess to be believers are encouraged to examine themselves lest they are found to possess only this temporary faith.[19] Beza declared that the reason God gives temporary faith to the reprobate is so that "their fall might be more grievous."[20] In Olmsted's opinion, Beza's teaching "comes perilously close to ascribing the matter to divine sadism."[21]

History shows that these doctrines produced a crippling anxiety in the later Calvinists and Puritans that drove them to an introspection which an objective observer might describe as pathological. John Bunyan's *Pilgrim's Progress* has blessed multitudes of Christians, but his spiritual autobiography, *Grace Abounding to the Chief of Sinners,* is disturbing. He recounts how, in his seemingly endless search for assurance of salvation, he was haunted by the question, "How can I tell if I am elected?"[22]

Kendall and Bell document the pastorally damaging results of the Puritan approach to assurance. Even those who disagree with Kendall's thesis concede that his "devastating critique" of the miserable travails produced by Puritan theology and practice is more or less "on the mark."[23] Kendall recounts the life and work of William Perkins (1558–1602), who

---

[19]See R. A. Muller, "Perkins' *A Golden Chaine:* Predestinarian System or Schematized *Ordo Salutis?*" *Sixteenth Century Journal* 60/1 (1978): 75. Perkins devised an elaborate chart that expounds a supralapsarian view of salvation. Under the heading of "A Calling Not Effectual," Perkins lists five evidences of the ineffectual work of the Holy Spirit: (1) an enlightening of the mind, (2) a penitence accompanied by a desire to be saved, (3) a temporary faith, (4) a taste of justification and sanctification that is accompanied by the heart-felt sweetness of God's mercy, and (5) a zeal for the things of religion. See also Kendall, "Calvin and English Calvinism," 67–76. Kendall quotes Perkins as saying that the quest for assurance ultimately requires a "descending into our own hearts" (75), which is a type of introspection that Calvin warned against.

[20]Cited in Kendall, *"Calvin and English Calvinism,"* 36.

[21]Olmstead, "Staking All on Faith's Object," 140–41.

[22]J. Bunyan, *Grace Abounding to the Chief of Sinners* (Chicago: Moody, 1959), 26.

[23]G. Harper, "Calvin and English Calvinism to 1649: A Review Article," *Calvin Theological Journal* 20 (November 1985): 257.

is often called the father of Puritanism. Perkins wrote extensively and almost exclusively on the subject of assurance, having devoted 2,500 pages to the topic. Unfortunately, the preaching and teaching of Perkins on assurance often had the opposite effect, creating more doubts than were resolved. Ironically, Perkins, like so many other Puritans of his day, died without a clear assurance of his own salvation.[24] In a similar fashion, Bell chronicles the struggle for assurance among the Scottish Calvinists. He says,

> It is well known, for example, that for generations many in the Scottish Highlands have refused to receive the communion elements because of the want of personal assurance of their salvation. Although believing that Jesus Christ is the Savior and the Son of God, self-examination fails to yield sufficient evidence of their election to salvation. Fearing that apart from such assurance they may eat and drink in an unworthy manner, and thereby incur the judgment of God, they abstain from receiving the Lord's Supper.[25]

The later Calvinists and Puritans employed two syllogisms, the practical syllogism and the mystical syllogism, in their attempt to ascertain assurance by way of logical deduction. They used the practical syllogism (*syllogismus practicus*) to determine whether or not they had believed and the mystical syllogism (*syllogismus mysticus*) to search for evidence of true faith.[26] The practical syllogism is as follows:

Major premise:	If effectual grace is manifested in me by good works, then I am elect.
Minor premise (practical):	I manifest good works.
Conclusion:	Therefore, I am one of the elect.

But how does one know the minor premise of the practical syllogism is true for him? The Puritans attempted to answer this question by an introspective self-examination using the mystical syllogism. The mystical syllogism is as follows:

---

[24]Kendall cites Thomas Fuller, the 19th-century historian, who reports that Perkins died "in the conflict of a troubled conscience." See Kendall, "*Calvin and English Calvinism*," 75.

[25]Bell, *Calvin and Scottish Theology: The Doctrine of Assurance*, 7.

[26]Beeke, *The Quest for Full Assurance*, 132–39.

Major premise:	If I experience the inward confirmation of the Spirit, then I am elect.
Minor premise (mystical):	I experience the confirmation of the Spirit.
Conclusion:	Therefore, I am one of the elect.

Beza concludes, "Therefore, that I am elect, is first perceived from sanctification begun in me, that is, by my hating of sin and my loving of righteousness."[27] The post-Reformation Calvinist and the Puritan believed that the basis of assurance is sanctification.

Of the three answers given to the question, "How does one know that he is genuinely saved?" only the second option, "Assurance is the essence of saving faith," provides certainty of salvation. Assurance of salvation must be based on Jesus Christ and His work for us—nothing more and nothing less.

COMPONENT # 2: EVENTUAL CERTAINTY
HOW SECURE IS ONE'S SALVATION?

Even if a believer knows he is saved, the question of perseverance is still unanswered. This brings us to the second aspect of assurance—how secure is one's salvation? Arminians have traditionally answered that apostasy is possible for the believer, while Calvinists have affirmed the perseverance of the saints. Some scholars have offered mediating positions arguing that while the Scriptures warn against the danger of apostasy, the possibility of apostasy does not exist for the genuine believer. Thomas Schreiner and Ardel Caneday's Means-of-Salvation position is one such midway proposal, and we will give additional attention to it.

---

[27]T. Beza, *A Little Book of Christian Questions and Responses* (Allison Park, PA: Pickwick Publications, 1986), 96–97.

Apostasy Is Possible	Apostasy Is Not Possible	Apostasy Is Threatened But Not Possible
Nonelect Believers Fall—Augustine	*Implicit Universalism*—Barth	*Irreconcilable Tension*—Carson
Nonpersevering Believers Fall—Moody	*Once Saved, Always Saved*—Grace Evangelical Society	*Means of Salvation*—Schreiner and Caneday
	Evidence of Genuineness—Demarest	*Middle Knowledge*—Craig

Augustinian and Arminian View: Apostasy Is Possible

Two positions accept the possibility that a believer may lose his salvation. Augustine believed that nonelect believers will fall from grace, while traditional Arminians argue that all believers are at risk of apostasy.

Nonelect believers fall. According to Augustine (354–430), only elect believers persevere and only God knows which believers are the elect.[28] God has not elected every believer whom He regenerates. A believer can lose his salvation and be placed back under the wrath of God by committing mortal sins. Augustine gives an example of two pious men, both "justified men" and both "renewed by . . . regeneration." Yet one perseveres and the other does not because God has chosen only one. God regenerates more than He elects. Why would God do this? Augustine answers, "I do not know."[29]

However, God grants repentance and perseverance to His elect. Since election is part of the hidden will of God, all believers must strive to endure until the end. On a practical level, the Augustinian perspective operates much like the Arminian one.

Nonpersevering believers fall. Arminians interpret the assurance passages in the light of the warning passages and understand salvation to be a present condition that a believer enjoys but could lose. Two recent

---

[28]B. Demarest, *The Cross and Salvation* (Wheaton: Crossway, 1997), 437–38.

[29]Augustine, *A Treatise on the Gift of Perseverance*, 21, in *Nicene and Post-Nicene Fathers*, vol. 5, ed. Philip Schaff. Available online at http://www.ccel.org/ccel/schaff/npnf105.xxi.iii.xxiii.html.

proponents of this position, Dale Moody and I. Howard Marshall, argue that the Scriptures are filled with explicit warnings to believers that they must persevere if they are to be saved.[30] Moody claims that because of preconceived theological positions, the full impact of these verses has been muted. He laments, "Yet cheap preaching and compromise with sin have made such texts forbidden for serious study."[31] He argues, "Eternal life is the life of those who continue to follow Jesus. No one can retain eternal life who turns away from Jesus."[32]

Schreiner points out that Moody solves the tension between the assurance passages and the warning passages by denying there is a tension.[33] Moody asserts that Calvinists have put so much emphasis on the assurance passages that they have bleached out the full force of the warning passages. However, he appears to have committed the same error in reverse when he ignores the unconditional nature of the promises of preservation and makes them subordinate to the warning passages.

Calvinist and Free Grace View: Apostasy Is Not Possible

Three positions argue apostasy is not possible and the believer's eventual salvation is guaranteed. The first position is the implicit universalism of Karl Barth based upon his view of election, while the Grace Evangelical Society advocates the second view—the Once-Saved-Always-Saved position—as a major plank of their doctrinal platform. Wayne Grudem argues for a third view, the Evidence-of-Genuineness position, which argues that saving faith manifests itself by perseverance.

Implicit Universalism. In a famous discussion in his *Church Dogmatics*, Karl Barth demonstrated that the Reformer's formulation for assurance stands upon an unstable platform. Beginning the search for certainty with the electing decree that is hidden in the secret will of God dooms the enterprise from the start. He argued that the Reformers

---

[30]Marshall, *Kept by the Power of God*; and D. Moody, *The Word of Truth: A Summary of Christian Doctrine Based on Biblical Revelation* (Grand Rapids: Eerdmans, 1981).

[31]Moody, *The Word of Truth*, 350.

[32]Ibid., 356. Moody defends his position by claiming that it is also the position of A. T. Robertson, the famed New Testament scholar at Southern Seminary.

[33]Schreiner, "Perseverance and Assurance," 33.

erred when they attempted to develop a doctrine of assurance with a Christological beginning and an anthropological ending.[34]

Barth resolved the question of assurance by utilizing his idiosyncratic view of election. According to Barth, Jesus Christ is both the electing God and the elected Man. God relates to the elect only through Christ, but Christ is also the rejected Man of the reprobate. Therefore, God relates to all—both elect and rejected—through Christ with the end result that God rejects the rejectedness of the reprobate. Barth solves concerns about assurance by placing all mankind in Christ.[35]

Barth never conceded that his position implied universalism. J. I. Packer observes that this was "a conclusion that Barth himself seems to have avoided only by will power."[36] However, his approach seems to conclude that a reprobate is someone who is elect but does not yet know it.

Once Saved, Always Saved. The Once-Saved-Always-Saved position rejects the traditional Reformed doctrine of the perseverance of the saints in favor of the doctrine of eternal security. Proponents of the view include Zane Hodges, Charles Stanley, Joseph Dillow, and R. T. Kendall.[37] Advocates of the Once-Saved-Always-Saved position, while not accepting Barth's view on election, agree with him that any attempt to arrive at assurance of salvation that involves looking at the believer's life for evidence or support will not succeed.

According to this view, assurance of salvation comes only by trusting the promises of the Word of God. The believer should manifest the fruit of salvation, but there is no guarantee that he will. At best, works provide a secondary, confirmatory function.[38]

---

[34]K. Barth, *Church Dogmatics* II/2 (Edinburgh: T&T Clark), 333–40.

[35]Ibid., 344–54. Randall Zachman and G. Michael Thomas currently advocate Barth's position. See Zachman, *The Assurance of Faith*, viii, 244–48; and Thomas, *The Extent of the Atonement,* 252–53.

[36]J. I. Packer, "Good Pagans and God's Kingdom," *Christianity Today* 30/1 (17 January 1986): 22–25.

[37]See Z. Hodges, *Absolutely Free!* (Grand Rapids: Zondervan, 1989); C. Stanley, *Eternal Security: Can You Be Sure?* (Nashville: Thomas Nelson, 1990); J. Dillow, *The Reign of the Servant Kings* (Haysville, NC: Schoettle, 1992), 187,194; R. T. Kendall, *Once Saved, Always Saved* (Chicago: Moody, 1983), 49–53.

[38]See the doctrinal statement of the Grace Evangelical Society at http://www.faithalone.org/. Stanley explains that "in all probability, a Christian who has expressed faith in Christ and experienced forgiveness of sin will always believe that forgiveness is found through Christ. But even if he does not,

Critics argue that this position has three weaknesses. First, it either ignores or explains away what seems to be the clear meaning of the warning passages directed to the saints. Second, it tends toward laxity in Christian commitment, and third, it gives false comfort to those who walk in disobedience to the commands of Scripture and who in fact really may not be saved.[39]

The advocates of the Once-Saved-Always-Saved position argue that the Bible provides plenty of motivation for Christian service without threatening the believer with eternal damnation.[40] First, the believer is moved to service by a sense of gratitude for his salvation. Second, the believer who fails to follow the Lord faithfully experiences the chastening hand of God, even to the point of death, if necessary. Third, in addition to divine chastening in this life, the disobedient believer experiences the loss of rewards at the judgment seat of Christ. The carnal believer enjoys the preservation of God even if he does not persevere in the faith.[41]

Evidence of Genuineness. The Evidence-of-Genuineness position, traditionally understood as the doctrine of the perseverance of the saints, agrees with the Once-Saved-Always-Saved view that the believer's salvation is eternally secure. They also agree that good works are not necessary to procure salvation. However, unlike those who advocate the doctrine of eternal security, the advocates of the Evidence-of-Genuineness position contend that the fruits of salvation will necessarily and eventually manifest themselves in the life of a believer.[42]

The Evidence-of-Genuineness proponents base their doctrine of perseverance on God's promises in Scripture that He will complete His work of salvation in the individual believer.[43] Even though a believer may fail miserably and sin terribly, he cannot remain in that condition. A Christian may fall totally, but his fall will not be final. The true believer will persevere.

---

the fact remains that he is forgiven!" (*Eternal Security*, 79). He likens salvation to a tattoo that a person may come to regret but cannot get rid of (p. 80). Also see pp. 74, 93–94.

[39]Moody, *The Word of Truth,* 361–65.

[40]See the section entitled "Motivation" of the Grace Evangelical Society at http://www.faithalone.org/.

[41]Stanley, *Eternal Security,* 92–100.

[42]Demarest, *The Cross and Salvation,* 439–44.

[43]Phil 1:6, "I am sure of this, that He who started a good work in you will carry it on to completion until the day of Christ Jesus."

The warning passages serve as litmus tests, according to the Evidence-of-Genuineness position.[44] Those who are not genuinely converted will eventually show their true colors. Therefore, the judgments threatened in those passages are not directed toward believers but are intended for false disciples, who for one reason or another are masquerading as real Christians.

Schreiner and Caneday agree with the advocates of the Evidence-of-Genuineness position that true believers will persevere, but they believe that the Evidence-of-Genuineness advocates have misinterpreted the warning passages in the New Testament. Schreiner and Caneday argue the warning passages are orientated toward the future, while the Evidence-of-Genuineness position turns the warnings into tests of past or present behavior.[45]

Mediating Views: Apostasy Is Threatened, but Is Not Possible

Some scholars understand the warning passages to be admonishing believers about the danger of eternal judgment, although a believer cannot apostatize. Three positions attempt to reconcile these two seemingly contrary concepts. The first view, the Irreconcilable Tension position, argues that the two types of passages are irresolvable and that a compatibilistic approach must be taken. Second, the Means-of-Salvation position argues that the warnings serve as an essential means by which the believer is preserved; and third, William Lane Craig argues that the Means-of-Salvation view is a middle knowledge approach.

Irreconcilable Tension. Certain scholars have given up any attempt to reconcile the assurance passages with the warning passages and have ascribed the whole matter to mystery. In his book, *Assurance and Warning*, Gerald Borchert concludes that the two types of passages are in irreconcilable tension and must be held in a "delicate balance."[46]

---

[44]See W. Grudem, "Perseverance of the Saints: A Case Study from the Warning Passages in Hebrews," in *Still Sovereign: Contemporary Perspectives on Election, Foreknowledge, and Grace*, ed. T. R. Schreiner and B. A. Ware (Grand Rapids: Baker, 2000), 133–82.

[45]Schreiner and Caneday, *The Race Set Before Us*, 29–35.

[46]G. L. Borchert, *Assurance and Warning* (Nashville: Broadman, 1987), 194.

D. A. Carson takes a similar tack when he argues for taking a compatibilist approach to the issue at hand. He defines compatibilism as,

> the view that the following two statements are, despite superficial evidence to the contrary, mutually compatible: (1) God is absolutely sovereign, but his sovereignty does not in any way mitigate human responsibility; (2) human beings are responsible creatures (i.e., they choose, decide, obey, disobey, believe, rebel, and so forth), but their responsibility never serves to make God absolutely contingent.[47]

Since we do not know how God operates in time, how God operates through secondary agents, or how God is both sovereign and personal at the same time, then we are not going to know how the two types of passages interface. In the end, we are left with a theological antinomy. Carson concludes, "So we will, I think, always have some mystery."[48]

Neither Schreiner nor Hodges are impressed with Carson's appeal to compatibilistic mystery. Schreiner cautions against appealing to mystery too quickly; otherwise we may be simply avoiding the hard labor and hard choices of doing theological work. He suspects that Borchert and Carson are using "tension" and "mystery" as code words for "contradiction."[49] Likewise Hodges argues that an assurance based on a mystery is not much of an assurance at all. He says, "If 'assurance' were indeed a mystery, then it would be a deeply disquieting mystery to those who need assurance the most. Does Dr. Carson know beyond question that he himself is regenerate? If so, let him tell us *how* he knows. The compatibilist cannot have a mystery and a confident answer, too!"[50]

Means of Salvation. In their book *The Race Set Before Us,* Thomas Schreiner and Ardel Caneday present a position they label the Means-of-Salvation view. They agree with the advocates of the Evidence-of-Genuineness position that a believer cannot apostatize. However, they argue that the warning passages, such as those found in the book of Hebrews, threaten believers with eternal damnation in hell if they fail to

---

[47]Carson, "Reflections on Christian Assurance," 22.
[48]Ibid., 26.
[49]Schreiner, "Perseverance and Assurance," 52.
[50]Z. Hodges, "The New Puritanism Part 1: Carson on Christian Assurance," http://www.faithalone.org/journal/1993i/Hodges.htm. Accessed 24 January 2002.

persevere. They reject the way proponents of the Once-Saved-Always-Saved position interpret 1 Cor 9:23–27 to mean that Paul was concerned about losing his qualifications for the ministry when he spoke of keeping his body in subjection so that he would not be cast away. Rather, they agree with Gordon Fee that Paul was warning the Corinthian Christians that without remaining faithful to the end even he would not go to heaven.[51] "Fear to become *adokimos* ["disqualified, reprobate"] motivates Paul to be diligent and deliberate in perseverance."

The Means-of-Salvation position contends that the New Testament is always referring to the gift of salvation when it speaks of the believer's reward.[52] Passages that exhort the elect to pursue crowns of life, glory, and righteousness are making reference to salvation itself, not to any subsequent reward that the believer may earn in addition to salvation. This is one of the central themes of their book.

> We have insisted throughout this book that the New Testament directs its admonitions and warnings to believers. We have also argued that these warnings do not merely threaten believers with losing rewards but that eternal life itself is at stake. Biblical writers frequently warn believers that if they turn away from Jesus Christ they will experience eternal judgment. If believers apostatize their destiny is the lake of fire, the second death, hell. These warnings cannot be waved aside and relegated to those who are not genuine Christians. They are directed to believers and must be heeded for us to be saved on the last day. We will win the prize of eternal life only if we run the race to the end. If we quit during the middle of the race, we will not receive eternal life.[53]

They also argue that obtaining eternal life requires not only continuing faith but also great effort. They conclude from 2 Pet 1:5–11 ("Make every effort to supplement your faith with goodness, . . . knowledge, . . . self-control, . . . endurance, . . . godliness, . . . brotherly affection, and . . . love. . . . [M]ake every effort to confirm your calling and

---

[51]Schreiner and Caneday, *The Race Set Before Us,* 179. Cf. G. Fee, *The First Epistle to the Corinthians,* New International Commentary on the New Testament (Grand Rapids: Eerdmans, 1987), 431–41. According to Fee, Paul understands that "he and they [the Corinthians] must persevere in the gospel to share in its promises" (p. 432) and that Christians must "exercise self-control lest they fail to obtain the eschatological prize" (440).

[52]Schreiner and Caneday, *The Race Set Before Us*, 89–95.

[53]Ibid., 268.

election. . . . For in this way, entry into the eternal kingdom of our Lord and Savior Jesus Christ will be richly supplied to you.") that

> Virtuous living is not encouraged simply because it makes life on earth more fulfilling, nor is the idea that living a godly life will lead to greater rewards in heaven. These virtues are imperative to escape the fate of the false teachers. That is, righteous living is necessary to obtain entrance into the kingdom of Jesus Christ.[54]

But Schreiner and Caneday argue that though the threats of damnation addressed to the saints are genuine, the possibility of apostasy is not. They affirm from passages such as 1 John 2:19 that "persevering in Christ is the mark of authenticity" because believers "have the promise of God that he will supply the necessary power" to persevere. "Thus, we can be certain that every believer will most certainly finish the race and obtain the prize."[55] This is because God uses means—including the warning passages—to fulfill His promise to save all who have trusted Jesus Christ as Savior. They claim that warning someone about certain behavioral consequences does not imply anything about the likelihood of their engaging in that behavior. "[C]onditional warnings in themselves do not function to indicate anything about possible failure or fulfillment. Instead, the conditional warnings appeal to our minds to conceive or imagine the invariable consequences that come to all who pursue a course of apostasy from Christ."[56] In assessing the warnings, they make a distinction between that which is conceivable and that which may or is likely to happen. They liken the warnings to road signs, which "caution against conceivable consequences, not probable consequences."[57] They further explain, "The truthfulness of a warning or admonition does not depend on whether or not the thing supposed may come to pass . . . . Rather, they function by supposing a particular course of action that has an invariable and inviolable consequence."[58]

---

[54]Schreiner and Caneday, *The Race Set Before Us,* 290. They also explain, "Peter summons the church to godly living so that they will enter the eternal kingdom," and they agree with Richard Bauckham that "the ethical fruits of Christian faith are objectively necessary for the attainment of final salvation" (p. 291).

[55]Ibid., 245.

[56]Ibid., 199.

[57]Ibid., 208.

[58]Ibid., 209.

The way Schreiner and Caneday see it, rather than causing conster-
nation in the elect, the threats of damnation produce encouragement and
confidence.

> The admonitions and warnings of the Scriptures threaten be-
> lievers with eternal judgment for apostasy, but these warnings
> do not violate assurance and confidence regarding final salva-
> tion. . . . The warnings do not rob us of assurance. They are sign-
> posts along the marathon runner's pathway that help us maintain
> our confidence.[59]

The tension between threats of judgment and signposts of confidence may be resolved, according to Schreiner and Caneday, by recog-
nizing the "already-but-not-yet" aspect of the gospel of the kingdom.
They argue that the advocates of the other positions have overlooked this
fundamental interpretative principle that is often referred to as inaugu-
rated eschatology.[60] With the resurrection of Christ, the end of the age
has begun, so all the blessings of the kingdom of God and its salvation on
behalf of the elect are an accomplished fact. However, our Lord has not
returned, so the full enjoyment of our salvation is not yet accomplished.
This sets up a tension in the world, in the church, and in the hearts of
individual believers that is expressed in the biblical record.

Schreiner and Caneday argue that the Once-Saved-Always-Saved position is particularly guilty of an over-realized eschatology that collapses
the "not yet" into the "already." They contend that those like Hodges and
Stanley have emphasized the conversion event to the point of making
salvation a completely past event. The opposite would be a theology in
which salvation is only a future possibility. The Means-of-Salvation view
teaches that saving faith is not just a one-time event but also a lifetime
journey. All the components and aspects of salvation have an "already–
not yet" orientation—even justification. They agree that justification is
primarily forensic,[61] but they also understand that "righteousness should

---

[59]Ibid., 269.

[60]Ibid., 46–86. "Both the present and future dimensions of salvation should be viewed as two
aspects of an indivisible whole" (p. 47). On this influential hermeneutical approach see G. E. Ladd, *The
Presence of the Future* (Grand Rapids: Eerdmans, 1974), 139.

[61]By "forensic" is meant that righteousness/justification terms use a legal or courtroom metaphor
describing the believer as one declared right before the divine judge. Schreiner's views on the forensic
nature of justification have evolved. Most recently, he stated, "[R]ighteousness and justification in Paul

be included in the already-but-not-yet tension that informs New Testament soteriology. Believers are righteous now, yet they still await the gift of righteousness that will be theirs on the day of redemption."[62]

As a way to understand the basis of assurance, Schreiner and Caneday present a three-legged stool.[63] The first leg is the promises of God, the second leg is the evidence of a changed life, and the third leg is the inward witness of the Holy Spirit. They admit that the analogy is an imperfect one, since the promises of God are primary for assurance,[64] but they deny that there can be a discontinuity between the first leg and the other two. They warn, "Even though the promises of God are primary in establishing our assurance, it would be a serious mistake to expel the necessity of believing obedience to confirm assurance." In fact, "a transformed life is evidence of and necessary for salvation."[65]

Schreiner and Caneday strongly affirm that a Christian can know he is saved based on God's promises, although various New Testament warning passages threaten him with final condemnation if he does not persevere in godly faith and life. Their attempt to explain the latter in terms of only "conceivable" rather than possible or probable consequences, however, seems to leave the two propositions in conflict. They affirm that the believer experiences forensic justification, full adoption, and divine regeneration as present realities. How then is it conceivable that a believer so positioned in Christ is in any danger of damnation? This objection does not arise merely from an over-realized eschatology, as they contend. In spite of their efforts to avoid it, they seem to sacrifice some of the "already" component of the "already–not yet" tension.

---

should be understood as forensic only." See T. R. Schreiner, *New Testament Theology* (Grand Rapids: Baker, 2008), 355. He further explains, "God's declaration about sinners is an end-time verdict that has been announced before the end has arrived. The verdict is effective in the sense that every verdict announced by God constitutes reality." Also, "By virtue of union with Christ believers already enjoy justification in this present evil age" (p. 361).

[62]Schreiner and Caneday, *The Race Set Before Us,* 77–79. They derive the future dimension of justification from passages such as Gal 5:5; and Rom 2:13; 3:20.

[63]Ibid., 276–305.

[64]They declare, "Our primary focus must be on the promises of God in Christ and his objective work on our behalf." Further, "The fundamental leg is the promises of God." Ibid., 283.

[65]Ibid., 283–84. They explain from 1 John that righteous living, love for fellow believers, and right belief about Christ "are necessary conditions to belong to the people of God, but they are not sufficient conditions" (p. 287). They also declare, "Assurance does not rest only on God's promises; it also is confirmed by the way we live" (p. 289).

Second, in their discussion of 1 Cor 9:27, Schreiner and Caneday say that Paul's "fear to become adokimos," that is, a castaway, motivated him to persevere. They say his fear was not of losing his salvation (although their wording sounds like it was), nor was it a fear of losing rewards.[66] What is the alternative except a fear that he might not be a genuine believer? If so, what kind of confidence is that? Their position seems to be unclear at this point. Dale Moody scoffs at the Means-of-Salvation view as Arminianism that has lost its nerve. In his opinion it ultimately "reduces the warnings to bluffing."[67]

Third, what can we say about those who do not persevere? Many who at one time professed faith in Christ later renounce their faith. Our authors acknowledge that the failure of such people to persevere indicates they were never truly saved.[68] So what the warning passages describe happens to false professors but not to the elect, and the Means-of-Salvation position seems to collapse into the standard Evidence-of-Genuineness view held by most Calvinist evangelicals.[69]

Fourth, as the first section of this chapter demonstrated, the Puritans employed an approach very similar to the Means-of-Salvation position and found it to be pastorally disastrous. Schreiner and Caneday acknowledge the experience of the Puritans and warn against it, but they give little reason to believe the same problems would not reoccur if the Means-of-Salvation view were to become widespread again.[70] The subtitle to their book is *A Biblical Theology of Perseverance and Assurance*, but the work seems to be long on perseverance and short on assurance. In discussing the function of the fruit of the Spirit in Christian assurance, they repeatedly say that the role is only to "confirm" the believer's as-

---

[66]Ibid., 179.

[67]Moody, *The Word of Truth,* 361.

[68] See Schreiner and Caneday, *The Race Set Before Us,* 214–44.

[69]This is, in fact, the position that Schreiner and Caneday take about those who lapse. See Schreiner and Caneday, *The Race Set Before Us,* 243. They acknowledge that "New Testament writers are also concerned about those who claim to believe and yet do not match their confession of faith with believing obedience" (p. 283). Such people "might presume upon God's grace" and "use the promises of Scripture to console their consciences" (p. 292). So it sounds like the warning passages apply more to false professors than to true believers.

[70]Ibid., 277–78.

surance derived from God's promises.[71] And yet the very nature of the Means-of-Salvation view seems to do just the opposite.

Fifth, at times it appears that the Means-of-Salvation proposal comes dangerously close to a works-salvation position, in spite of their declarations to the contrary.[72] Graciously enabled works are still works. Most Evangelicals agree that true saving faith works, but it is still faith alone and not faith plus godliness that is the means of salvation. Yet Schreiner and Caneday state, "Perseverance is a necessary means that God has appointed for attaining final salvation."[73]

Calvin addressed this approach in his response to the Council of Trent when he stated,

> Here there is no dispute between us as to the necessity of exhorting believers to good works, and even stimulating them by holding forth a reward. What then? First, I differ from them in this, that they make eternal life the reward; for if God rewards works with eternal life, they will immediately make out that faith itself is a reward which is paid, whereas Scripture uniformly proclaims that it is the inheritance which falls to us by no other right than that of free adoption.[74]

Even though they are careful to insist that the works done by the believer are actually accomplished by the grace of God, their position is difficult to reconcile with the Reformation principle of *sola fide*. Perhaps Schreiner and Caneday could address this concern by giving a clear definition of what they mean when they use the word "perseverance." Do they understand it to be an undying faith (that produces good works), or a continuing in godly behavior?[75]

Middle Knowledge. Does the Means-of-Salvation view inadvertently abandon the traditional Reformed understanding of divine sovereignty

---

[71]Ibid., 283–99.

[72]Ibid., 86. But see Zuck, "Review of *The Race Set Before Us*," 142. It is interesting that in his argument that salvation begins with faith but is completed by works, A. P. Stanley cites Schriner and Caneday for support. See *Did Jesus Teach Salvation by Works?* (Eugene, OR: Pickwick, 2006), 244.

[73]Ibid., 152.

[74]Calvin, "Acts of the Council of Trent with the Antidote," 144–45.

[75]After I wrote this chapter, Dr. Schreiner was kind enough to send me a draft of his upcoming book *Run to Win the Prize* (InterVarsity). In it he clarifies his position and provides a helpful response to many concerns expressed by me and others. Most helpful is his description of perseverance, which he defines as "persevering in faith"—a definition with which I agree wholeheartedly. However, I remain unconvinced that the warning passages of the New Testament threaten believers with damnation.

and instead hold a Molinist position? William Lane Craig believes that
it does. He argues that the Means-of-Salvation position implicitly employs middle knowledge. Craig asks that if the believer's will is so over-
whelmed by God's grace, then why does God give the warnings at all?
And if the warnings themselves bring about perseverance, does this mean
that the believer is capable of apostasy, even if he does not apostatize?
Hypothetically, at least, the elect can fall away, but God, using middle
knowledge, has chosen to actualize a world in which scriptural warnings
will operate as means to keep His children from apostasy. This is a novel
understanding of perseverance, but it appears to be the view argued by
those who hold to the Means-of-Salvation position.[76] Craig states,

> The classical defender of perseverance must, it seems, if he is to
> distinguish his view from Molinism, hold to the intrinsic efficacy
> of God's grace and, hence, the causal impossibility of the believ-
> er's apostasy. But in that case, the warnings of Scripture against
> the danger of apostasy seem to become otiose and unreal.[77]

Craig concludes that the Means-of-Salvation view is, in fact, a Molinist perspective and represents an abandonment of the classic Reformed
doctrine of perseverance.

Schreiner and Caneday's response to Craig's article seems to indicate they miss the point to his argument. In an appendix to their book,
The Race Set Before Us, they contend that Craig misunderstands the difference between his view of how God's grace works in the human will
and the view of Reformed theology.[78] Since Craig assumes a "false dis-
junction" between God's grace that overwhelms the believer's will and
the warnings themselves, he thinks the efficacy of the warnings reside
merely in themselves. Schreiner and Caneday claim Craig wrongly attributes his own view to the proponents of the Means-of-Salvation position, and "thus his whole argument against the Reformed view takes a
trajectory that misses its mark."[79]

---

[76]W. L. Craig, "'Lest Anyone Should Fall': A Middle Knowledge Perspective on Perseverance and
Apostolic Warnings," *Philosophy of Religion* 29 (1991): 65–74.

[77]Ibid., 72.

[78]Schreiner and Caneday, *The Race Set Before Us,* 332–37.

[79]Ibid., 337.

However, Craig does fully realize the difference between the Reformed view and the Molinist view of God's use of means. That is exactly his point. If God is using the warnings as the means to insure perseverance, then either the saints would fall without the warnings (which is contrary to how Reformed theology understands how God's grace works in the believer) or the saints would persevere even without the warnings (which would make the warnings superfluous). Either way, the Means-of-Salvation position seems to depart from standard Reformed soteriology.

A MODEST PROPOSAL: A VARIATION OF THE EVIDENCE-OF-GENUINENESS POSITION

The model for assurance offered over the next few pages is very close to the Once-Saved-Always-Saved view. However, it differs in that it simultaneously affirms both God's preservation of the redeemed and their persistent, persevering faith, so it is more accurately described as a variant of the Evidence-of-Genuineness view. This position has four points: (1) the only basis for assurance is the objective work of Christ; (2) assurance is the essence of saving faith; (3) saving faith perseveres; and (4) God offers rewards available to the believer subsequent to salvation.

The Four Tenets of a Modified Evidence-of-Genuineness View	
1. *The only basis for assurance is the objective work of Christ.*	Christ is the foundation of assurance; good works merely support and confirm.
2. *Assurance is the essence of saving faith.*	A certain knowledge of salvation is simultaneous with being saved. Subsequent doubts may come, but a core conviction remains.
3. *Saving faith perseveres or remains until the day when it gives way to sight.*	Perseverance is a faith that cannot be annihilated. Perseverance is more a promise than it is a requirement.
4. *There are rewards that are subsequent to salvation for the believer to win or lose.*	Believers will be judged and rewarded according to their service.

First, *the only basis for assurance is the objective work of Christ.* Any doctrine of assurance that includes introspection as a component will produce anxiety in the hearts of the very people it is intended to encourage. Barth is right when he points out that no system that has a Christological beginning and an anthropological ending can provide genuine and sustained assurance.

This is why Schreiner and Caneday's analogy of a three-legged stool for assurance fails. They admit the analogy is imperfect because they view the leg of God's promises as preeminent over the other legs of sanctification and the inward testimony of the Spirit. Nevertheless, a stool that has one leg that is longer, stronger, and sturdier than the others is an inherently unstable platform. To change metaphors, when it comes to providing assurance, Christ is the soloist and evidences are just members of the back-up choir.

A close corollary to the premise that Christ is the only basis for assurance is the necessity to reaffirm the doctrine of *sola fide*. Perseverance cannot be understood in terms of good works and great effort without having the result of dismantling the Reformation. The doctrine of perseverance must be formulated so that it does not create the impression that the Scriptures contradict themselves about grace and works.[80]

Second, *assurance is the essence of saving faith.* The very nature of conversion and regeneration guarantees that certain knowledge of salvation is simultaneous with being saved. Subsequent doubts and fears may come, but a core conviction about one's relationship with God will remain.

Good works and the evidences of God's grace do not provide assurance. They provide warrant to assurance but not assurance itself. Perhaps a good analogy is how a Christian knows the love of God. He experiences the love of God every day in a myriad of ways. However, all those countless blessings merely affirm what the Christian already knows—God loves him. Even during those times when the good favor of God seems to be circumstantially absent and the Christian's confidence is tested, he still knows that God loves him the same way he has always known this—

---

[80]Rom 11:6, "And if by grace, then it is no longer of works; otherwise grace is no longer grace. But if it is of works, it is no longer grace; otherwise work is no longer work" (NKJV).

by the promises of God. So it is with the assurance of salvation. Good works play the mere supporting role of confirmation.

Third, *saving faith perseveres or remains until the day when it gives way to sight.* Perseverance should be understood as a faith that cannot be annihilated and therefore persists. This persistent faith eventually and inevitably exhibits itself in the believer's life in such a way as to bring glory to God. The point of Hebrews 11 is that saving faith manifests itself by the journey of discipleship. One may stumble and falter but never leave the trail. Perseverance should be viewed more as a promise than a requirement.

I cannot agree with Schreiner and Caneday when they contend that the Evidence-of-Genuineness position makes the mistake of turning the forward-looking warning passages into retrospective tests. Rather, the warning passages that look forward (such as those found in the book of Hebrews) are pointing out the obvious: genuine belief will not turn back. Warnings about future behavior can be tests of genuineness without being retrospective.

Some passages teach that past behavior can be an indicator of genuineness. The genuinely saved person hungers and thirsts for righteousness, even when he is struggling with temptation or even if he stumbles into sin. In fact, I am not as concerned about the destiny of those who struggle as I am about those who do not care enough to struggle. Indifference is more of a red flag than weakness.

The absence of a desire for the things of God clearly indicates a serious spiritual problem, and a continued indifference can possibly mean that the person professing faith has never been genuinely converted. God is infinitely more dedicated to our salvation than we are, and He will not fail to finish that which He has begun. If a believer engages in willful disobedience or deliberate indifference, our heavenly Father promises him decisive and appropriate action. The indwelling of the Holy Spirit insures that no peaceful backslider exists.

Fourth, *there are rewards that are subsequent to salvation for the believer to win or lose.* One of the great weaknesses of the Schreiner and Caneday proposal is the necessity to deny that there are any subsequent rewards available for the believer and that all promises of reward must be references to salvation itself. Their position is difficult to reconcile with many biblical passages. For example, 1 Cor 3:12–15 speaks of one Christian's work remaining while another Christian's work burns. The believer whose work remains receives a reward while the other believer suffers loss. Schreiner and Caneday admit the passage teaches "some will be saved that have done shoddy work."[81] This admission undermines the major plank of their position—that persevering in good works is a necessary means by which our salvation is completed. A better understanding of the role of works in believers' lives is to hold that we will be judged and rewarded according to our service.

In the end, assurance comes from depending on Christ alone. I agree with Calvin's retort to the Catholic controversalist Albert Pighius, "If Pighius asks how I know I am elect, I answer that Christ is more than a thousand testimonies to me."[82]

---

[81] Schreiner and Caneday, *The Race Set Before Us*, 51.
[82] J. Calvin, *Concerning the Eternal Predestination of God* (Louisville: Westminster John Knox, 1997), 321.

CHAPTER 7

ROSE**S**

IS FOR SINGULAR REDEMPTION

"He Himself is the propitiation for our sins, and not only for ours,
but also for those of the whole world."
—1 John 2:2

EVIDENTLY, OF THE five points of TULIP, limited atonement is the most difficult to defend. A significant number who consider themselves "Reformed" call themselves "four-point" Calvinists. Of these, it is understood that it is the "L" they have dropped. Four-point Calvinism is often labeled *Amyraldianism*, after Moise Amyraut (1569–1664), the French Calvinist theologian who argued for unlimited atonement.

Even Calvinists who hold to all five points express regret over the term "limited atonement." In his introductory essay to John Owen's *The Death of Death in the Death of Christ*, J. I. Packer delivers a polemic in which he declares that adherence to limited atonement is necessary for "the recovery of the gospel."[1] However, years later, Packer explains that the term does more harm than good. To make his point, Packer quotes Reformed theologian Roger Nicole:

> The language of limited atonement describes inadequately and
> unfairly the view which is held by Reformed people. The problem
> is that it seems to place emphasis upon limits. It seems to take
> away from the beauty, glory and fullness of the work of Christ.
> We seem to say that it does not go quite as far as it could or
> should go. . . . what we need to say is that the atonement is defi-
> nite, that it is related to a particular people whom God has cho-
> sen. This helps us psychologically. Because if you say, "I believe
> in limited atonement," the one who disagrees with you will say,

---

[1] J. I. Packer, "Introductory Essay," in *The Death of Death in the Death of Christ* (Edinburgh: Banner of Truth, [1647] 1959), 1.

"I believe in *unlimited* atonement." He appears to be the one who exalts the greatness of the grace of Christ. . . . Why put ourselves at a disadvantage? On that account, I will gladly send the tulips flying! You see, I am not Dutch; I am Swiss, and I do not care so much about the tulips. I do not care about acronyms. I care about the precious faith of the Reformed church . . . and I do not think that "limited atonement" represents me. I want to say "definite atonement" or "particular redemption," and I would encourage other people to do so also.[2]

Packer then concludes, "Surely this is wise advice. I wish I had taken it earlier in life."[3]

In addition, many Calvin scholars argue that Calvin himself did not hold to limited atonement. Kevin Kennedy has compiled an impressive list of quotes by Calvin in which the reformer asserts that Christ died for all humanity. For example,

God commends to us the salvation of all men without exception, even as Christ suffered for the sins of the whole world.

When he says "the sins of the world," he extends this kindness indiscriminately to the whole human race that the Jews might not think that the Redeemer has been sent to them alone. . . . Now it is for us to embrace the blessing offered to all, that each may make up his own mind that there is nothing to hinder him from finding reconciliation in Christ if only, led by faith, he come to Him.

Our Lord Jesus was offered to the world . . . suffered for all.[4]

If Calvin did not hold to limited atonement, it would not automatically mean that the doctrine was wrong. But it would call into question whether or not the TULIP paradigm was the proper way to present any soteriology that went by the name of Calvinism.[5]

---

[2]J. I. Packer, "The Love of God: Universal and Particular," in *The Grace of God, the Bondage of the Will,* vol. 2, ed. T. R. Schreiner and B. A. Ware (Grand Rapids: Baker, 1995), 424.

[3]Ibid.

[4]John Calvin, quoted by K. Kennedy, *Union with Christ and the Extent of the Atonement in Calvin* (New York: Peter Lang, 2002), 28–31.

[5]The proceedings of the Synod of Dort reveal a wide diversity of opinion among the delegates concerning the extent of the atonement. See S. Strehle, "The Extent of the Atonement and the Synod of Dort," *Westminster Theological Journal* 51:1 (Spring 1989): 1-23.

This chapter argues for what Timothy George calls *singular redemption*, that Christ did not die for all in general but for each person in particular. Singular redemption affirms the slogan most Calvinists also affirm: Christ's atonement is *sufficient* for all but *efficient* only for those who believe. But I, like many moderate Calvinists, do not believe that the affirmation of penal substitution of Christ's death requires holding to a limited atonement. The Bible teaches that the benefits of the atonement are not applied until a person is converted. Adhering to this distinction resolves the apparent dilemma that exists between the *extent* of the atonement and its *intent*.

THE DIVINE PURPOSE OF THE ATONEMENT

The question under consideration is, "What exactly did the death of Christ accomplish?" What did the Father intend by offering His Son as a sacrifice? Arminians generally hold to a general atonement, Dortian Calvinists argue for limited atonement, and moderate Calvinists (and some Arminians) hold to a view of unlimited atonement that Timothy George calls "singular redemption."[6] Robert Lightner gives three terms to help distinguish between the three views: *obtained*, *secured*, and *provided*.[7] The general atonement position sees the death of Christ as *obtaining* redemption for all but securing it for none. The limited atonement view understands Christ's death to *secure* salvation for the elect—but only for the elect. The singular redemption position understands Christ's death to *provide* salvation for all humanity, but the benefits of the atonement are secured only for those who believe, and those benefits are applied at the time of their conversion.

---

[6]T. George, *Amazing Grace: God's Initiative—Our Response* (Nashville: Lifeway, 2000), 80–83.

[7]R. Lightner, *The Death Christ Died,* 2nd ed. (Grand Rapids: Kregel, 1998), 45–46.

Three Views of the Extent of the Atonement		
General Atonement	**Limited Atonement**	**Singular Redemption (Unlimited Atonement)**
Redemption is ob-tained—salvation is obtained for all but secured for none.	*Redemption is se-cured*—salvation is secured for and only for the elect.	*Redemption is pro-vided*—salvation is provided for all, but applied only to those who believe.
Governmental view of the Atonement	Penal Substitutionary view of the Atonement	Penal Substitutionary view of the Atonement

The General Atonement View

Arminians, or more specifically, Wesleyan-Arminians, believe that Christ's death *obtained* salvation for all but secured it for none.[8] The idea is that Christ purchased a general pardon for humanity, but did not die for any individual in particular. Rather, Wesleyan-Arminians argue for a *governmental view* of the atonement, which understands the atonement as a general amnesty. In a passage complaining that too many Arminians were being influenced by Calvinists, Wesleyan theologian J. Kenneth Grider gives the following explanation of the governmental view:

> A spillover from Calvinism into Arminianism has occurred in recent decades. Many Arminians whose theology is not very precise say that Christ paid the penalty for our sins. Yet such a view is foreign to Arminianism, which teaches instead that Christ suffered for us. Arminians teach that what Christ did he did for every person; therefore what he did could not have been to pay the penalty, since no one would then ever go into eternal perdition. Arminianism teaches that Christ suffered for everyone so that the Father could forgive those who repent and believe; his death is such that all will see that forgiveness is costly and will strive to

---

[8]Arminius himself did not hold to the governmental theory but rather subscribed to the penal substitutionary view, which we will discuss in the next section. Most Arminians today follow John Wesley in his advocacy of the governmental position. Many Arminians who adhere to the penal substitutionary view refer to themselves as Reformed Arminians. See S. M. Ashby, "A Reformed Arminian View," in *Four Views on Eternal Security,* ed. J. M. Pinson (Grand Rapids: Zondervan, 2002), 140-43.

cease from anarchy in the world God governs. This view is called
the governmental theory of the atonement.[9]

As Grider makes clear, Wesleyan-Arminians believe that Christ died
for *us*, not for our *sins*. God, as Judge of the universe, chose to accept
the death of Christ instead of the demands of the Law. Jesus' death demonstrates the seriousness of sin but did not pay for our sins. He suffered
for us, but He was not punished for us. For those who place their trust in
Christ, God grants them amnesty from the Law and accounts their faith
as righteousness. In this view, our sins were not paid for at Calvary; they
were overlooked.

Yet, the governmental view cannot be squared with what Scripture
actually says about the death of Christ. Paul clearly states that "Christ
died for our sins" (1 Cor 15:3) and that "Christ has redeemed us from
the curse of the law by becoming a curse for us, because it is written:
Everyone who is hung on a tree is cursed" (Gal 3:13). John declares that
Jesus "Himself is the propitiation for our sins, and not only for ours, but
also for those of the whole world" (1 John 2:2). The testimony of the
Bible is that Jesus was punished and that His suffering was payment for
our sins.

The Limited Atonement View

Calvinists such as John Owen (1616–1683) and John Murray (1898–
1975) held that Christ's death *secured* salvation for the elect alone. Christ
not only made it possible for the elect to be saved, He saved them. Proponents of the limited view understand it to be a logical corollary of the *penal substitutionary* theory of the atonement.[10] Christ offered Himself as a
sacrifice and substituted Himself for us. He actually bore the punishment
which should have been ours and, in so doing, satisfied the Father and
reconciled God and man. Jesus died for the sins of particular individuals. So the Bible presents the atonement as a finished accomplishment,
and all for whom Christ died are saved. Since not everyone is saved,

---

[9]J. K. Grider, "Arminianism," in *Evangelical Dictionary of Theology,* 2nd ed. (Grand Rapids:
Baker, 2001), 97–98.

[10]S. Waldron, "The Biblical Confirmation of Particular Atonement," in *Calvinism: A Southern
Baptist Dialogue* (Nashville: B&H, 2008), 140–44.

advocates of the limited atonement position conclude that Jesus did not atone for those who die without Christ.

Some Calvinists view adherence to limited atonement as essential for the other four points. The early Packer states, "For the five points, though separately stated, are really inseparable. They hang together; you cannot reject one without rejecting them all, at least in the sense in which the Synod meant them."[11]

The Singular Redemption View

The singular redemption view, held by moderate Calvinists and Reformed Arminians, agrees with the limited view that Christ paid a propitiatory atonement but argues that this payment was made for all humanity. This view holds that the atonement was unlimited and universal. Christ *provided* salvation for all, but the benefits of the atonement are *applied* only to those who believe. The key distinction of the singular redemption view is that it sees a temporal difference between the provision and the application.

The Bible teaches that Christ provided redemption for all universally (John 3:16; 2 Cor 5:19; 2 Pet 2:1; 1 John 2:2). The death of Christ is the basis for the salvation of all men. But Scripture does not call upon men to believe in a salvation they already have; rather they are to receive the forgiveness they desperately need. The gospel does not simply inform the elect that they are saved; it exhorts all to repent and believe so that they will be saved.

In addition to universal provision, the Bible also teaches that there is a limiting aspect to redemption: the death of Christ secures salvation only for those who believe. A number of passages emphasize that the atonement is effectual exclusively for those who belong to Christ (John 10:15; Eph 5:25). So what about those for whom the Savior died who yet reject Him? In their case, the atonement testifies against them, and serves

---

[11]Packer, "Introductory Essay," 6. R. C. Sproul Sr. also takes a dim view of four-point Calvinism. He states, "I have often thought that to be a four-point Calvinist one must misunderstand at least one of the five points. It is hard for me to imagine that anyone could understand the other four points of Calvinism and deny limited atonement. There always is the possibility, however, of the happy inconsistency by which people hold incompatible views at the same time." R. C. Sproul Sr., *Chosen by God* (Wheaton: Tyndale, 1986), 204.

as the basis of condemnation. As John declares, "Anyone who does not believe is already condemned, because he has not believed in the name of the One and Only Son of God" (John 3:18b).

Therefore, in the words of Robert Lightner, the singular redemption view can be summed up thusly: "Christ died to make possible the salvation of all men and to make certain the salvation of those who believe."[12] Many Calvinists have advocated the unlimited provision/limited application position: Moise Amyraut, Richard Baxter, Bruce Ware, Millard Erickson, and Bruce Demarest, to name a few. Significantly, a number of Arminians, such as Robert Picirilli and Matthew Pinson, have also adhered to the singular redemption view rather than the general atonement view.[13]

ARGUMENTS FOR LIMITED ATONEMENT

Advocates of the limited atonement view present a number of arguments. *First, they note those passages of Scripture that speak of Christ dying for His own or those that describe the atonement in less than universal language.* The Bible several times refers to the people for whom Jesus died in limited terms.[14] When the angel spoke to Joseph in a dream about Mary's virgin conception, he told Joseph that her Son would "save His people from their sins" (Matt 1:21). In John 10, Christ taught that the Good Shepherd gives His life for His sheep (vv. 3–4,14–16,25–27). In Paul's farewell address to the pastors of Ephesus, he declared that Jesus purchased "the church of God . . . with His own blood" (Acts 20:28). To the church at Rome Paul wrote that "Christ died for us" (Rom 5:8),

---

[12]Lightner, *The Death Christ Died*, 47.

[13]For Calvinists who hold to an unlimited atonement, see B. Armstrong, *Calvinism and the Amyraut Heresy: Protestant Scholasticism and Humanism in Seventeenth-Century France* (Madison, WS: Univ. of Wisconsin, 1969); G. M. Thomas, *The Extent of the Atonement: A Dilemma for Reformed Theology from Calvin to the Consensus* (Carlisle: Paternoster, 1993); B. Demarest, *The Cross and Salvation* (Wheaton: Crossway, 1997), 189-94; M. Erickson, *Christian Theology,* 2nd ed. (Grand Rapids: Baker, 1998), 846-52; and J. D. Moore, *English Hypothetical Universalism: John Preston and the Softening of Reformed Theology* (Grand Rapids: Eerdmans, 2007). For a discussion of universal penal substitution from a Reformed Arminian perspective, see R. Picirilli, *Grace, Faith, Free Will* (Nashville: Randall House, 2002), 103-22.

[14]Attention is also often given to the particularistic language of Isa 52:13–53:12: "He Himself bore our sicknesses, and He carried our pains" (53:4), "He was pierced because of our transgressions, crushed because of our iniquities; punishment for our peace was on Him, and we are healed by His wounds" (53:5), "the LORD has punished Him for the iniquity of us all" (53:6), "My righteous Servant will justify many, and He will carry their iniquities" (53:11), and "He bore the sin of many" (53:12).

and "for us all," that is, for "God's elect" (Rom 8:32–35). In describing
Christ's relationship with the Church by means of the marriage metaphor,
Paul declared, "Christ loved the church and gave Himself for her" (Eph
5:25). Proponents of the limited view see these passages as implying that
those not included in these groups are not those for whom Jesus died.

In addition, there are passages which speak of Christ dying for
"many" rather than for "all." For example, Matthew records the Lord as
stating that "the Son of Man did not come to be served, but to serve, and
to give His life—a ransom for many" (Matt 20:28; also Isa 53:11–12).
Owen understands the Savior to be making a distinction between the
"many" (i.e., the elect) and the rest of humanity.[15]

However, verses like those above which highlight the effects of the
atonement do not indicate the extent of its provision. For example, Paul
declared, "The life I now live in the flesh, I live by faith in the Son of
God, who loved me and gave Himself for me" (Gal 2:20). When Paul
says that Christ died for him, no one understands the apostle to be claiming that Jesus died *only* for him. Rather than delimiting the atonement,
such passages seem to be extolling the special love Christ has for His
own.

As for the passages such as Matthew 20:28 and Mark 14:24 that
speak of Christ dying for "many," it is worth noting that Calvin did not
understand these verses to be teaching limited atonement. In fact, it is
just the opposite. Calvin comments:

> The word "many" does not mean a part of the world only, but
> the whole human race: he contrasts "many" with "one," as if to
> say that he would not be the Redeemer of one man, but would
> meet death to deliver many of their cursed guilt. No doubt that in
> speaking to a few Christ wished to make His teaching available
> to a larger number. . . . So when we come to the holy table not
> only should the general idea come to our mind that the world is
> redeemed by the blood of Christ, but also each should reckon to
> himself that his own sins are covered.[16]

---

[15]John Owen, *The Death of Death in the Death of Christ* (Edinburgh: Banner of Truth, [1647] 1959), 63–64.

[16]John Calvin, quoted by Kevin Kennedy, *Union with Christ*, 33.

In other words, he understood the "many" to be in contrast to the "One" who died for them. The One—Jesus Christ—died for everyone else. Calvin did not see these passages to be limiting the atonement's extent at all.

Second, limited atonement proponents argue that if the atonement really is unlimited, then a great deal of Christ's work was wasted. Since the majority of humans who reach the age of moral accountability turn down the gospel (Luke 13:22–25), it appears the unlimited position teaches that, for the most part, the sufferings of Christ were a futile effort.

Advocates of singular redemption typically give two responses. First, it is noted that God often provides more than we appropriate, which is something Calvinists also recognize. God provides common grace (Acts 14:17; 17:27) and general revelation (Psalm 19) to all humanity. But according to Paul (Rom 1:18–23) all such universal displays are uniformly twisted, suppressed, and ignored.

But second, the unresponsiveness of lost humanity to God's worldwide exhibitions of power, mercy, and goodness does not mean such demonstrations are "wasted." Rather, they act as testimonies against humanity's willful unbelief. Similarly, Christ's offering acts as the basis of condemnation against all who reject the Lord Jesus (John 3:18).

Third, limited atonement advocates contend that since Christ's intercession as our High Priest is limited, so the atonement must be limited also. John Owen was the first to make this argument, and many modern proponents for the limited view echo him.[17] They note that Jesus prayed, "I pray for them. I am not praying for the world but for those You have given Me, because they are Yours" (John 17:9).

Indeed, Christ's priestly prayer in John's gospel was only on behalf of the saints. But as Lightner points out, the Bible does not equate the two—Christ's atonement and his priestly role—in extent.[18] Intercession relates to believers, and only after the exercise of faith. Christ's intercession for His Church illustrates that the blessings of the atonement are experienced only by those who place their trust in the Son of God.

---

[17] Owen, *The Death of Death in the Death of Christ*, 64–65.
[18] Lightner, *The Death of Christ*, 103–4.

A fourth argument made by advocates of limited atonement is that adherence to unlimited atonement leads to universalism. Reformed theologian Lorraine Boettner argued that "universal redemption means universal salvation."[19] In other words, if Christ paid for the sins of everyone, then everyone will be saved. In response, singular redemption proponents point out that this objection seems to carry weight only if the biblical necessity of faith is ignored. As we saw in the chapter on overcoming grace, the Bible presents faith as the condition for receiving eternal life.

Proponents of limited atonement often make a fifth argument, which is that unlimited atonement cannot be reconciled with God's sovereignty. However, Lightner points out that this is a problem only for those who hold to a single decree of double predestination.[20] In the chapter on sovereign election, we saw that even most Calvinists reject the idea that God actively predestined the lost to hell. This objection requires that one understands God's sovereignty to be incompatible with contingency or conditionality. Yet in chapter one I argued that a proper understanding of God's sovereignty requires contingency, especially when considering the matters relating to creation, election, and evil. The doctrine of limited atonement seems to be a case of adherence to necessity run amok.

A sixth argument made by limited atonement proponents could be called the double jeopardy argument: if Christ died for some who die lost, then their sins are paid for twice. In other words, if Christ died as a substitutionary atonement for everyone who has ever lived, then it would be unjust of God to send anyone to hell. John Owen seems to be the first to make this argument, and modern Calvinists often repeat it. Reformed theologian Sam Waldron puts it this way: "Will a just God punish the same sins twice? It cannot be. Double jeopardy is as unjust in the divine court as it is in human courts."[21]

In response, Anthony Badger points out that the double jeopardy argument assumes what it wishes to prove: that the death of Christ actually secures salvation for the elect and applies the benefits to them prior

---

[19]L. Boettner, *The Reformed Doctrine of Predestination* (Philadelphia: P&R, 1965), 156.
[20]Lightner, *The Death Christ Died,* 98–100.
[21]Waldron, "The Biblical Confirmation of Particular Atonement," 140.

to the exercise of faith.[22] However, salvation is provided at Calvary but applied when the sinner believes. Until faith is exercised, an elect person is just as lost as the nonelect. Once a person believes, and receives the forgiveness of sins, then he is protected from double jeopardy. So the double jeopardy argument makes the case for a believer's security, not limited atonement. Beza applied the double jeopardy argument to believers struggling with a sense of God's condemnation. He advised them to tell the devil that God "is content with one payment."[23]

The double jeopardy argument is a legal argument rather than an exegetical one. And it just so happens there is a legal precedent to answer this question. In the 1830s, a federal court found a man named George Wilson guilty of robbing the U.S. mail and sentenced him to death.[24] President Andrew Jackson granted Wilson a pardon. However, Wilson refused to admit he was guilty and subsequently rejected the presidential pardon. The case went all the way to the Supreme Court, with his lawyers arguing the double jeopardy principle that a man who had been pardoned could not be punished. The Court disagreed, with Chief Justice Marshall delivering the ruling:

> There is nothing peculiar in a pardon which ought to distinguish it in this respect from other facts; no legal principle known to the court will sustain such a distinction. A pardon is a deed to the validity of which delivery is essential, and delivery is not complete without acceptance. It may then be rejected by the person to whom it is tendered, and if it be rejected, we have discovered no power in a court to force it on him.
>
> It may be supposed that no being condemned to death would reject a pardon, but the rule must be the same in capital cases and in misdemeanors. A pardon may be conditional, and the condition may be more objectionable than the punishment inflicted by the judgment.[25]

---

[22]Anthony Barger, "TULIP: A Free Grace Perspective Part 3: Limited Atonement," in *Journal of the Grace Evangelical Society* available at http://www.faithalone.org/journal/2004ii/badger.pdf. Calvinists, however, generally do not explicitly claim that the benefits of salvation are *applied* to the elect prior to faith.

[23]See G. M. Thomas, *The Extent of the Atonement: A Dilemma for Reformed Theology from Calvin to the Consensus (1536–1675)* (Carlisle: Paternoster, 1997), 57.

[24]See *United States v Wilson, 32 U. S. 150 (1833)*, available at http://supreme.justia.com/us/32/150/case.html.

[25]Ibid.

In other words, the Supreme Court ruled that principles of double jeopardy did not apply. President Jackson provided forgiveness for George Wilson, but Wilson refused the provision. Wilson was executed. Similarly, though Christ secured our forgiveness at infinite cost, we still must accept His pardon if we are to enjoy its benefits.

ARGUMENTS FOR SINGULAR REDEMPTION

The singular redemption position, in a nutshell, holds that when Jesus Christ died at Calvary he provided atonement for each and every individual in the world, but the benefits of this provision are enjoyed only by those who repent from their sins and place their trust in the Savior. Some passages of Scripture speak of the atonement's universal provision; others highlight its limited application. This distinction between provision and application means that Christ provided a particular redemption that is universal in scope.

First, the Scriptures present the atonement as to include all humanity. As we saw in the previous section, the arguments for limited atonement are primarily theological rather than exegetical, and they rest on certain assumptions that are difficult to justify with Scripture. In fact, the most powerful argument for the unlimited atonement position of singular redemption is to note the straightforward declarations of the Bible. Lightner notes four types of passages: those which say Christ died for the world, those which invite "whoever" [or "everyone" or "anyone"] to come, those which say Christ died for "all" or its equivalent, and those that distinguish between those for whom Christ died and those who are saved.[26]

At numerous places, the Scriptures declare that Christ died for the "world." A representative sampling are:

> The next day John saw Jesus coming toward him and said, "Here is the Lamb of God, who takes away the sin of the world!" (John 1:29)

---

[26]Lightner, *The Death Christ Died*, 62–65.

> For God loved the world in this way: He gave His One and Only
> Son, so that everyone who believes in Him will not perish but
> have eternal life. For God did not send His Son into the world
> that He might condemn the world, but that the world might be
> saved through Him. (John 3:16–17)

> For we have heard for ourselves and know that this really is the
> Savior of the world. (John 4:42)

> That is, in Christ, God was reconciling the world to Himself.
> (2 Cor 5:19)

> He Himself is the propitiation for our sins, and not only for ours,
> but also for those of the whole world. (1 John 2:2)

> The Father has sent the Son as Savior of the world. Whoever con-
> fesses that Jesus is the Son of God—God remains in him and he
> in God. (1 John 4:14)

Advocates of the limited atonement position sometimes argue that
"world" can designate a group more limited than "everyone" (e.g., Luke
2:1–2), and therefore can refer to the "world of the elect." However, instead of "world" referring to the elect, the biblical writers distinguish the
elect from the world. This is particularly true with the apostle John (e.g.,
John 17:9; 1 John 2:15–17).

A long list of biblical passages make indiscriminate, blanket offers
of the gospel, using the word "whoever" or "everyone/anyone who" to
invite the hearers to come to Christ. A few examples will suffice:

> Whoever calls on the name of the Lord will be saved. (Acts 2:21)

> For everyone who calls on the name of the Lord will be saved.
> (Rom 10:13)

> Whoever desires should take the living water as a gift.
> (Rev 22:17)

Lightner points out that "whoever" is used at least 110 times in the New
Testament and always with "unrestricted meaning."[27]

---

[27]Ibid, 63. Lightner makes his argument based on the times "whosoever" (rather that "whoever")
is used in the King James Version.

A third type of passage that points to the universality of the atonement are those verses which say Christ died for "all" or its equivalent. For example:

> If One died for all, then all died. And He died for all so that those who live should no longer live for themselves, but for the One who died for them and was raised. (2 Cor 5:14–15)

> Who gave Himself—a ransom for all, a testimony at the proper time. (1 Tim 2:6)

> We have put our hope in the living God, who is the Savior of everyone, especially of those who believe. (1 Tim 4:10)

> But we do see Jesus—made lower than the angels for a short time so that by God's grace He might taste death for everyone. (Heb 2:9)

There are times when it is evident the biblical writers do not mean "all" or "everyone" in an absolute or literal sense. For example, Paul instructs the believers at Rome to "try to do what is honorable in everyone's eyes. If possible, on your part, live at peace with everyone" (Rom 12:17-18). Context indicates whether "all" or "everyone" should be understood literally or as hyperbole. As for the many passages which speak of the atonement in universal terms, generally there is nothing in their respective contexts that would restrict the scope.

Finally, there are some passages that distinguish between those for whom Christ died and those who are saved. The most noteworthy is found in 2 Peter, where the apostle warns:

> But there were also false prophets among the people, just as there will be false teachers among you. They will secretly bring in destructive heresies, even denying the Master who bought them, and will bring swift destruction on themselves. (2 Pet 2:1)

Generally, limited atonement proponents respond by arguing that at times universal words such as "all" are used by the biblical writers in ways that clearly have a limited sense. For example, Luke says that in the days of Caesar Augustus a decree went out that "all the world" should be taxed (Luke 2:1 ESV). Obviously, the apostle does not intend for us

to understand "all the world" literally (HCSB renders it "the whole em-
pire"). Advocates of limited atonement argue that "all" in such passages
as I have cited should be understood as "all without distinction" rather
than "all without exception." However, many Reformed theologians acknowledge that such explanations fail. Timothy George admits, "This
is a strained exegesis which is hard to justify in every case. Unless the
context clearly requires a different interpretation, it is better to say that
'all means all,' even if we cannot square the universal reach of Christ's
atoning death with its singular focus."[28]

*Second, it is much easier to reconcile the limiting verses to the uni-
versal ones than vice versa.* As we noted earlier, no one thinks Paul is
claiming that Christ died only for him when he says "[Christ] loved me
and gave Himself for me" (Gal 2:20). A more straightforward understanding would be that some verses focus on the provision of the atonement,
while others emphasize its application to the redeemed. Some verses,
such as Gal 2:20, refer to a subset of those for whom Christ died.

Those who deny the universal extent of the atonement have a much
more difficult task. When read through the lens of limited atonement,
many passages seem strange. Lightner points out that 2 Cor 5:19 has
to be understood to say that God was in Christ reconciling *the elect* to
Himself, and Heb 2:9 that Jesus came to taste death for all the elect, and
1 John 2:2 that Christ is the propitiation for our [the elects'] sins, and not
only for ours, but also for all the elect people in the world.[29] And Lightner is not guilty of caricaturing the view. The post-Reformation Calvinist
theologian Francis Turretin spends four pages of his *Institutes of Elenctic
Theology* trying (in vain) to make the case that John 3:16 speaks only
about the elect.[30] Lightner observes, "In all honesty, we must ask, 'Why
did not these writers say what they meant? If they mean elect people,
why not say that, since those who will never be saved are also *lost* and
ungodly?'"[31]

---

[28]George, *Amazing Grace: God's Initiative—Our Response*, 82.

[29]Lightner, *The Death Christ Died*, 69.

[30]F. Turretin, *Institutes of Elenctic Theology* (Phillipsburg, NJ: P&R, 1992), 1:405–08. In his discussion, Turretin acknowledges that his interpretation of John 3:16 was contrary to that of Calvin's.

[31]Lightner, *The Death Christ Died*, 70 (emphasis original).

A third argument in favor of the unlimited nature of the atonement is the symmetry between the extent of Adam's sin and the extent of Christ's atonement. For example, Isaiah states, "We all went astray like sheep; we all have turned to our own way; and the LORD has punished Him for the iniquity of us all" (Isa 53:6). Isaiah used the word "all" twice in that verse: the first "all" describes the scope of sin, while the second "all" gives the parameters of the atonement. As Calvin said when preaching on this passage, "So we must take careful note of these words of the Prophet when he says that the correction of our peace was on our Lord Jesus Christ; seeing that by His mediation God is satisfied and appeased, for He bore all the wickednesses and all the iniquities of the world."[32]

Paul makes the clearest case for the parallel, symmetric relationship between the imputation of Adam's sin and Christ's atonement in Romans 5. The apostle contrasts Adam and Jesus in a number of ways, basically arguing that the destruction wrought by Adam was undone by Christ. For example, Paul states, "For if by the one man's trespass the many died, how much more have the grace of God and the gift overflowed to the many by the grace of the one man, Jesus Christ" (v. 15). The "many" who died in Adam are the same "many" for whom the grace of God overflowed in Jesus Christ. (Here is a clear instance where "many" is intended to be understood in universal terms.)[33]

Again, Paul declares, "So then, as through one trespass there is condemnation for everyone, so also through one righteous act there is life-giving justification for everyone" (v. 18). In his discussion of this verse, John Murray tried to argue that the guilt of Adam's race was not imputed to Christ, but rather only the guilt of a subset—the elect—was laid upon the Savior. He contended that the "everyone" in the second part of the verse does not have the same meaning as the "everyone" in the first part.[34] However, he provides no exegetical justification for his claim. It would seem that if a word used twice in the same verse changes

---

[32]J. Calvin, *Sermons on Isaiah's Prophecy of the Death and Passion of Christ* (London: James Clarke, 1956), 74.

[33]Again I find myself in agreement with Calvin, who in his comments on Isa 53:12 ("yet He bore the sin of many"), states, "It is evident from other passages, and especially from the fifth chapter of the Epistle to the Romans, that 'many' sometimes denotes 'all.'" See J. Calvin, *Commentary on the Prophet Isaiah,* vol. 4 (Grand Rapids: Eerdmans, 1956), 131.

[34]J. Murray, *Redemption Accomplished and Applied* (Grand Rapids: Eerdmans, 1955), 60.

meanings with nothing in the context to indicate a change, then all hope of doing exegesis is lost.[35]

So if Paul teaches in Rom 5:12–20 that the effects of Adam's sin and of Christ's atonement are symmetric and equal in extent, was Paul arguing for universalism? No, because the apostle stipulates the requirement of faith for receiving Christ's benefits. The atonement is applied to "those who receive the overflow of grace and the gift of righteousness" (v. 17).

Fourth, the doctrine of limited atonement is logically inconsistent with the "well meant" offer of the gospel. The doctrine of limited atonement leads certain Calvinists, such as David Engelsma, to deny that the gospel is offered to the non-elect.[36] The reprobate, according to Engelsma, may happen to be where the gospel is proclaimed and may happen to hear the message of the good news, but it is not for him. Engelsma declares that the "well-meant" offer is contrary to apostolic preaching and practice. He states, "As a predestinarian, [Paul] did not believe, nor did he ever preach, that God loved all men, was gracious to all men, and desired the salvation of all men, that is, he did not believe, teach, or give the well-meant offer of the gospel."[37] Engelsma continues, "Reformed preaching will not approach the audience with the declaration: 'God loves all of you, and Christ died for all of you.'"[38] He concludes bluntly, "This message is a lie."[39]

In contrast to Engelsma, other Calvinists, such as Sam Waldron, simultaneously hold to limited atonement and a well-meant offer. But Waldron admits that he cannot say to an individual lost person, "Christ died for you."[40] The most he can say is that "Christ died for sinners" in

---

[35]By contrast, Calvin understands Rom 5:18 to be clearly teaching that Christ died for all. In his comments on this verse, he states, "Paul makes grace common to all men, not because it in fact extends to all, but because it is offered to all. Although Christ suffered for the sins of the world, and is offered by the goodness of God without distinction to all men, yet not all receive Him." See J. Calvin, *The Epistles of Paul the Apostle to the Romans and to the Thessalonians* (Grand Rapids: Eerdmans, [1540]1960), 117-8.

[36]David Engelsma, *Hyper-Calvinism and the Call of the Gospel: An Examination of the "Well-Meant" Offer* (Grandville, MI: Reformed Free, 1994).

[37]Ibid, 70.

[38]Ibid, 88.

[39]Ibid.

[40]Waldron, "The Biblical Confirmation of Particular Atonement," 149.

a generic sense, but he would not know if Christ died for a particular person until after God regenerates that person.

The issue of the well-meant offer brings us back to the question addressed in chapter 2: does God love all men or does He not? Does He desire the well-being of all humanity, or is He eternally opposed to those whom He has not chosen? The issue is not whether God has a special love for His elect (He does), but whether He has any love *at all* for the entire world. As Lightner asks, "Would we attempt to restrict any other perfections of God to the elect only?"[41]

Fifth, the limited-view seems to teach that the nonelect are condemned for rejecting Christ when in fact He did not die for them. Men cannot reject what does not even exist. However, the singular redemption position agrees with Calvin's argument that those who refuse the Savior are doubly guilty. Calvin makes the double guilt case during his discussion of John 3:16:

> That, then, is how our Lord Jesus bore the sins and iniquities of many. But in fact, this word "many" is often as good as equivalent to "all." And indeed our Lord Jesus was offered to all the world. For it is not speaking of three or four when it says: "God so loved the world, that he spared not His only Son." But yet we must notice what the Evangelist adds in this passage: 'That whosoever believes in Him shall not perish but obtain eternal life.' Our Lord Jesus suffered for all and there is neither great nor small who is not inexcusable today, for we can obtain salvation in Him. Unbelievers who turn away from Him and who deprive themselves of Him by their malice are today *doubly culpable*. For how will they excuse their ingratitude in not receiving the blessing in which they could share by faith?[42]

SUMMARY

Exegetically speaking, proponents of the limited atonement position are in a difficult spot. They must reject what appears to be the clear

---

[41]Lightner, *The Death of Christ*, 113.

[42]J. Calvin, *Sermons on Isaiah's Prophecy of the Death and Passion of Christ* (London: James Clark, [1559] 1956), 141 (emphasis added). This quote was brought to my attention by a paper presented by David Allen at the *John 3:16 Conference*, November 2008.

meaning of such words as "all" and "world." It is easier to reconcile the limited verses with the unlimited and not vice versa.

By contrast, the singular redemption position is able to affirm that the Bible speaks of the atonement in both universal and limited ways. The atonement is sufficient for all, but efficient only for those who believe. Many Calvinists hold that this position is more consistent with Calvin himself.

The key to reconciling the universal passages with those that speak of a limited application is to acknowledge the role of exercising personal faith. "If it be acknowledged that God's design in the death of His Son was to provide redemption for all, conditioned upon the reception of it by individual faith, the problems vanish. This we believe to be the clear and consistent testimony of Scripture."[43]

***

As we come to the end of this book, what shall we conclude? Taking a Molinist view of divine sovereignty and employing a soft libertarian understanding of human choice, we have fleshed out a theology of salvation. Two biblical principles come through clearly: certainty and contingency. This, in turn, respectively provides two great motivations: confidence and urgency. We have confidence because of the certainty of God accomplishing His sovereign plan (Rom 9). Human rebellion and wickedness cannot and does not thwart His will. We can have confidence "that He who started a good work in [us] will carry it on to completion until the day of Christ Jesus" (Phil 1:6). At the same time, because of the genuine contingency of events and situations in our lives, we are to conduct our service for the Lord with real urgency.

That the certainty/contingency pairing produces the confidence/urgency coupling impacts our approach to evangelism. We can undertake the task of winning the lost with the same confidence Paul enjoyed in his mission to Corinth. There the Lord told him, "Don't be afraid, but keep on speaking and don't be silent. For I am with you, and no one will lay a hand on you to hurt you, because I have many people in this city" (Acts 18:9–10). Receiving God's promise that "many people" would be

---

[43]Lightner, *The Death Christ Died*, 104.

converted, Paul threw himself with abandon into the work. Later, the apostle described his ministry to the Corinthians like this: "I planted, Apollos watered, but God gave the growth. So then neither the one who plants nor the one who waters is anything, but only God who gives the growth" (1 Cor 3:6–7). Because salvation is the work of God, we can launch into evangelism, missions, and witnessing with that same enthusiastic certainty and confidence.

However, the Bible also teaches that choices and events are truly contingent, and this fact adds to the task of evangelism the urgency of human responsibility. When God commissioned Ezekiel, he also warned him,

> "Son of man, I have made you a watchman over the house of
> Israel. When you hear a word from My mouth, give them a warn-
> ing from Me. If I say to the wicked person, "You will surely die,"
> but you do not warn him—you don't speak out to warn him about
> his wicked way in order to save his life—that wicked person will
> die for his iniquity. Yet I will hold you responsible for his blood."
> (Ezek 3:17–18)

Notice the contingent, conditional nature of God's charge. It really does matter that we pray, share the gospel, and do missions. *If* we fail to obey the Great Commission, *if* we are indifferent to the desperate need of the world, and *if* we do not share the gospel with others, then people we could have impacted for eternity will die lost. The real, contingent nature of our choices and actions should instill a sense of urgency and obligation upon all of us.

The Molinist model of salvation and the sovereignty of God endeavors to maintain the biblical balance of certainty and contingency, confidence and urgency. Our sovereign God saves. Despite that God granted genuine freedom to us; despite that we promptly abused that freedom to descend into darkness and death; despite that, as fallen creatures, we loved our sin and were without love for Him—despite all these things— God is perfectly accomplishing His plan of salvation. And He is doing so in a way that maintains His perfect integrity from evil and does not turn humans, who He created in His image, into robots. Salvation is of the Lord, all of grace and for His glory.

BIBLIOGRAPHY

Armstrong, Brian G. *Calvinism and the Amyraut Heresy: Protestant Scholasticism and Humanism in Seventeenth-Century France*. Milwaukee: The University of Wisconsin Press, 1969.

Baker, Lynne Rudder. "Why Christians Should Not Be Libertarians: An Augustinian Challenge." *Faith and Philosophy* 20:4 (October 2003): 460–78.

Barth, Karl. *Church Dogmatics*. Vol. II/2. Edinburgh: T&T Clark, 1957.

Basinger, David, and Randall Basinger, eds. *Predestination and Free Will: Four Views of Divine Sovereignty and Human Freedom*. Downers Grove: InterVarsity, 1986.

Bavinck, Herman. *Reformed Dogmatics*. Vol. 2. Trans. John Vriend. Grand Rapids: Baker, 2004.

Bell, M. Charles. *Calvin and Scottish Theology: The Doctrine of Assurance*. Edinburgh: Handsel, 1985.

Berkhof, Louis. *Systematic Theology*. Grand Rapids: Eerdmans, 1938.

Berkouwer, G. C. *Divine Election*. Grand Rapids: Eerdmans, 1960.

Beza, Theodore. *A Little Book of Christian Questions and Responses: In Which the Principal Headings of the Christian Religion Are Briefly Set Forth*. Trans. Kirk M. Summers. Allison Park, PA: Pickwick Publications, 1986.

Bloesch, Donald. *Christian Foundations*. Vol. 7: *The Last Things*. Downers Grove: InterVarsity, 2004.

Brand, Chad Owen, ed. *Perspectives on Election: Five Views*. Nashville: B&H, 2006.

Calvin, John. *The Bondage and Liberation of the Will*. Edited by A.N.S. Lane. Trans. G. I. Davies. Grand Rapids: Baker, [1543] 1996.

———. *Concerning the Eternal Predestination of God*. Trans. J. K. S. Reid. Louisville: Westminster John Knox, [1552] 1961.

———. *Sermons on Isaiah's Prophecy on the Death and Passion of Christ*. Trans. T. H. L. Parker. London: James Clarke, 1956.

———. *Commentary on the Prophet Isaiah*. Vol. 4. Grand Rapids: Eerdmans, 1956.

————. *Commentaries on the First Twenty Chapters of the Book of the Prophet Ezekiel.* Vol. 2. Trans. Thomas Myers. Grand Rapids: Baker, 1999.

————. *The Epistles of Paul the Apostle to the Romans and to the Thessalonians.* Trans. Ross MacKenzie. Grand Rapids: Eerdmans, 1960.

————. *Commentaries on the Catholic Epistles.* Vol. 22. Edited by John Owen. Grand Rapids: Baker, 1999.

Carson, D. A. *Divine Sovereignty and Human Responsibility.* Atlanta: John Knox, 1981.

————. *The Difficult Doctrine of the Love of God.* Wheaton, IL: Crossway, 2000.

Ciocchi, David M. "Human Freedom." In *Christian Perspectives on Being Human: A Multidisciplinary Approach to Integration.* Edited by J. P. Moreland and David M. Ciocchi. Grand Rapids: Baker, 1993.

Clairvaux, Bernard of. *On Grace and Free Choice: De gratia et libero arbitrio.* Trans. Daniel O'Donovan OCSO. Kalamazoo, MI: Cistercian, 1988.

Craig, William Lane. *The Only Wise God.* Baker : Grand Rapids, 1987.

————. "'No Other Name': A Middle Knowledge Perspective on the Exclusivity of Salvation Through Christ." *Faith and Philosophy* 6:2 (April 1989): 172–88.

————. "Middle Knowledge, Truth-Makers, and the 'Grounding Objection'." *Faith and Philosophy* 18:3 (2001): 337–52.

————. "The Middle Knowledge View." In *Divine Foreknowledge: Four Views.* Edited by James K Beilby and Paul R. Eddy. Downers Grove: InterVarsity, 2001.

————. *The Problem of Divine Foreknowledge and Future Contingents from Aristotle to Suarez.* New York: E. J. Brill, 1988.

Daane, James. *The Freedom of God: A Study of Election and Pulpit.* Michigan: Eerdmans, 1973.

Demarest, Bruce. *The Cross and Salvation: The Doctrine of Salvation.* Wheaton: Crossway, 1997.

Dowe, Phil. "A Counterfactual Theory of Prevention and 'Causation' by Omission." *Australasian Journal of Philosophy* 79:2 (June 2001): 216–26.

Edwards, Jonathan. *Freedom of the Will*. Edited by Paul Ramsey. New Haven: Yale Univ. Press, 1957.

Engelsma, David. *Hyper-Calvinism and the Call of the Gospel*. Grand Rapids: Reformed Free Publishing Association, 1994.

Feinberg, John S. *No One Like Him: The Doctrine of God*. Wheaton: Crossway, 2001.

Fesko, J. V. *Diversity Within the Reformed Tradition: Supra- and Infralapsarianism in Calvin, Dort, and Westminster*. Greenville, SC: Reformed Academic Press, 2001.

Flint, Thomas P. "Two Accounts of Providence." In *Divine and Human Action: Essays in the Metaphysics of Theism*. Edited by Thomas V. Morris. Ithaca: Cornell Univ. Press, 1988.

———. *Divine Providence: The Molinist Account*. Ithaca: Cornell University Press, 1998.

Geisler, Norman. *Chosen But Free*. Minneapolis: Bethany, 2001.

———. *Systematic Theology*. Vol. 3. Minneapolis: Bethany, 2004.

Geivett, R. Douglas. "Divine Providence and the Openness of God: A Response to William Hasker." *Philosophia Christi* 4 (2002): 377–96.

George, Timothy. "Southern Baptist Ghosts." *First Things* 93 (May 1999): 18–24.

———. *Amazing Grace: God's Initiative—Our Response*. Nashville: Lifeway, 2000.

Guelzo, Allen. *Edwards on the Will: A Century of American Theological Debate*. Middletown: Wesleyan University Press, 1989.

———. "From Calvinist Metaphysics to Republican Theory: Jonathan Edwards and James Dana on Freedom of the Will." *Journal of the History of Ideas* 56 (July 1995): 399–418.

Helm, Paul, and Oliver D. Crisp, eds. *Jonathan Edwards: Philosophical Theologian*. Burlington, VT: Ashgate, 2003.

Hubmaier, Balthasar. "Freedom of the Will." In *Balthasar Hubmaier: Theologian of Anabaptism*. Trans. and edited by H. Wayne Pipkin and John H. Yoder. Classics of the Reformation series, vol. 5. Scottsdale, PA: Herald, 1989.

Humphreys, Fisher, and Paul E. Robertson. *God So Loved the World: Traditional Baptists and Calvinism*. New Orleans: Insight, 2000.

Jewett, Paul K. *Election and Predestination*. Grand Rapids: Eerdmans, 1985.

Kane, Robert. "Introduction: The Contours of Contemporary Free Will Debates." In *The Oxford Handbook on Freewill*. Edited by Robert Kane. Oxford: Oxford, 2002.

———. *The Significance of Free Will*. New York: Oxford University Press, 1998.

Kendall, R. T. *Calvin and English Calvinism to 1649*. Oxford: Oxford University Press, 1979.

Kennedy, Kevin Dixon. *Union with Christ and the Extent of the Atonement in Calvin*. New York: Peter Lang, 2002.

Koons, Robert C. "Dual Agency: A Thomistic Account of Providence and Human Freedom." *Philosophia Christi* 4 (2002): 397–410.

Lee, Sang Hyun, and Allen C. Guelzo. *Edwards in Our Time: Jonathan Edwards and the Shaping of American Religion*. Grand Rapids: Eerdmans, 1999.

Lightner, Robert P. *The Death Christ Died: A Biblical Case for Unlimited Atonement*. Rev. ed. Grand Rapids: Kregel, 1998.

Luther, Martin. *The Bondage of the Will*. Great Britain: The Camelot Press Ltd., London and Southampton, [1525] 1957.

MacGregor, Kirk R. *A Molinist-Anabaptist Systematic Theology*. Lanham, MD: University Press of America, 2007.

Marshall, I. Howard. "Predestination in the New Testament." In *Grace Unlimited*. Edited by Clark Pinnock, 127–43. Minneapolis: Bethany, 1975.

McGrath, Sarah. "Causation by Omission: A Dilemma." *Philosophical Studies* 123 (2005): 125–48.

Molina, Luis de. *On Divine Foreknowledge (Part IV of the Concordia)*. Trans. Alfred J. Freddoso. Ithaca, NY: Cornell University Press, 1988.

Moore, Jonathan D. *English Hypothetical Universalism: John Preston and the Softening of Reformed Theology*. Grand Rapids: Eerdmans, 2007.

Moreland, J. P., and William Lane Craig. *Philosophical Foundations for a Christian Worldview*. Downers Grove: InterVarsity, 2003.

Morris, Thomas V. *The Logic of God Incarnate*. Ithaca, NY: Cornell University Press, 1986.

Muller, Richard. *Post-Reformation Reformed Dogmatics: The Rise and Development of Reformed Orthodoxy, ca. 1520 to ca. 1725*. Vol. 3. Grand Rapids: Baker Academic, 2003.

Murray, John. *Redemption Accomplished and Applied*. Grand Rapids: Eerdmans, 1955.

O'Connor, Timothy, ed. *Agents, Causes, and Events: Essays on Indeterminism and Free Will*. New York: Oxford University Press, 1995.

Oden, Thomas. *The Transforming Power of Grace*. Nashville: Abingdon, 1993.

Owen, John. *The Death of Death in the Death of Christ*. Edinburgh: Banner of Truth, 2007.

Packer, J. I. *Evangelism and The Sovereignty of God*. Downers Grove: InterVarsity, 1961.

———. "The Love of God: Universal and Particular." In *The Grace of God, the Bondage of the Will*. Vol. 2. Edited by Thomas R. Schreiner and Bruce A. Ware. Grand Rapids: Baker, 1995.

Pelikan, Jaroslav, and Valerie Hotchkiss, eds. *Creeds and Confessions of Faith in the Christian Tradition*. 4 vols. New Haven: Yale University Press, 2003.

Peterson, Robert A., and Michael D. Williams. *Why I Am Not an Arminian*. Downers Grove: InterVarsity, 2004.

Picirilli, Robert E. "Foreknowledge, Freedom, and the Future." *Journal of the Evangelical Theological Society* 43 (2000): 259–71.

———. *Grace, Faith, Free Will*. Nashville: Randall House, 2002.

Pinnock, Clark, ed. *Grace Unlimited*. Minnesota: Bethany, 1975.

———, ed. *The Grace of God, the Will of Man: A Case for Arminianism*. Grand Rapids: Zondervan, 1989.

Pinson, J. Matthew, ed. *Four Views on Eternal Security*. Grand Rapids: Zondervan, 2002.

Piper, John. *God's Passion for His Glory: Living the Vision of Jonathan Edwards*. Wheaton: Crossway, 1998.

Plantinga, Alvin. *The Nature of Necessity*. Oxford: Clarendon, 1974.

Richards, Jay Wesley. *The Untamed God: A Philosophical Exploration of Divine Perfection, Simplicity and Immutability.* Downers Grove: InterVarsity, 2003.

Schreiner, Thomas R., and Ardel B. Caneday. *The Race Set Before Us: A Biblical Theology of Perseverance and Assurance.* Downers Grove: InterVarsity, 2001.

Schreiner, Thomas R., and Bruce A. Ware, eds. *The Grace of God, the Bondage of the Will: Biblical and Practical Perspectives on Calvinism.* 2 vols. Grand Rapids: Baker, 1995.

Shank, Robert. *Elect in the Son.* Minneapolis: Bethany, 1989.

Shedd, W. G. T. *Calvinism: Pure and Mixed.* Carlisle, PA: Banner of Truth, 1986.

Sproul, R. C. Sr. *Chosen by God.* Wheaton: Tyndale, 1986.

———. *Willing to Believe: The Controversy over Free Will.* Grand Rapids: Baker, 1997.

Sproul, R. C. Jr. *Almighty Over All: Understanding the Sovereignty of God.* Grand Rapids: Baker, 1999.

Storms, Sam. *Chosen for Life: The Case for Divine Election.* Wheaton: Crossway, 2007.

Strehle, Stephen. "The Extent of the Atonement and the Synod of Dort." *Westminster Theological Journal* 51:1 (Spring 1989): 1–23.

Stump, Eleonore. "Augustine on Free Will." In *The Cambridge Companion to Augustine.* Edited by Eleonore Stump and Norman Kretzmann. Cambridge: Cambridge University Press, 2007.

Thomas, G. Michael. *The Extent of the Atonement: A Dilemma for Reformed Theology from Calvin to the Consensus (1536-1675).* Carlisle: Paternoster, 1997.

Thomson, Judith Jarvis. "Causation: Omissions." *Philosophy and Phenomenological Research* 66:1 (January 2003): 81–103.

Timpe, Kevin. "Grace and Controlling What We Do Not Cause." *Faith and Philosophy* 24:3 (July 2007): 284–99.

Toon, Peter. *The Emergence of Hyper-Calvinism in English Nonconformity, 1689-1765.* London: The Olive Tree, 1967.

Turretin, Francis. *Institutes of Elenctic Theology.* Vol. 1. Edited by J. T. Dennison Jr. Trans. G. M. Griger. Phillipsburg, NJ: P&R, 1992.

Walls, Jerry L. "Divine Commands, Predestination, and Moral Intuition." In *The Grace of God, the Will of Man: A Case for Arminianism.* Edited by Clark H. Pinnock. Grand Rapids: Zondervan, 1989.

———. "Is Molinism as Bad as Calvinism?" *Faith and Philosophy* 7:1 (January 1990): 85–98.

Walls, Jerry L., and Joseph R. Dongell. *Why I Am Not a Calvinist.* Downers Grove: InterVarsity, 2004.

Ware, Bruce A. "The Place of Effectual Calling and Grace in a Calvinist Soteriology." In *The Grace of God, the Bondage of the Will.* Vol. 2. Edited by Thomas R. Schreiner and Bruce A. Ware. Grand Rapids: Baker, 1995.

Ware, Bruce A. *God's Greater Glory: The Exalted God of Scripture and the Christian Faith.* Wheaton: Crossway, 2004.

Wegner, Daniel M. *The Illusion of Conscious Will.* Cambridge, MA: Bradford, 2002.

White, James. *The Potter's Freedom: A Defense of the Reformation and a Rebuttal to Norman Geisler's Chosen But Free.* Amityville, NY: Calvary, 2000.

Zanchius, Jerom. *The Doctrine of Absolute Predestination.* Trans. Augustus M. Toplady. Grand Rapids: Baker, 1977.

NAME INDEX

SUBJECT INDEX

SCRIPTURE INDEX